THREE MESSENGERS FOR ONE GOD

Three Messengers for One God

ROGER ARNALDEZ

translated by

GERALD W. SCHLABACH

with

MARY LOUISE GUDE, C.S.C

and

DAVID B. BURRELL, C.S.C

UNIVERSITY OF NOTRE DAME PRESS
Notre Dame London

First published as *Trois Messagers Pour Un Seul Dieu*

Manufactured in the United States of America
Composition by Kelby Bowers, Compublishing, Cincinnati, Ohio

Grateful acknowledgment is made to the Ministry of Culture of France for financial assistance in the translation of this work.

Library of Congress Cataloging-in-Publication Data

Arnaldez, Roger.
[Trois messagers pour un seul Dieu. English]
Three messengers for one God / by Roger Arnaldez; translated by Gerald W. Schlabach with Mary Louise Gude and David B. Burrell.
p. cm.
Includes bibliographical references.
ISBN 0-268-01885-5 (alk. paper)
1. Religions — Relations. 2. Monotheism. 3. Christianity — Essence, genius, nature. 4. Islam — Essence, genius, nature. 5. Judaism — Essence, genius, nature. I. Title.
BL410.A7613 1994
291.1'72 — dc20 93-42512
CIP

∞ *The paper used in this publication meets the minimum requirements of the American National Standard for Information Sciences — Permanence of Paper for Printed Library Materials, ANSI Z39.48-1984.*

CONTENTS

PREFACE

We are invited, in our time, on a voyage of discovery stripped of colonizing pretension: an invitation to explore the *other* on the way to discovering ourselves. The world into which we have been thrust asks nothing less of us; those of us intent on discovering our individual vocations cannot proceed except as partners in such a variegated community. And as that journey enters the domain of faith, our community must needs assume interfaith dimension. What once were boundaries have become frontiers which beckon to be broached, as we seek to understand where we stand by expanding our minds and hearts to embrace the other. Put in this fashion, our inner journey can neither be syncretic nor procrustean: assimilating or appropriating. What is rather called for is a mutuality of understanding and of appreciation, a critical perception which is already incipiently self-critical. Rather than reach for commonality, we are invited to expand our horizons in the face of diversity. The goal is not an expanded scheme, but an enriched inquirer: discovery of one's own faith in encountering the faith of another.

But a journey so extensive and so freighted with promise needs a guide; nor could it be a journey of discovery if there were no dangers, no fear. Trustworthy guides allay our fears, however, not by understating the risks but by helping us discriminate between real pitfalls and those we set for ourselves. Faith always involves risks, and if we consent to a journey of faith we will invariably encounter obscure passages and our self-deceptions writ large. So a guide is indispensable. We are fortunate to have one in Roger Arnaldez, a believing Christian who has spent a lifetime of study of Islam and of Judaism. Recently retired from the chair of Islamics at the Sorbonne of Paris, Professor Arnaldez offers us the fruit of his reflections in negotiating a comparative appreciation of Judaism, Christianity, and Islam. His approach is the opposite of reductionist and colonizing; it is rather moved by an appreciation that helps dissolve fear. Moreover, his presentation moves at a level designed to include readers of each faith, and to engage inquirers who may think themselves unprepared as well as those who deemed themselves schooled in interfaith matters.

We have moved as a team at the University of Notre Dame to prepare this English version of *Trois messagers pour un seul Dieu* (Paris: Albin Michel, 1983). Gerald Schlabach (of the department of Theology) crafted the initial text in English, which was then vetted by Mary Louise Gude, C.S.C. (of the department of Romance Languages) and myself. We have utilized the New Jerusalem Bible, unless otherwise noted, for biblical citations (though substituting "the LORD" for their use of "Yahweh"), have adapted the Pickthall version of the Qur'an (*The Meaning of the Glorious Koran* [Boston: George Allen and Unwin, 1976]), and employed English editions of other works cited, whenever possible. Footnotes added by the translators are enclosed in brackets. We are grateful to the author for the enthusiasm with which he has sustained our project, and for the reception which he and Madam Arnaldez have given us personally. We are also indebted to the French publisher, Albin Michel, in the person of Jacquéline Favero, for permission to translate, as well as to the University of Notre Dame Press and its director, James Langford, for encouraging this endeavor. We are confident that the insight and judgment of Professor Arnaldez will shine through whatever infelicities remain in this English rendering.

David B. Burrell, C.S.C.

Theodore M. Hesburgh C.S.C. Professor in Philosophy and Theology
University of Notre Dame

1

THREE MESSENGERS AND THREE MESSAGES

Distinguer pour unir
—J. Maritain

Moses, Jesus, and Muhammad: three messengers of the one, the only God! And yet: three different messages, three religions standing against one another in their dogmas, sometimes in their spirit and in their conceptions of the One who sent their founder! How do we understand and justify such divergence if the God whom they invoke is the same?

In order to produce a helpful study, we must avoid all confusion from the very beginning and take care to avoid a hasty syncretism, for syncretism is a degeneration of thought. Now, a marked tendency can be observed these days in those who are enamored of unity and ecumenism. They tend to assume that since God is one there cannot be a plurality of messages. As a consequence everything opposed to this view is situated outside authentic revelation. It is a human creation which must be rejected in order to cling to the essential: the existence of one God, the Lord and Creator of all things, who guides humanity through His Word and who realizes the ultimate goals of people. The Qurʾan (3:64) already set forth this point of view: "Say: O People of the Book! Come to an agreement between us and you: that we shall worship none but God, and that we shall ascribe no partner unto Him, and that none of us shall take others for lords besides God." Accompanying this exhortation is a reprimand against Jews and Christians (9:31): "They have taken as lords besides God their rabbis and monks." Muslim commentators do not fail to conclude from that assertion that Jewish and Christian beliefs do not result from divine teaching, but from human speculations by the doctors of the Law and the Fathers of the Church.

Still, if one were held to the letter of these verses, the one God of the three monotheisms would hardly be distinguished from the one God of the philosophers. Since Greek thinkers, moving beyond civic polytheism, were able to conceive of a supreme master of the universe and thereby to reduce the different divinities to mere powers, one can conclude that human reason can establish a true monotheism by itself without recourse to any revelation. In this case one will no longer need the messengers; Islam, along with Judaism and Christianity, will lose all distinctive value.

Only for the sake of preserving the revealed religions would wishful thinking suppose that the philosophers were inspired by the prophets. So believed Philo of Alexandria and Abū Sulaymān al-Sijistānī (4th century A.H./10th century C.E.).[1] The latter wrote in *The Cabinet of Wisdom* that all the "sages" of Greece had received light from the "Niche of prophecy," and based his claim on the famous verse in the Sūrah *al-Nūr* (24:35): "God is the Light of the heavens and the earth. The similitude of His light is as a niche wherein is a lamp. The lamp is in a glass. The glass is as it were a shining star. [This lamp is] kindled from a blessed tree, an olive tree neither of East nor West, whose oil would almost glow forth [of itself] though no fire touched it. Light upon light, God guides unto His light whom He will." From this verse is drawn the idea of the niche of prophesy. Nevertheless, if the All-Powerful enlightens whom He will, it seems a bit audacious to use this verse to establish the idea that the light from this niche touched the philosophers.

But the God of Islam is no more identical to the God of the philosophers than is the God of Judaism or of Christianity. Doubtless a superficial knowledge of the Qur'an can create this illusion; such superficiality characterizes the judgment of certain "*philosophes*" of the eighteenth century who saw in Islam the expression of "natural religion." But in fact, Muslim theology does not recognize natural law, natural morality, or natural religion. What it has called *fiṭra*—sometimes translated "nature"—is in reality only the mark of creation on the creature, the opening of human beings to their Creator. Reason is given in order to receive and understand the Word of God, not to engage in autonomous speculations. Finally, the Qur'an brings a positive law, a set of commandments whose sole justification is the absolute will of God, who legislates as He will. Nothing is farther removed from a natural law.

Consequently, from this point of view, it would falsify Islam to reduce it to a kind of common denominator among all monotheisms, for the Qur'an preaches more than the unicity of God, His omnipotence, His omniscience, and other attributes—truths that are in fact already present within the Old and New Testaments. Islam teaches a law that is not that of the Bible, and less still that of the Gospels—a law that repeals all those preceding it and will never be repealed. Islam calls for obedience to a prophet whom neither Jews nor Christians recognize; moreover the definition of prophet and of prophecy varies among the three religions.

Hence, the problem of the diverse messages stubbornly remains. There is no way of reducing it to a common core so long as we situate ourselves within one of the three religious families. One must be Jewish, Christian, or Muslim, adhering to a faith that excludes the other two. If we want to extract some monotheism-in-itself, a monotheistic theology or morality as such, we must simultaneously depart from the three monotheistic religions and place ourselves outside or above them. To put it most forcefully, we would have to neglect the particularities of their messages, ignore the characteristics of each, and repress the very notion of a Messenger.

THE GOD OF ISRAEL

It is good to note, moreover, that the doctors of the three monotheisms, reflecting on their sacred texts, have not failed to take up this delicate question, either directly or indirectly, in their controversies. Their positions are clear. The Jews have the advantage of being the first: the Bible is and remains the only source from a historical point of view, and a constant reference from a doctrinal point of view. The one God, the first to be worshipped in a clear and explicit fashion, is the God of the Jews—of Abraham, of Isaac and of Jacob—who brought His people out of Egypt, who led them to the promised land, who made a covenant with them in perpetuity, and who sent them, through Moses, an immutable law that distinguishes them from all others as the people He has elected. This people almost certainly worshipped this one God as the only God from the beginning. In other words, unlike all the peoples around them the Hebrews rejected polytheism and had only one God, whom they honored as their defender, more powerful than the gods whom their enemies invoked.

Henotheism was the first form of monotheism and the sacred texts carry its traces. J. Giblet recounts in the *Dictionary of Biblical Theology*: "This monotheism of faith had long been able to reconcile itself with representations involving the existence 'of other gods,' for example Chemosh in Moab." In fact, it is written: "Will you not keep as your possession whatever Chemosh, your god, has given you?" (Judges 11:24).

One can find numerous testimonies to this ancient conception in the Psalms: "Had we forgotten the name of our God and stretched out our hands to a foreign god [*ʾēl zār*], would not God have found this out . . . ?" (44:20–21 [Hebrew 44:21–22]). "What god [*ʾēl*] is as great as our God?" (77:13 [Hebrew 77:14). "For the LORD is a great God [*ʾēl*], a king greater than all the gods [*ʾelōhîm*]" (95:3). The word *ʾelōhîm* is a plural, and, taken as such, it applies to the gods of paganism. But the Bible likewise employs it to set apart the only God of Israel. In its plural meaning, commentators have suggested that it signifies the angels; doubtless this displays a purely monotheistic reaction against a simple henotheistic reading. Moreover, in reading the Bible one finds passage after passage developing an ever more accentuated evolution toward the idea of one God, creator and lord of all things, and in turn, God of all people.

The Bible reduces the gods of paganism to idols: "Great is the LORD, worthy of all praise, more awesome than any of the *ʾĕlōhîm*, for all the *ʾĕlōhîm* of the nations are idols [*ʾĕlîlîm*]" (96:4–5). Other verses employ the word *ʿāṣāb*, which means the statue of an idol: "Their idols [*ʿăṣabêhem*] are silver and gold, made by human hands" (115:4). Parallel to this evolution, the God of Israel becomes the God of all humanity: "The LORD protects the stranger, He sustains the orphan and the widow" (146:9). God is the providence of all the beings whom He created: "All look to You in hope and You feed them with the food of the season. And, with generous hand, You satisfy the desires of every living creature" (145:15–16). Thus the God of Israel becomes the God of all. At the beginning Emmanuel (God with us) is "our God," God for us, the sons of Abraham, and not for you, the strangers (hence, the "we" is exclusive—we ourselves and not you). But He becomes the God who is with us all, with all human beings (so the "we" becomes inclusive).

Nevertheless, even when the Bible recognizes Him as the universal God, He remains the God of Abraham, of Isaac and of Jacob. All nations are called to recognize Him as such. They must do more than simply confess God's existence and unicity: they must hear His Word and recognize the covenant He has made and renewed with the patriarchs of His people. For humanity, this people is the witness to the covenant. They witness to it by observing the Law. God said to Abraham: "All nations on earth [*kōl gôyê hā-āreṣ*] will bless themselves by your descendants, because you have obeyed my command" (Genesis 22:18). Hence, the covenant relates strictly to the Law. God orders Moses to speak to the people on His behalf: "So now, if you are really prepared to obey me and keep my covenant, you, out of all peoples, shall be my personal possession" (Exodus 19:5). And when Moses had received the Law, "taking the Book of the Covenant [*sēper hab-bĕrît*], he read it to the listening people, who then responded, 'We shall do everything that the LORD has said; we shall obey'" (Exodus 24:7). Likewise, the second book of the Kings (23:3) reads: "The king [Josiah] then, standing on the dais, bound himself by the covenant before the LORD, to follow the LORD, to keep his commandments, decrees and laws with all his heart and soul, and to carry out the terms of the covenant as written in this book."

We must note the expression, "with all his heart and soul" (*bĕ-kol lēb ûbĕ-kol nepeš*). In fact, as the Psalms repeatedly attest, for the servant of God the Law is an object of love. "Your commandments fill me with delight, I love [*ʾāhābtî*] them dearly" (Psalm 119:47). "I love your law" (*tôrātkā ʾāhābtî*) (Psalm 119:113, 163). In turn, "God takes pleasure in those who fear him, in those who trust in His grace" (Psalm 149:4).[2]

In sum, it is the Law that places humanity and God in relation. The love uniting them is realized within the Law. As a result, Jewish monotheism is based on worship of the only God, who is the God of Abraham, of Isaac and of Jacob, the God of an elect people, the people of the promise and of the Covenant. This God is in principle the God of all creation and all humanity. But foreign nations will only have access to His blessings by recognizing Him as the God of Israel and observing the Law of Moses. We cannot discover and worship the true God outside of this eternal Law.

We are therefore far removed from the abstract universality of the philosophers' God. And we must underscore an important particularity of the biblical revelation concerning God. Never is He described or defined by means of general concepts taken in themselves; He always emerges through His dealings with the concrete history of His people or of select individuals who have received the responsibility of leading them. What systematic theology will call "attributes of God," for example, only appear through the interventions of God within this history. Even though Genesis begins with the account of creation, the God of the Bible is not primarily and essentially present as Creator—the cause of the existence of heaven and earth. He is above all the God who brought His people out of the land of Egypt, who divided the floods of the sea to make them pass through, who fed them in the desert, and who later freed them from captivity in Babylon. The Psalms ceaselessly recall the wonders God has done for His people: "Yes, the Lord did great deeds for us" (Psalm 126:3) and these wondrous actions are what have disclosed His bounty, His power, His grace, His mercy, His knowledge, His wisdom, His greatness, His long-suffering, etc. The God of Israel is not the object of speculative theology but the one who engenders a unique experience, lived within history. Such is the true God, the only God. Once again, one would be unable to discover such a one outside of His ways, and one cannot recognize His ways without recourse to the testimony of those whom He has faithfully accompanied on the byways of their history.

Under these conditions, the fact that Christianity and Islam preach monotheism, which they have borrowed broadly from the Torah, the Prophets, the Writings and the Psalms, is all meaningless in the eyes of Judaism. As long as one has not received the Law, one has no contact with the true God who only reveals Himself to His people, within His people, and through His people. The messianic hope is that in the last days, as the prophet Micah announces (4:2), "many nations will come and say, 'Come, we will go up to the LORD's mountain, to the Temple of the God of Jacob, so that he may teach us his ways and we may walk in his paths; for the Law issues from Zion and the LORD's word from Jerusalem."

THE CHRISTIAN PERSPECTIVE

Christianity places itself in direct continuity with Judaism. The existence of Jewish-Christian communities from the beginning clearly proves this. Even if certain facts of history have opened a breach between the two religious traditions, it is no less true that intimate relations continue to link them to each other. The God of the Christians is, by their own confession, the One who revealed Himself to Abraham, Isaac, and Jacob, and whose presence the chosen people continue to celebrate, by giving thanks to Him for his immense blessings. But from the Christian perspective the teaching of the Bible, while expressing pure religious truths, is a pedagogue destined to form the human spirit in a people chosen for this purpose, by preparing them to receive the definitive revelation brought by Christ.

Jesus said: "Do not imagine that I have come to abolish the Law or the Prophets. I have come not to abolish but to complete them. In truth I tell you, till heaven and earth disappear, not one dot, not one little stroke, is to disappear from the Law until all its purpose is achieved"

(Matthew 5:17–18). The Greek word translated as "to complete" is the verb *plērōsai*, which means "to fill up" or "to fill in." We do not know which Aramaic term Christ might have employed. But the Syriac Peshitta uses the verb *mallē*, which has the same meaning—that of filling up and completing. It seems therefore that the idea of completing the Law supposes that one is filling in its framework, thereby completing the Law with an inner content so that one interiorizes that content. And in Matthew this is exactly what stands out in the rest of the text: "For I tell you, if your uprightness does not surpass that of the scribes and Pharisees, you will never get into the kingdom of Heaven" (5:20). What should one understand by scribes and Pharisees? The entire Gospel explains: it refers to jurists and the strict observers of the Law who are intent on determining all the material details of what one must do or not do, and who fulfill their duty—nothing more—with a tranquil and satisfied conscience.

Still, in denouncing this danger, which is inherent in the practice of any law, Jesus will be introducing new and essential elements. One need only look again at chapter 5 of Matthew, beginning the Sermon on the Mount: "You have heard how it was said to our ancestors, You shall not kill. . . . But I say this to you, anyone who is angry with a brother will answer for it before the court" (5:21–22). The rest is familiar. Christ wants the Law to express the demands of an extremely sensitive conscience, which repels even the subtlest nuance of evil. That is why he does not credit the letter of a legislation which one can observe without being purified from within, to say nothing of violating sacred laws under the cover of a decreed and written law. So it is that he cures illnesses, even on the Sabbath, and permits his disciples to pluck grain on that day in order to eat (Matthew 12:1–5). On this occasion he responds to those who would accuse him of violating the Law by citing Hosea (6:6): "And if you had understood the meaning of the words: *Mercy* [eleos] *is what pleases me, not sacrifice,* you would not have condemned the blameless." The word *eleos* translates the Hebrew *ḥesed,* which means bounty, grace, love, and which very often designates the compassionate love of God toward those who fear Him. For example, it is said (Psalm 86:15): "But you, Lord, God of tenderness and mercy [or love: *wĕ-rab ḥesed*], slow to anger, rich in faithful love and loyalty, turn to me. . . ." Moreover numerous passages of the Bible declare that the interior dispositions of the heart are more precious in the eyes of God than the exterior rites of sacrifice. In this vein Samuel says: "Is the LORD pleased by burnt offerings and sacrifices or by obedience to the LORD's voice? Truly, obedience is better than sacrifice" (1 Samuel 15:22). Or in the celebrated oracle of Isaiah (1:11ff.): "'What are your endless sacrifices to me?' says the LORD. 'I am sick of burnt offerings of rams and the fat of calves. I take no pleasure in the blood of bulls. . . . Your hands are covered in blood, wash, make yourselves clean. Take your wrong-doing out of my sight!'"

Jesus does not destroy the Law; he preaches its interiorization and its spiritualization, so that one might truly say: "Your Law, my God, is deep in my heart" (Psalm 40:8). Whoever follows the preaching of Jesus step by step reaches that fundamental teaching. In response to a Pharisee, a doctor in the Law, who asked him which is the greatest commandment, he responds: "You must love the Lord your God with all your heart, with all your soul, and with all your mind. This is the greatest and first commandment. The second resembles it: You must love your neighbor as yourself. On these two commandments hang the whole Law, and the Prophets too" (Matthew 22:37–40).

So then, the Law that Christ brings is the Law of love: this Law "completes" the Law of Moses by releasing in it the spirit whose significance is not merely symbolic—as one might think when contrasting the spirit and the letter—but rather a powerful wind, capable of regenerating, animating, and intensifying the moral and religious life of humanity. This is the Law the psalmist loved, which ceases to be a set of precepts in the grip of jurists. This Law truly becomes an active presence of God in us, so that God really is with each of us, perfectly interiorizing the meaning of Emmanuel.

Now, can anyone love a text as such, fine though it may be? Can a text fill up a human life? Yes, but on one condition and only one: if it bears the imprint of a loved one. This was certainly the thought of the psalmist: in his love for the Law, it is God whom he loves.

But the revelation of Christ goes farther still: he is himself the way, the truth, and the life—three terms that designate the Law. He is himself the Law, in its deep reality, the Law of love. In fact, Christianity sees in Christ the eternal Word, the eternal Verb of God become man in flesh in order to dwell among us. *Kai ho logos sarx egeneto,* says Saint John (1:14), which one translates as: And the Word is made flesh. But the Greek word *sarx* (flesh) very plausibly translates the Hebrew word *bāśār*, which does mean "flesh" but also means "the man of flesh" (just as we would say "flesh and blood" in order to emphasize the human reality). The Syriac Peshitta employs a word with the same root and the same sense: *besārō*.

To love the Law is, from now on, to love Christ, the Word of God. In the hearts of believers Christ replaces the Law by subsuming it within the law of love. "It is Christ who lives in me!" writes Saint Paul, corresponding exactly to: "Your Law is deep in my heart." But to love Christ is to love God, for Christ is God. And God Himself, teaches Saint John, is love (1 John 4:8).

Especially after what Paul had said, one can understand why Jews refused to follow Christians in a direction that in their eyes was leading to the destruction of their Law. The apostle's arguments are well known. First he remarks that Abraham did not live under the Law when God made the promise to him: "For the promise to Abraham and his descendants that he should inherit the world was not through the Law, but through the uprightness of faith" (Romans 4:13). Later he shows that in commanding good the Law discloses evil, and in itself offers no help for struggling against the "law of sin," the evil tendencies of the body: "We are well aware that the Law is spiritual: but I am a creature of flesh and blood sold as a slave to sin" (7:14). "In my inmost self I dearly love God's law, but I see that acting on my body there is a different law which battles against the law in my mind. So I am brought to be a prisoner of sin which lives inside my body" (7:22–23). Meanwhile, "The real Jew is the one who is inwardly a Jew, and real circumcision is in the heart, a thing not of the letter but of the spirit" (2:29). Interior purification cannot be the work of the Law. Rather, in its spirituality the Law calls forth a grace that frees man from the law of sin, and that is a fruit of faith and hope in Jesus Christ: "When law came on the scene, it was to multiply the offenses. But however much sin increased, grace was always greater; so that as sin's reign brought death, so grace was to rule through saving justice that leads to eternal life through Jesus Christ our Lord" (5:20–21). It is in and by Jesus Christ that one manages to live the interior spirituality of the Law, which is then revealed as the Law of love. Such speculations could not help but pain Jews profoundly.

But on the other hand, one can understand how Christians believed, in good faith, that they were remaining faithful to the teaching of the Torah and the Prophets, and that they were within a line of thought that was developing the spiritual values of Judaism. So they interpreted the books of the Bible in a way that made the force of these values erupt everywhere, by showing that they could not be realized outside of Christ. They combed the texts for the announcement or foretelling of his coming, and they saw figures of this Christ in many biblical figures. From the point of view of the historical truth of the texts, this kind of exegesis may rightly be criticized, and Jews have been able to repudiate it easily. The New Testament had offered an example of such interpretation, and the Church Fathers did not fail to follow it. There is therefore a Christian reading of the Bible that Jesus would not accept, even if, for their part, they had their own well-developed use of allegory and symbol. Such Christian readings often seem purely and simply to evade the Law, whereas we have seen how the position of Saint Paul on this point is much more nuanced. In any case, when taken in themselves and stripped of their supporting teaching, many of these commentaries have elaborated religious ideas that can hardly leave a Jewish reader indifferent.

Furthermore, Christianity began to thrive right in the middle of Judaism: the apostles and the first disciples were Jews. Christ himself declared that he was sent to the Children of Israel; his response to the pagan Syro-Phoenician who begged him to heal her demon-possessed daughter was very harsh: "The children should be fed first, because it is not fair to take the children's food and throw it to the little dogs" (Mark 7:27). So it is that the teaching of Christ does not address idolaters as such, but a people who worships the only true God, to apprise them that the Law which they had received must be fulfilled within the Law of love, the Law of the heart. The pagans will be saved through this Law, through faith, in the love of Christ, who is the basis of their hope, as Saint Paul says. Or as the conclusion of the episode reported by Mark clearly highlights (7:28–29): "'Ah yes, sir,' she replied, 'but little dogs under the table eat the scraps from the children.' And he said to her, 'For saying this you may go home happy, the devil has gone out of your daughter.'" The same sharp contrast recurs everywhere: the universalism of Jewish monotheism implies recognition of the Law of Moses by all the nations, whereas the universalism of Christian monotheism amounts to the shining of the Law of love upon all humanity love through faith and hope in the Christ who incarnates it.

ISLAM'S POINT OF VIEW IN RELATION TO JUDAISM

Islam preaches the existence of one God—the Creator and Providence of His creation, All-powerful, Omniscient, and Living—who sends prophets to human beings in order to reveal these fundamental truths to them and bring them a law. The Qur'an calls to mind the mission of the biblical "prophets" as well as the mission of Christ. In doing so it presents not the sustained narrative found in the Bible but only the peak moments (*awqāt*) in the life of Abraham, of Isaac, of Jacob, of Moses, of Jesus, the son of Mary.

These signal and discontinuous moments comprise those in which God reveals that He is the one God, the Lord of the worlds and Master of the Day of Judgment, as one can read in the introductory sūrah of the Qurʾan, the *Fātiḥa.* For example, it is written (2:258): "when [*idh*] Abraham said: My Lord is He who gives life and causes death . . ." and again (6:75): "(Remember) when [*idh*] Abraham said unto his father Azar: Do you take idols for gods?" Or similarly, concerning Moses, one reads (2:53): "And when We gave unto Moses the Scripture . . ." or (5:20): "And (remember) when Moses said unto his people: O my people! Remember God's favor unto you, how He placed among you Prophets. . . ." One can give numerous other examples of the particle *idh* being employed to indicate an important event that takes place in a privileged moment. Moreover the verses concerning the "prophets" and the ancient law are disseminated in fragments throughout the Qurʾan and never form a sustained recitation. As a result the history of the people of Israel, which forms the framework of the biblical accounts is utterly deconstructed and destroyed. The same holds for the verses about Jesus.

What counts for the Qurʾan is not human history, but rather the intervention of God, who, from the height of His transcendence, "causes His word to descend" (*tanzīl, inzāl*) upon one or another of His prophets. This word falls vertically, so to speak, at distinct points in time, without ever unfolding within the horizontal continuity of historical immanence. Qurʾanic revelation is punctiliar, and so acknowledges the divine Absolute, a foreigner to temporality. This contrasts with the conception of divinity in Judaism, where God reveals Himself through His promise and renews it from one generation to another. "From generation to generation, Your faithfulness!" (*lĕ-dōr wā-dōr ʾĕmûnāteḳā*) (Psalm 119:90);[3] "He remembers his covenant for ever, the promise he laid down for a thousand generations" (*lĕ ʿelep dôr*) (Psalm 105:8). "You guided your people like a flock by the hand of Moses and Aaron" (Psalm 77:20). This continuity of divine action within time, modeled upon the historic continuity of the life of His people, is absent from the qurʾanic recitation.

Islam recognizes that God intervenes in history, since nothing is ever outside of divine power. But even when they concern events in the life of the prophet Muhammad, these interventions are evoked in a fragmentary way, in passing, and outside of all chronological continuity, sometimes even by a mere allusion. Thus it is written (8:9): "When [*idh*] ye sought help of your Lord and He answered you (saying): I will help you with a thousand of the angels, rank on rank." This verse recalls, according to commentators, the help that God gave Muslims in the battle of Badr against the Quraysh of Mecca. Again we note the presence of the particle *idh* in this text, just as in those that we have cited concerning Abraham and Moses. This particle condenses duration into an instant and suddenly releases the pure religious truth that God wants to teach—in this case, that God comes to the aid of those who combat in His way. So it is written elsewhere (47:7): "O all who believe! If you help God, He will help you and will make your foothold firm." It is this truth that matters, rather than the battle itself with its episodes. In fact the Qurʾan does not even name the battle explicitly, but reduces it to a punctual event, in other words, to a point where revelation intersects. It becomes one of the occasions for revelation to descend (*asbāb al-nuzūl*).

With the biblical narration, in contrast, real-life events are the frame upon which revelation is woven into historical time. To choose one example from a thousand, the second book of Samuel (5:23–25) also involves a battle, but here one sees the God's action extending within the story according to the successive moments of human action: "David consulted the LORD, who replied, 'Do not attack them from the front; go round to their rear and engage them opposite the balsam trees. When you hear the sound of footsteps in the tops of the balsam trees, advance, for that will be the LORD going out ahead of you to defeat the Philistine army.' David did as the LORD had ordered and beat the Philistines from Gibeon to the Pass of Gezer." So it is that the qurʾanic recollection (*dhikr*) of events told in the Bible denies Jews their history, and their historic relation to their God. Indirectly, it also antagonizes Christians.

But there is something even more serious: the Abrahamic covenant and most especially the promise that accompanies it are absent from the Qurʾan. Several verses evoke the importance of the patriarch, whom the Qurʾan calls the Friend of God (*Khalīl Allāh*, 4:125). But the story of the foreign visitors who announce the birth of Isaac to Abraham (51:24–30) is not linked to any promise. It relates the episode in chapter 18 of Genesis, but detaches it from chapter 17 and totally omits the account of where God makes His covenant with Abraham: "And I shall maintain my covenant between myself and you, and your descendants after you, generation after generation, as a covenant in perpetuity, to be your God and the God of your descendants after you." In Genesis the Lord announces to Abraham that through his wife Sarah he will have a son, Isaac, in whom the promise is being renewed, to the exclusion of Ishmael, the son of the servant Hagar: "Yes, your wife Sarah will bear you a son whom you must name Isaac. And I shall maintain my covenant with him, a covenant in perpetuity, to be his God and the God of his descendants after him. For Ishmael too I grant you your request. I hereby bless him and will make him fruitful . . . and I shall make him into a great nation. But my covenant I shall maintain with Isaac, whom Sarah will bear you at this time next year" (17:19–21).

If we place this account next to the qurʾanic verses which retain only the story in Genesis 18, we see that the Qurʾan reports the latter this way: "Has the story [*ḥadīth*] of Abraham's honored guests reached you (O Muhammad)? When they came in unto him and said: Peace! [*salām*] he answered Peace! (and thought): Folk unknown (to me). Then he went apart unto his housefolk so that they brought a fatted calf; And he set it before them, saying: Will you not eat? Then he conceived a fear of them. They said: Fear not! and gave him tidings of (the birth of) a wise son. Then his wife came forward, making moan, and smote her face, and cried: A barren old woman! They said: Even so says your Lord. Lo! He is the Wise, the Knower." Within the qurʾanic perspective, the single goal of this recitation is to teach that God knows what must be, for that which must be depends solely on His omnipotence and His will. The announcement of the birth of Isaac is identical to that of the birth of John the Baptist and of Jesus. "So (it will be). God does what He will," is the response given to Zachariah (3:40) and to Mary: "So (it will be). God creates what He will. If He decrees a thing, He says unto it only: Be! and it is (3:47). Or again: "So (it will be). . . . It is easy for Me" (19:21). The difference in tone between the verses of the Qurʾan and the verses of either the Bible or the Gospels is on this point obvious. The qurʾanic revelation bursts from the height of heaven like a clap of thunder; the biblical revelation seeps into human history and spreads along with it.

Moreover, if Islam recognizes Isaac as a prophet, it accords Ishmael a place that is at least equal. It is with the son of Hagar that Abraham laid the foundations of the temple of Mecca, the Kaʿba: "And We imposed a duty[4] upon Abraham and Ishmael, (saying): Purify My house [temple or *bayt*] for those who go around [*liʾ l-tāʾafin*: allusion to a right of pilgrimage that consists in turning (*tawāf*) around the Kaʿba] and those who meditate therein and those who bow down and prostrate themselves (in worship)" (2:125). Very often the Qurʾan cites Ishmael with his father, next to Isaac, Jacob, and the twelve Tribes of Israel.

To be sure, God's covenant with the Israelites (*Banū Isrāʾīl*) is recognized as genuine, but not exclusive or eternal. "And (remember) when (*idh*) We made a covenant with the Children of Israel . . ." (2:83). Again we find the particle *idh* which confers on the event a simple punctiliar reality. Indeed, the commentators of the Qurʾan make no mistake about it: this covenant, they explain, is for a time. On this point the contrast between Islam and Judaism is irreducible.

The contrast shows up again just where their agreement would seem the closest: on the conception of revelation as the sending of a law. The Torah offers an eternal law; so too the Qurʾan. But for Islam, the qurʾanic law repeals all others and will never be repealed. The Mosaic law, as we have seen, is linked to the covenant, and God is faithful to His promise. But the God of Islam never enters into history, any more than He enters into the order of His creation. Just as the Creator can at any moment modify the physical laws that govern material beings, so too can he repeal, and does repeal, the religious laws that he imposes on peoples through the course of centuries. The only promise (*waʿd*) that God reveals and upholds is associated with a threat (*waʿīd*), but it does not concern the world here-below. Rather, it concerns the "afterlife"—the promise of Paradise for the faithful, and the threat of Hell for the infidels. Therefore, if divine transcendence is as absolute in Jewish monotheism as in Muslim monotheism, Islam presents it with an abstract rigor that is much more pronounced. This "abstraction," etymologically, signifies the total detachment of God, His perfect separation, in His isolation from all creatures in the beyond. He is present to them only in and through His creative act.

Now the creative act, according to numerous Muslim theologians, is not a causal act of the sort that necessarily supposes a certain immanent relation of resemblance between the cause and the effect. Rather, what God creates bears no semblance to Him at all: "Naught is as His likeness" (42:11). The idea that man is created in the image and likeness of God is foreign to orthodox Islam. Therefore as God, He is above all the all-powerful Creator who does as He wills. In the first verse revealed to Muhammad (96:1) it is said: "Read: In the name of thy Lord who creates." For the Jews, God is first of all the One who brought His people out of Egypt; the Bible never ceases to allude to this event. The difference is profound if one considers the two revelations from this angle, that is to say, by comparing them to each other according to the idea each has of God.

Verses revealing this absolute will of God are numerous. One can cite, among others (2:253): "And if God had so willed it (*law shaʾa*), those who followed after them would not have fought one with another . . . but God does what He will (*ma yuridu*)." Or later (5:48; 16:93): "Had God willed He could have made you one community." To believe in one God doubtlessly presupposes that His will alone is efficacious. But must it therefore follow that this will is arbitrary, that it takes nothing but itself into account? The Bible certainly has expressions very close to those found in the Qurʾan. Thus it is written (Job 23:13): "To Him, all is of a piece (*bĕ-ʾeḥād*), and what will turn Him back? His soul both desires (*wĕ-napšô ʾiwwĕtâ*), and He does (what He pleases)."[5] Is this not arbitrary? Yes, but only in the formula Job employs—not in God's. In fact, the evils with which God afflicts His servant result from a veritable wager with Satan, who accused Job of not serving His Lord freely (*hinnām*). In order to prove the contrary God removes all He has given Job. But Job sees to it that God wins the wager, and so is rewarded. The lesson here is not so much the absoluteness of the divine will as the graciousness of the divine gift, which the LORD Himself articulates clearly at the end of the poem (41:3): "Who has gone before me, for what I have rendered to them?"[6] But the idea of such a wager is absent from the Qurʾan. Indeed, it is inconceivable from the Islamic point of view, even if one so wanted to interpret in this sense the verse where God, despite the angels' objection, declares that He is going to establish Adam, the man, as His vicar upon the earth (2:30). The contexts are entirely different, and as numerous commentators note, the Qurʾan wants above all to show that God picks out from among His creatures those whom He will, and that while the angels are made of light, and humans of clay, this does not grant angels any superior rights. Moreover, when God accords to Iblīs a delay until the Day of the Resurrection, and Iblīs declares that he will cause a great number of people to stumble, God, instead of wagering on humanity's behalf, threatens and says to the demon: "As for such of them as follow you, surely I will fill hell with all of you!" (7:18). The difference in tone is startling and the theological consequences are great.

Another example: it is described in the Qurʾan (2:117; 3:47; 16:40; 19:35; 36:82): "When He decrees a thing, He says unto it only: Be! and it is." In an analogous sense, Isaiah has said (55:11): ". . . so it is with the word that goes from my mouth: it will not return to me unfulfilled or before having carried out my good pleasure [or will: *hapasti*] and having achieved what it was sent to do." And one reads in the Psalms (33:9): "For, the moment he spoke, it was so, no sooner had he commanded, than there it stood!" Both series of texts equally recognize that the will of God is efficacious. Yet here again, it is easy to see how, in the Qur᾽an, God speaks of His will in an "abstract," general and absolute fashion, whereas, in the Bible, the will of God is woven into the events of human life. In fact, the words of Isaiah turn on a comparison (55:10): "For, as the rain and the snow come down from the sky and do not return before having watered the earth, fertilizing it and making it generate to provide seed for the sower and food to eat, so it is with the word that goes from my mouth. . . ." And the entire passage ends with this happy announcement (55:12): "Yes, you will go out with joy and be led away in safety [or peace]." The same remark applies to the immediate context of verse 9 in Psalm 33: "The LORD's own plan stands firm for ever, his heart's counsel from age to age. How blessed the nation whose God is the LORD, the people he has chosen as his heritage" (33:11–12). In conclusion one can say that the Bible and the Qur᾽an agree in confessing the all-powerful will of God, who decides without needing a counselor (Isaiah 40:13) and has no one associated with His sovereignty (Qur᾽an 17:111; 25:2). But while the Bible demonstrates this will concretely at work in human affairs, the Qur᾽an affirms it abruptly, as a theological truth in itself. The Qur᾽an presents itself as a guide to conduct (*hudā*), that has descended from heaven; the Bible shows human conduct on earth to be under divine guidance, for the people God has chosen. The Qur᾽an attains universality immediately through the abstract formation that the word of God acquires; the Bible reaches out toward the universal—toward the recognition of the God of Israel by all nations; but it remains a poignant call that resounds throughout history.

ISLAM'S POINT OF VIEW IN RELATION TO CHRISTIANITY

The opposition of Islam to Christianity is even more pronounced, and it essentially turns on dogmatic questions that are pointless to develop. The Qur᾽an definitively rejects the Trinity and the Incarnation. It recognizes Jesus as a prophet; it attests the virginal conception; it affirms the reality of the miracles of Christ, the Messiah (*al-masīḥ*), in particular the gift that he received to heal illnesses and raise the dead. But he remains only a man. He preached a law that is contained in the Gospel: this law softens the rigor of the Mosaic Law. But this Gospel (in the singular: *injīl*) has been altered, and must not be confused with the four Gospels that are a human creation. (We note as well that the Torah of the Jews has undergone an analogous alteration.) Finally, Islam denies that Jesus was crucified, a denial that amounts to negating [the Christian understanding of] redemption. The contrast is radical, therefore, and bears upon essential points. There is no need to argue any further.

QURʾANIC POLEMIC

Generally speaking, Islam reproaches both Jews and Christians for believing that they are exclusive possessors of the truth. For the mere fact that the latter are in disagreement manifestly proves their error. "And the Jews say the Christians follow nothing (true), and the Christians say the Jews follow nothing (true). . . . God will judge between them . . ." (2:113). For this reason God has cast "enmity and hatred" (*al-ʿadāwa waʾl-baghdāʾ*) into each of their camps, "until the Day of Resurrection" (5:14 and 5:64). If the "People of the Book" were sincere, they would accept the qurʾanic revelation as confirming (*musaddiq*) the truth contained in their own Scriptures. But they do not acknowledge it, because they have falsified their scriptures. In effect, Islam believes that the Bible and the Gospel had announced the mission of Muhammad. Thus their commentators apply the sending of the Paraclete in Saint John (15:26 and 16:13) to the Prophet. As for the Bible, one thinks of Deuteronomy (18:18), where God says: "From their own brothers I shall raise up a prophet like yourself; I shall put my words into his mouth and he will tell them everything I command him." The prophecy of Isaiah likewise comes to mind (42:1): "Here is my servant whom I uphold, my chosen one in whom my soul delights. I have sent my spirit upon him, he will bring fair judgement to the nations." (We note that Christians, of course, apply this text to Christ.)

On the other hand, Islam binds itself directly to the faith of Abraham. Here the Qurʾan uses the kind of argument we have already seen in Saint Paul, but presents it under a still more radical form. Saint Paul remarked that at the time of the covenant the patriarch was not under the Law of Moses. Now God says in the sūrah *Al ʿImrān* (The Family of ʿImrān) (3:65,67): "O People of the Book! Why will you argue about Abraham, when the Torah and the Gospel were not revealed till after him? . . . Abraham was not a Jew, nor yet a Christian: but he was an upright man [*ḥanīf*] who had surrendered (to God) [*Muslim*]. . . ." And He adds (3:68): "Lo! those of mankind who have the best claim to Abraham are those who followed him, and his Prophet [Muhammad]." Therefore, quite apart from the relationship of Arabs to Abraham as descendants of Ishmael, anyone who shares his faith can claim him.

Finally, Islam claims to recognize all the prophets, whereas Jews exclude Jesus and Muhammad, and Christians, Muhammad. As a result, Islam is the most inclusive religion. But having said that, Islam does not take into account that Judaism has its own conception of prophecy: Moses transmitted the Law, and the function of the prophets of Israel consists in calling the people back to the Law. Christians, on the other hand, have their own notion: the prophets recall the covenant, understood in a purely spiritual way, and through it they announce Jesus Christ. The Islamic conception differs from both of these notions: all the prophets recall the unicity of God and the obligation to worship Him exclusively; those assigned to be messengers (*rusul*) convey a law to their people, a law that will be repealed as each subsequent messenger offers a new one, until the law of Muhammad repeals all the others, being in itself the definitive one.

Islam, having appeared last in history, has no problem recognizing all the previous prophets, just as Christianity recognizes Moses and all the biblical prophets. Islam can have its own reading of the Torah and the Gospel, just as Christianity has its own reading of the Old Testament. In this sense, Christians, in the presence of Islam, resemble Jews in the presence of Christianity. The sole difference—a considerable one—is that the revelation of Christ incorporates the Bible, intact, exactly the way it is transmitted through Judaism, whereas because of the Qurʾan, which God dictated word for word and is thereby law, Islam speaks of a Torah and a Gospel which, as a kind of pre-Qurʾan, do not correspond to the books now in the hands of Jews and Christians. Islam insists that their texts have been altered, for as God revealed to Muhammad in numerous verses: "Some of those who are Jews change words from their context" (4:46). "And with those who say: 'Lo! we are Christians,' We made a covenant, but they forgot a part of that whereof they were admonished" (5:14). This "displacement" of meaning is called *taḥrīf*, and the verb *ḥarrafa* (to change words, to falsify meaning) is employed in order to blame the People of the Book in later verses (2:75; 5:13; 5:41). Such a claim is characteristic of the attitude of Islam.

Still, since the qurʾanic revelation arrived after the other two, Islam has before its eyes an overall view of monotheism, and that is why it is written in the Book (29:46): "Our God and your God is One." In reality this formula possesses, above all, an apologetic value: it is an argument for leading the People of the Book to Islam. The eternal Word of God, having come down to the Prophet Muhammad, cannot contradict itself. Putting aside the diversity of precepts, whatever is contained in the authentic Bible and Gospel is also found in the Qurʾan. All monotheists can and should recognize the purity of their own faith within the Muslim faith. Under these conditions their God and the God of Islam will be found to be the one and only God. The context of the preceding citation clearly illustrates this: "And argue not with the People of the Book unless it be in (a way) that is better [that is to say, according to the commentators, by citing the qurʾanic verses] . . . and say: We believe in that which has been revealed unto us and revealed unto you; our God and your God is One [God] and unto Him we surrender [*muslimūn* = Muslims]."

These are the profound differences separating the three monotheisms. Even so, we have avoided underscoring dogmatic contrasts. We have been content to reflect upon the character of the three revelations, as each appears throughout the texts. One can then wonder whether these revelations are of the same nature, whether the God whom they reveal is the same, or whether each of the monotheisms has its proper God.

Under these conditions how and where are we to find any common ground at all? This is the inquiry we must undertake. It is not easy. But its difficulties must not be concealed or minimized by vague and superficial congruences. The latter risk being merely verbal or subjective; they cannot be recognized by everyone and fade upon closer examination. Let us move forward then, basing our hope on the marvelous saying of Maritain: *Distinguish in order to unite.*

2

MESSENGERS, MESSAGES, AND ADDRESSES

If God exists and is one, it would seem obvious that all those who believe in Him worship the same God. This point of view is certainly very abstract, indeed too abstract. In reality, unless one addressed Him through a purely philosophical cult, one could not pray to God without creating a particular idea of Him for oneself, and it is this very idea that varies throughout the three messages.

The pure historian of religions could easily resolve the problem posed here, insofar as he or she understands "message" to be what a thinker says and communicates to others. In this sense we may speak of a writer's or a poet's message, and of the *inspiration* from which it springs. In this case we can understand that there are successive and diverse approaches to a reality in need of unveiling, that there are different languages and various points of view—visions more or less well understood and more or less complete; inspirations more or less broad and more or less profound. This is the historian's approach, and those who are sensitive to certain human problems and certain religious values can grasp it by reading the Bible, the Gospels, and the Qur'an. Such people will indeed grasp it all the better if they are neither Jews, Christians, or Muslims, since then they will not be troubled by dogmatic divergence, but recognize themselves simply as men and women who aspire to the summits of what they consider the thought of humanity.

GOD SENDS THE PROPHETS

A position of this sort is altogether respectable. An open culture demands this attitude and the scientific work of historians is beholden to its methodology. However this attitude is not totally satisfying, insofar as it neglects faith, and what is more, the specificity of faith. Now, for believers, the notion of a message does not boil down to the figurative meaning that a desacralized world may confer upon it. As Victor Hugo put it, this world seeks a substitute for the sacred in the words of its "Magi." But in the eyes of faith, the messenger really is an envoy of God, and the message really comes from God.

In Exodus (3:10), the LORD says to Moses: "So now I am sending you [*wĕ-ʾešlāḥăkā*] to Pharaoh, for you to bring my people the Israelites out of Egypt." And a little later (3:13–15): "Moses then said to God, 'Look, if I go to the Israelites and say to them, "the God of your ancestors has sent me [*šĕlāḥanî*] to you," and they say to me, "What is his name?" what am I to tell them?' God said to Moses, 'I am he who is [*ʾehyeh ʾăšer ʾehyeh*].' And he said, 'This is what you are to say to the Israelites, "I am has sent me to you."' God further said to Moses, 'You are to tell the Israelites, "[He who is called *I am* . . .] has sent me [*šĕlāḥanî*] to you."'"

The prophets of Israel, who are disciples of Moses, are also envoys. Upon grasping his vision, Isaiah understood the voice of the Lord saying (Isaiah 6:8): "Whom shall I send [*ʾet-mî ʾešlaḥ*?" He responded: "Here I am, send me [*šĕlāḥēnî*]." We can cite another verse: "Jeremiah then came back from Topheth [the place where children were burned in honor of Moloch] where the LORD had sent him to prophesy [*lĕ-hinnābēʾ*; cf. *nabîʾ*, Arabic *nabiʾ*: prophet]" (Jeremiah 19:14). "Son of man, I am sending you [*šôlēaḥ ʾănî ʾôtkā*] to the Israelites" (Ezekiel 2:3). The same God says to Amos (7:15): "Go, and prophesy [*hinnābēʾ*] to my people Israel." Where the verb *šālaḥ*, to send, is not used, one finds the imperative *lēkh* (go!), or *qûm* (up!). See, for example, Jonah (1:2 and 3:2): "Up! Go to Nineveh."

Jesus likewise proclaims that he has been sent. In the Gospel of Luke (4:18–20), he applies the prophecy of Isaiah (61:1) to himself: "The spirit of the LORD is on me. . . . He has sent me [*šĕlāḥanî—apestalken me*] to bring the news to the afflicted. . . ." In the Gospel of John, Jesus says (16:5): "But now I am going to the one who sent me [*pros ton pempsanta me*] . . ." and in his prayer to the Father, he says (17:23): so "that the world will recognize that it was you who sent me [*hoti me apesteilas*]." The Greek employs two different verbs, *apostellein* and *pempein*, where the Hebrew only has one. But the meaning remains one of sending forth.

Islam affirms the same idea. Muhammad is the One Sent by God (*Rasūl Allāh*), according to the testimony of both the Profession of faith, the well-known *shahāda* formula—*lā ilāha illā ʾllāh, wa Muhammad Rasūl Allāh*—and many other verses. In the Qurʾan God recalls having sent different prophets who succeeded one another over the ages: "We sent Noah (of old) unto his people" (7:59; 11:25; 22:23, etc.). "And verily We sent Moses with Our revelations and a clear warrant" (11:96; 40:23;

etc.). "And We verily sent until Thamūd their brother Ṣāliḥ" (27:45). "And We verily sent Noah and Abraham and placed the Prophethood and the Scripture among their seed" (57:26). Finally, He sent Muhammad: "Lo! We have sent you (O Muhammad) with the truth, a bringer of glad tidings and a warner" (2:119; 25:56; 35:24). "We have sent [*arsalnāka*] you (Muhammad) as a messenger unto mankind and God is sufficient as witness" (4:79).

Consequently, lest we neglect the reality which is the existence of religious beliefs, it is indispensable to take these envoys, these missions and these prophetic messages in their proper sense. But then someone will object that no conciliation is possible. If one admits that Moses was in fact sent by God in order to bring a Law that is the sign of an eternal Covenant with the Children of Israel and that all nations will one day recognize—one must be a Jew. If one admits that Christ is the One Sent from the Father, His eternal incarnate Word sent to save humanity through the Law of love given by the God who is Love—then one must be Christian. Finally, if one admits that Muhammad is the One Sent from God, the Seal of the prophets (*khātam al-nabiyyīn*, 33:40) who brings to the world a Law that is definitive because it repeals all others, and that the Qurʾan is the eternal and uncreated Word of God—one must be a Muslim. Yet to rest with the claim that Jews, Christians and Muslims worship the same God through messages that are different—and worse yet opposed on essential points—offers a very unsatisfying solution.

What then can we say? That only one of the three messages is authentic and comprehensive, while the others are false or incomplete? Doubtless this will be the conviction of each believer, who is persuaded of the truth of his own religion. How could it be otherwise for the believer? Furthermore, even if we place ourselves above the debate, either the three discordant messages must all be false, or only one of them is true. Yet this remark, coming at the point when we are just about to lose all hope, will perhaps show us the path to pursue.

In fact, if there is one truth, it can be unique only inasmuch as it is true in itself. Consequently, if one considers that the messages bear textually formulated truths or errors, then they exclude each other, and the messages cannot all have been sent by one and the same God in order to proclaim multiple and different truths. But does there not exist another genuine dimension of the message which we could, without excluding the first, consider apart from it—a message possessing its own truth, a truth of another order, not formulable via opposing dogmas, but rather, open and communicable? The idea merits attention, even though the question is most delicate.

THE MYSTICAL OPENING

We were speaking of people endowed with a certain religious sense who—without adhering to any of the three religions, or while adhering to one of them—can be culturally sensitive to the values of the Bible, the Gospel, and the Qur᾿an, simply because they are human beings. However interesting such an attitude may be, it veers toward a certain dilettantism and is not, at any rate, the one we are researching.

Let us hone in more precisely: Is it possible for a Jew not only to be sensitive to Christian and Muslim values but to appropriate them and come to live by them? Are such people capable of living them at the very heart of their Judaism, within meditation on Jewish values? Is it likewise possible that a Christian have an identical experience with respect to Jewish and Muslim values, and a Muslim with respect to Jewish and Christian values?

To this question we would respond that such an experience is not only possible, it exists; it suffices that all these values be known by all. Nurtured by the message they have received from one of the three messengers, persons in each of the three religions have known and lived amazing experiences. They have spoken about and described them, and their accounts ultimately concur, to the point that one can often place the language which contains them side by side. Such are the mystics.

Certainly all mystics refer to their own texts and their own beliefs—indeed, to their own appointed and formulated dogmas. But far from reflecting pure and simple dogmatic oppositions, what they say about what they have lived within their respective faiths presents profound and often identical affinities. Will someone object that this accord does not imply the accord of the messages among themselves? This is obvious and no one can claim the contrary. But it is no less objectively true that from these messages the mystics have drawn life-giving values that correspond and harmonize with each other. These values are implicitly contained within the messages. So what are we to think? That they are what is essential in the three messages and that dogmatic oppositions are only superficial accidents owing to historical conditions and their transmission?

Admittedly, this is one possible attitude. In many minds, especially these days, this attitude feeds on a hatred of theological speculation, hatred of any doctrinal formulation, and even in certain cases, hatred of the ancient ideal of a truth in itself—one that is sharp, immutable, the declared fruit of atemporal and universal reason, as was once sought in sacred texts.

But such is not the attitude of believers in each religion, and if adopted, one would find oneself in a situation analogous to the one we have already exposed: one risks destroying the integral nature of the message properly speaking; for then the messengers would not transmit solely the word of the God who sent them. Otherwise there would be agreement at all levels on what they transmit to people. One would in turn have texts clothed with an exterior meaning due to circumstances of time and place and which as such reveal nothing of the divine message, even though they present themselves as revealed. But in the end, beyond the evident meaning of these texts, one would discover a concealed meaning, everywhere identical, which dogmatic formulas cannot adequately express, a meaning constituted by values one must live out and not just think about. That is where the unique message would be found. There the messengers would meet. But is this how the messages are received by believers?

CHARACTER OF THE BIBLICAL AND GOSPEL MESSAGES

In fact, if one considers the Bible, it is clear that it reflects historical events that had no need to be revealed. The lived tradition and experience of a people sufficed to explain everything. But in reporting these events, the biblical texts interpreted them by giving them religious meaning. In this way the political hopes of the Jewish nation became messianic hopes, and upheld hope in God. The prophets announced the end of servitude and the victory of the Children of Israel. God revealed to Isaiah (44:26): it is "I . . . who confirm the word of my servant and make the plans of my envoys succeed; who say to Jerusalem, 'You will be inhabited,' and to the towns of Judah, 'You will be rebuilt. . . .'" We see by this text that thanks to the guarantee of God, the Lord's messengers enjoy a certain autonomy; they are men engaged in the affairs of this world. The light they receive is colored by their human preoccupations, but it simultaneously elevates and turns them toward transcendent realities and values. There is a kind of concurrence, a collaboration between God and His messengers.

We find an analogous state of affairs, although less marked, in the Gospels. It is very clear, for example, when Jesus reproaches the towns where he had accomplished the greatest miracles for not having repented (Matthew 11:20–24; Luke 10:13–15): "Alas for you Chorazin! Alas for you, Bethsaida! For if the miracles done in you had been done in Tyre and Sidon, they would have repented long ago. . . . And as for you, Capernaum, did you want to be raised high as Heaven? You shall be flung down to hell." This is an episode in the life of Jesus. But the threat he makes against the cities is only an accessory circumstance to the essential message which consists in teaching how great an evil is pride and how repentance is good.

Without multiplying examples, it is clear that the Bible and the Gospels lend themselves to discriminating between a chance meaning that is superficial and does not constitute the message itself, and a real meaning both profound and spiritual. The fundamental reason for this is that while the prophets of Israel relate what God says, they are still the ones who speak: "The words of Jeremiah . . . the word of the LORD came to him. . . . The word of the LORD came to me, saying . . ." (Jeremiah 1:1–4). One finds the same thing exactly in Ezekiel 6:1. Amos (1:1 and 3) is content to say: "Words of Amos. . . . The LORD says this. . . ." So too Obadiah (1:1): "Vision of Obadiah: about Edom. The Lord GOD says this. . . ." The prophet Jonah (1:1) begins with the words: "The word of the LORD was addressed to Jonah" (*ʾel-yônâh*); the same to Micah (*ʾel-mîkâ*), to Zephaniah (*ʾel-ṣĕpanyâ*), and to Zechariah (*ʾel-zĕkaryâ*). The announcement of the prophecy of Haggai is still more characteristic (1:1): "[T]he word of the LORD was addressed through [literally, by the hand or intermediary, *bĕ-yad*] the prophet Haggai to Zerubbabel" (*ʾel-zĕrubbābel*). The idea that the prophet is an intermediary between God and man emerges clearly here. It is likewise found at the beginning of the book of Malachi (1:1): "A message. The word of the LORD to Israel through [*bĕ-yad*] Malachi." As for the texts of the Gospels, they are the work of evangelists, who report the words of Christ in the course of their narration.

CHARACTER OF THE QURʾANIC MESSAGE

But matters are entirely different for the Qurʾan, which is the very Word of God, sent down to Muhammad and dictated literally by the angel Gabriel. According to the Arabic of the Qurʾan "to reveal," *anzalla* or *nazzala*, means "to make come down." Even more precisely, the Qurʾan says it comes down from "next to God" (*min ʿindiʾllāh*). God speaks directly, either using the royal "we" or addressing the hearer in the third person singular. But the prophet himself never reports what He says.

The revelation falls from on high like a bolt of lightning; this image is characteristically qurʾanic; in fact, it is written concerning infidels (2:19): "Or like a rainstorm from the sky, wherein is darkness, thunder and the flash of lightning. They thrust their fingers in their ears by reason of the thunderclaps, for fear of death." And one can read in the commentary of Jalālayn: "Thus, when God makes the Qurʾan come down where he calls unbelief to mind, comparing it to darkness, along with the threat which weighs upon it and is compared to thunder, as well as to the ringing demonstrations that are compared to lightning, these infidels plug their ears so as not to understand. So the threats and demonstrations do not reach them, for they might then incline toward the true faith and abandon their (false) religion, which in their eyes would be a death." These men, deaf to the Word of God, pursue their lives and their ancestral habits while following the example of their fathers who preceded them in history. They evade the promises and threats that come from on high, grounded within in the transcendence of God rather than in the immanence of beliefs and customs transmitted from generation to generation.

The Qurʾan is the only revealed Scripture where God speaks like this. The Prophet need only preach word-for-word what has been dictated to him; he has only to repeat without adding anything of his own; his is but to pass on (*tablīgh*) the message just as he received it. Even on this subject God gives precise instructions to the Prophet: "And hasten not (O Muhammad) with the Qurʾan before its revelation has been perfected unto you" (20:114). The commentator Qurṭubī explains this verse by saying that God teaches the Prophet how he must learn the Qurʾan. In fact, according to Ibn ʿAbbās, an important transmitter of *ḥadīth*s, Muhammad "got ahead of Gabriel, meaning that he began to recite a verse before the Angel had finished revealing it to him, out of a desire to memorize it, out of consideration for the Qurʾan and for fear of forgetting it. God forbids him from proceeding in this way by revealing this warning." Again, one can cite (75:16–17): "Stir not your tongue herewith to hasten it [i.e., the Qurʾan]. Lo! upon Us (rests) the putting together thereof [in your heart, add the commentators] and the reading thereof."

As a result, the One Sent by God is completely supplanted in the wake of the message he bears and which must be received to the letter. When certain *ḥadīth*s relate the circumstances in which a particular verse has been revealed, they only register a coincidence; although such events, while they remain outside the revelation itself, can certainly help us understand the Word that came down at the moment they occurred. Yet those events do not enter into the fabric of the message itself. Without them the content, impact, and formulation of the message would remain the same. Moreover, God never specifies the circumstances of revelation. We saw this in the text where God recalls the aid given to believers: commentators say that this reminder concerns the battle of Badr, but nowhere does the Qurʾan speak overtly of this battle. In the Bible, on the other hand, it is in the very course of a battle, or in reporting it, that the sacred writer raises his thought toward the help the LORD brings to His people. Moreover the Qurʾan alludes to an event in the life of the Prophet in order to evoke reflection about him later, so that the marks of divine action in him may be made visible to the eyes of believers who have participated in that event.

One finds a very clear example of this procedure at the beginning of sūrah 59 (verse 2). This text is very difficult to translate, however, so one is forced to choose among numerous interpretations. Here is how it can be rendered: "He it is Who has caused those of the People of the Book who disbelieved to go forth from their homes unto the first exile [the first gathering, *li-awwal al-ḥashr*]. You deemed not that they would go forth, while they deemed that their strongholds would protect them from God. But God reached them from a place whereof they reckoned not, and cast terror in their hearts so that they ruined their houses with their own hands and the hands of the believers. So learn a lesson, O all who have eyes!" Most commentators understand the word *ḥashr* to mean a gathering in anticipation of a departure for some country or for the army; this meaning is confirmed by the great dictionary of Ibn Manẓūr (d. 711/1311) entitled *Lisān al ʿArab*, which actually cites this verse. Therefore one can translate this term either as exile, or as mobilization. But since the word *ḥashr* designates in particular the ingathering of humanity on the Day of Judgment, one must consider whether it here constitutes the final gathering. This possibility led R. Blachère to translate *li-awwal al-ḥashr* as "in a prelude to their ingathering (for the last Judgment)." M. Hamidullah chose another exegesis and translated the phrase as "from the first mobilization"; in fact one finds this explanation in the commentator Fakhr al-Dīn al-Rāzī: "The sense is that God makes them leave their homes when, for the first time, He reassembles them for the battle that they had had to lead, for it is the first battle that the one sent from God wages against them." But the sense of exile, expulsion, evacuation (*jalāʾ*) is the one most frequently retained.

We see then the kind of difficulty one encounters when attempting to achieve an exact comprehension of the Qurʾan. In any case, to which event does God allude in this verse? Note what Rāzī, among others, writes on this subject: "The Banūʾl-Naḍīr [a Jewish tribe of Medina] had made peace with the One Sent from God in the sense that they were neither against him, nor for him. Now, when the battle of Badr had taken place [a Muslim victory], they said: 'This man is the prophet that the Torah describes with the attributes of victory.' But when the Muslims had routed them in the battle of Uḥud [Ohod], they had doubts and they broke their agreements. Kaʿba b. al-Ashrah [of the clan of Banūʾl-Naḍīr on his mother's side] set out toward Mecca at the head of forty knights; they made, under an oath outside of the Kaʿba, an alliance with Abû Sufyân [chief of the Qurayshite clan of the ʿAbd Shams, the most ferocious adversary of Muhammad, ancestor of the Umayyad caliphs]. Then the One Sent by God gave an order to Muhammad b. Maslama al-Anṣārī, who killed Kaʿb through cunning. . . . Then the Prophet said to the Banūʾl-Naḍīr: 'Leave Medina!' They responded: 'We would rather die!' And they held a meeting among themselves for the purpose of making war. It is said that they asked the One Sent by God for a delay of ten days in order to prepare themselves to depart. ʿAbd Allah b. Ubayy [a powerful leader of Yathrib, before the hijra, who had done homage to Muhammad, but who plotted against him on this occasion] made them say that they would not leave the fortress: 'If the Muslims attack you, we will be with you, we will not abandon you. And if you go out, we will go with you.' So they retrenched and the Prophet laid siege against them for twenty-one days. Then, when God had cast terror into their hearts, they despaired of the victory of the hypocrites [Ibn Ubayy and his partisans] and they sued for peace. The Prophet refused them, unless they agreed to go into exile."

This example is typical. Concrete historical development is entirely neglected in the qurʾanic text, which only preserves an allusion to the facts known about Muhammad and his companions, later transmitted by the tradition. God uses them in order to provide a lesson, or more precisely, to see to it that believers themselves draw out the lesson from the "reminder" that he makes to them, through a kind of divine version of the events. Curiously, the traditions that commentators use to elaborate what these verses express so concisely, are accounts that report the facts and human exploits without ever mingling God in the unfolding of their enterprises: they show people acting as though God did not exist, as though they led and accomplished their affairs by themselves. The accounts only name God at the end, at the moment one falls back on the qurʾanic citation to be explained and that one sought to reinforce.

So it is always God who speaks, God who teaches; human beings are only recipients; they do not find their God within the lived experience of things in this world. Creation is certainly full of signs (*āyāt*). But they are discerned only after God has revealed their existence and significance. Thus one can read, among many passages: "Therewith He causes crops to grow for you, and the olive and the date-palm and grapes and all kinds of fruit. Lo! herein is indeed a portent [or sign] for people who reflect" (16:11). Again we can feel the stark difference in tone that distinguishes the qurʾanic message from the biblical message, and even more from the Gospel message.

Under these conditions, within the Qurʾan there is no room at all for any thought of separating those exterior elements relating to historical, political, social, and hence contingent situations, from some deeper essential meaning that would correspond to an interior word addressed by God to his messenger, a word constituting God's only real message.

Actually, the distinction between an apparent or exoteric sense (*ẓāhir*) and a hidden or esoteric sense (*bāṭin*) belongs to the repertoire of Islamic thinkers, whether speculative theologians or mystics. But this does not correspond to the idea of the contingent and the essential. It arises above all in relation to the Law. The commandments of God suppose on the part of human beings an obedience relative to the different levels of their being: people have bodies whose members (*jawāriḥ*) must perform certain actions and avoid others; thus for example the different postures in canonical prayer (*ṣalāt*), the prohibition of certain foods, or again, abstinence during the fast of Ramadan. There are also words that the tongue (*lisān*) has to pronounce; but a human being also has a heart (*qalb*) and obedience of heart is likewise required, if not more so. The formulation of the Law that addresses the obedience of the body reiterates an appeal to a more intimate adhesion, which addresses obedience of heart. So then, beneath the literal meaning lies the outline of a spiritual sense that results in an interiorization of the Law. But this *ẓāhir* and this *bāṭin* articulate each other, and neither goes without the other. Interior worship through spiritual values does not suppress exterior worship, for that would risk becoming an anarchic subjectivism that is incompatible with the notion of obedience. Obedience to the Law through well-defined exterior observances is the guarantor of obedience of heart. Therefore, the qurʾanic revelation, in both its literal and spiritual meanings, is equally the word of God, a divine commandment, and a guide willed for human beings by their all-powerful Lord. One would depart from Islam if one disassociated these two aspects, above all if only the second, spiritual, one were retained. Certain mystic extremists who have committed this error have been considered infidels.

For all these reasons, the qurʾanic message is absolutely exclusive. It admits no compromise and if it calls the People of the Book to conciliation, it does so by inviting them to recognize the truth of Islam purely and simply. Besides, since the Qurʾan comes after the other revealed Scriptures, it is in a good position to criticize Judaism and Christianity, without even considering the fact that it abolishes their Law. Christ attacked the scribes and Pharisees, but he did not teach that the Bible had been altered. He identified with the Jewish tradition, which he interpreted without destroying. If the Jews attacked him, or attacked his doctrine, he countered from within the tradition and denounced only the clash between their words and their deeds. On the other hand, it goes without saying that the Gospels could not launch a war against Islam. As for the Bible, it could not possibly contain controversies against Christianity or Islam. Conversely, the Qurʾan is a polemical revelation: it vigorously and continuously calls to account the People of the Book, Jews and Christians. God asks them to return to the faith of Abraham, whom the authentic Torah, the authentic Gospel (*injīl*) and the Qurʾan all call to mind. If there are three messengers, there is only one message, or at least three messages that concur.

A polemical text evokes polemical responses. Jews and Christians have not failed to reply. Muslims have had to defend themselves and the controversy has been venomous. It is altogether pointless to engage one another today in this way. We will limit ourselves to noting that the openness of Islam is only apparent. If Islam recommends obedience to the Torah, it is not to the book the Jews have in their hands, for the latter has been altered; if it praises the Gospel, it does not speak of the four Gospels that Christians read, for they are human works. If it recognizes all the prophets, it is after having Islamized them (and it does not speak of the prophets of Israel—Isaiah, Ezekiel, Jeremiah and the others—

though it does treat Jonah as a special case). The position of Islam is unassailable, but on one and only one condition, which is major: to confess that the Qurʾan is the eternal and uncreated Word of God, revealed word for word to the prophet Muhammad. Now this is precisely what Jews and Christians refuse to admit, for the simple reason that Jews do not recognize themselves in the Judaism of the qurʾanic Moses, just as Christians do not recognize themselves in the Christianity of the qurʾanic Christ. This is a fact. That much said, we will end the discussion there.

Thus it is clear that if one can extract a spiritual and essential message from the sacred books of Jews and Christians, a message that they hold or nearly hold in common, the Qurʾan refuses any such strategy. Still, given these conditions, how is one to explain the profound agreement that unites Muslim mystics with those of the other two religions? Must we admit—along with numerous doctors of Islam, who are attached above all to the Law and moved by a spirit that is exclusively legalistic—that the Sufis are suspect, that we can doubt the purity of their Muslim faith, and that they have introduced elements originally alien to Islam into their thoughts and into their practices? Here we have come up against a new and very grave difficulty. We will be tempted to dismiss it by showing that the more illustrious representatives of *taṣawwuf* (Sufiism) have, above all else, meditated on the texts of the Qurʾan and reflected on certain key terms. Nonetheless, we must not forget that there is always some hostility to the mystical in Islam, whether latent or declared, and that this attitude remains very widespread in our day.

THE ADDRESSEES OF THE MESSAGES

There is no question that Jewish, Christian, and Muslim mystics exist and that their testimonies do not exclude one another—far from it, although they begin with an effort to integrate into their life three different and often opposed messages. This fact sets our task before us: to discover what these messages were *for them.* Until now we have only considered the one God who sent His Messengers, the Messengers themselves, and their messages. We must now focus on those to whom the Messengers were sent and to whom the message was addressed. We will do this first more generally, and then from the particular perspective of the mystics.

MESSAGE AGAINST IDOLATRY

From a general viewpoint, it is easy to see that the Torah and the Qur᾽an first address people who live in a milieu of polytheistic idolatries. Thus, the affirmation of the unicity and the immateriality of God becomes all-important. As disciples of Moses, the prophets of Israel highlight this. One reads in Isaiah 45:5: "I am the LORD, and there is no other, there is no other God except me [*zûlâthî*]," which corresponds exactly to the qur᾽anic revelation (16:2; 20:14): "There is no God save me [*illā anā*]." We further note Isaiah 43:11: "I, I am the LORD, and there is no other Saviour but me." And Hosea 13:4: "you knew no god but me [*zûlâthî*], since you had no one else [*biltī*] to save you." The savior, in the Bible, is first of all the God who saves His people from their enemies and liberates them from captivity. The idols of metal are incapable of this. There is an analogous idea in the Qur᾽an, when for example God speaks to Noah (23:28–29): "And when you are on board the ship, you and whoever is with you, then say: Praise be to God Who has saved us [*najjānā*] from the wrongdoing folk! And say: My Lord! Cause me to land at a blessed landing place, for You are best of all who bring to land." So too God reminds the Jews what He has done for them, with these words (7:141): "And (remember) when We did deliver [*idh anjawnākum*] you from Pharaoh's folk. . . ."

The overall idea of divine help, alone efficacious, is just as qur᾽anic as biblical. In the Qur᾽an God gives the word of the prophet Shuᶜeyb (11:88) by way of example: "My welfare is only in God. In Him I trust and unto Him I turn (repentant)." Finally, one can quote in this sense the verse (59:23): "He is God, than whom there is no other God, the Sovereign Lord, the Holy One, Peace [*Salām*]. . . ." The meaning of the divine name of *Salām* has indeed been discussed. Qurṭubā, in his commentary, distinguishes three meanings. First, God is "safe" (*Salīm*), that is to say, exempt (*barī᾽*) from all imperfection. Second, He greets His followers in Paradise, according to what is written (26:57): "The word from a Merciful Lord (for them) is: Peace!" Third, God preserves his servants from all evil. Only the last meaning corresponds to the biblical notion of Savior: it makes the name of *Salām* an attribute of action (*ṣifat al-fiᶜl*), whereas the first makes of it an attribute of essence (*ṣifat al-dhāt*). Through His acts God gives peace, security and deliverance. Conversely, the idols are incapable of offering the slightest help.

The Bible and the Qur᾽an set about convincing their worshipers of the powerlessness of these false gods. Jeremiah grills them (2:28): "Where are your gods you made for yourself? Let them get up if they can save you when trouble comes!" (cf. Jeremiah 11:12). And the Qur'an reports that Abraham said to his father and his people (26:70f): "What do you worship? They replied: We worship idols, and are ever devoted unto them. He said: Do they hear you when you cry? Or do they benefit or harm you?" And one reads a few verses later (26:92–93): "And it will be said unto them: Where is (all) that you used to worship instead of God? Can they [these idols] help you or help themselves?" The same idea is expressed in (29:17): "You serve instead of God [*min dūni'llāh*] only idols of wood or stone, and you only invent a lie. Lo! those whom you serve instead of God own no provision for you." This makes one think of Jeremiah, who denounces "those who say to a piece of wood, 'You are my father,' and to a stone, 'You gave birth to me'" (2:27). And along with him, Isaiah writes of the idolater with irony (44:14–17): "He has cut down cedars. . . . Once it is suitable to burn, he takes some of it to warm himself; having kindled it, he bakes bread. But he also makes a god and worships it; he makes an idol from it and bows down before it. Half of it he burns on the fire, over this half he roasts meat, eats it and is replete; at the same time he warms himself and says, 'Ah, how warm I am, watching the flames!'"

In the biblical perspective, the one God affirms His existence and His power by elevating Himself on the predicted ruin of the cult of idols, on the overthrow of their altars: " . . . and the LORD alone will be exalted, on that day; when the idols all disappear . . . (Isaiah 2:17–18). The destruction of false gods and their altars is linked to the chastisement of idolatrous peoples; and the children of Israel fall under this law of annihilation when they turn away from the true God. Only through the worship of the one Lord can a particular people, and human beings generally, live and subsist: "Announce it to the nations, proclaim it: . . . 'Babylon is captured, Bel [a current name of Marduk, or Merodoch] disgraced, Marduk shattered. (Her idols are disgraced, her obscenities shattered)'" (Jeremiah 50:2). "For it is a country of idols [of suspect images: *pĕsilîm*], and they are mad about those bogeys of theirs!" (*ibid.*, 50:38). "At this everyone stands stupefied, uncomprehending, every goldsmith blushes for his idols; his castings are but delusion, with no breath in them. They are futile, a laughable production, when the time comes for them to be punished, they will vanish" (*ibid.*, 51:17–18). One could multiply quotations of this sort.

The Qur'an explains the same idea in its own way (26:94–95):

"Then they will be hurled therein [into hell, those who are lost in polytheism], they and the seducers [*al-ghāwūn*] and the hosts of Iblîs, together." The commentators generally understand the *al-ghāwūn* to be the divinities of the idolaters (*al-āliha*); they wonder why these statues would be cast into hell; the response, according to Rāzī, is that they will be fuel to sustain the fire.

In these two messages then, the affirmation of one God stands out against the denial of the existence of false gods. This is emphasized in both Hebrew and Arabic through the use of particles of exception: *zûlâth* and *illā*; *biltī* and *min dūnī*. L. Massignon said that God is the supreme exception. It is true that the biblical revelation begins with the one Savior and moves toward the one God. For God is first the all-powerful One who delivered His people from Egyptian slavery, then from exile, who has led them throughout their history and sustained them in their battles; therefore, He is the creator of humanity and of the whole universe: "That day, a man will look to his Creator and his eyes will turn to the Holy One of Israel" (Isaiah 17:7). "The LORD is the everlasting God, he created the remotest parts of the earth. He does not grow tired or weary, his understanding is beyond fathoming. He gives strength to the weary, he strengthens the powerless" (*ibid.*, 40:28–29).

In the qurʾanic message, on the other hand, it is the creator God who comes before all else. According to Muslim tradition, the first verses that descended on the Prophet are 96:1 and following: "Recite: In the name of your Lord who creates, creates man from a clot. . . ." As Creator, God is all-powerful, king and master of all creatures, and therefore there is no help, security, and peace except in Him.

But in both cases, biblical and qurʾanic, the result is the same. One reads in Islamic scripture a verse (2:255) that naturally evokes the one from Isaiah quoted earlier: "God! There is no God save Him, the Alive, the Eternal. Neither slumber [*sina*] nor sleep [*nawm*] overtakes Him. Unto Him belongs whatsoever is in the heavens and whatsoever is in the earth." God does not tire and has no need of rest: "Do they not see how God produces creation, then reproduces it? Lo! for God that is easy. . . . None of you can escape (from Him) in the earth or in the sky, and beside God there is for you no friend nor helper." God does not cease to create and actively sustains this creation at every moment.

Muslim thinkers, taking Genesis 2:2 literally, have criticized the idea of God resting on the seventh day. It is nonetheless clear that the verse does not mean that God no longer acts once creation is accomplished. God finished creating what He wanted to create and His work ends with humanity; but this work does not subsist by itself, and the Creator continues to work in order to conserve it in being and above all to watch over His creatures. That is why one can read in Psalm 121:3–4: "May he save your foot from stumbling; may he, your guardian, not fall asleep! You see—he neither sleeps [*lōʾ yānûm*] nor slumbers [*wĕ-lōʾ yîšōn*], the guardian of Israel." The two verbs *nwm* (slumber) and *yšn* (sleep) of the Hebrew correspond exactly to the two Arabic nouns of the qurʾanic verse: *nawn* (slumber) and *sina*, from the root *w s n* (Hebrew *yšn*). Consequently, on this point the two messages are in essential agreement.

CHRISTIAN MESSAGE TO JEWS

In contrast, the message of Christ is addressed to the Jews and it is preached in a monotheistic milieu. Therefore the existence of one God and of one savior does not have to be affirmed against a background where idols are negated. This is why Christianity announces the unicity of God in a non-polemical fashion. Its teaching focuses on this requires; it does not simply proclaim an exterior profession of faith and worship that excludes all pagan ritual. Rather it proclaims an interior disposition corresponding to such a profession. For persons who are fragmented by all that attracts them—and so by a multiplicity contrary to the unity of God—cannot truly interiorize belief in a single lord and savior. Monotheism truly lived out implies a concentration of heart; it is necessary to be unified oneself in order really to worship the One. It is necessary therefore to struggle against such fragmentation, given the innumerable enticements of the world.

The "world" that Saint Paul attacks replaces the idolatrous "nations" of the Old Testament. "Now, the Spirit we have received is not the spirit of the world but God's own Spirit, so that we may understand the lavish gifts God has given us" (1 Corinthians 2:12). "Do you not see how God has shown up human wisdom [or the wisdom of the world] as folly?" (*ibid.* 1:20). "[I]t is the world's kind of distress that ends in death" (2 Corinthians 7:10). "Because this world as we know it is passing away" (1 Corinthians 7:31).

Saint John likewise denounces the deceptions of the world and, above all, he reports the words of Christ to his apostles (14:27): "Peace I bequeath to you, my own peace I give you, a peace which the world cannot give, this is my gift to you;" and later, in commending his disciples to the Father, Jesus says (17:11 and 14): "I am no longer in the world, but they are in the world. . . . [T]hey belong to the world no more than I belong to the world" (cf. 15:18–20).

Now this world has its idols, most especially money. "No one can be the slave of two masters: he will either hate the first and love the second, or be attached to the first and despise the second. You cannot be the slave both of God and of money [Mammon]" (Matthew 6:24). For "the lure of riches choke the word and so it produces nothing" (*ibid.* 13:22). Christ curses riches. What about the rich? These are the ones who love the world: "Do not love the world or what is in the world . . . because everything there is in the world—disordered bodily desires, disordered desires of the eyes, pride in possession—is not from the Father but is from the world" (1 John 2:15–16). Wealth in itself is not cursed: "It is a gift of God," according to the biblical conception, "to those who obey His voice" (cf. Deuteronomy 28:1–14); moreover, it allows the poor to benefit. What is evil is attachment to wealth, the idolatry of wealth.

Without denying the originality of Christ's teaching when placed within the body of Christian doctrine, one must remember that the Old Testament proclaims identical values. Wealth turns people away from God. Thus, it is written in Deuteronomy (8:11 ff.): "Be careful not to forget the LORD your God. . . . When you have eaten all you want . . . when you have seen your flocks and herds increase, your silver and gold abound and all your possessions grow great, do not become proud of heart. Do not then forget the LORD your God who brought you out of Egypt. . . ." The prophet Hosea takes up the same idea (13:6): "I pastured them, and they were satisfied; once satisfied, their hearts grew proud, and therefore they forgot me."

Anxiety about the goods of this world is as dangerous as their possession: "[W]hen they gash themselves over the grain and new wine, they are still rebelling against me" (Hosea 7:14). One can hardly help thinking of the words of Christ: "Do not store up treasures for yourselves on earth, where moth and woodworm destroy them. . . . But store up treasures for yourselves in heaven. . . . So do not worry; do not say, 'What are we to eat? What are we to drink? What are we to wear?' It is the gentiles who set their hearts on all these things. Your heavenly Father knows you need them all. Set your hearts on his kingdom first, and on God's saving justice, and all these other things will be given you as well" (Matthew 6:19–20 and 31–33). One recalls what Jesus said to Martha (Luke 10:41–42): "[Y]ou worry and fret about so many things, and yet few are needed, indeed only one. . . ."

CONVERGENCE WITH THE QURʾAN

On this point, the convergence between the Bible and the Gospel extends to the Qurʾan. Islamic revelation brands polytheism with the name of *shirk*, which means association: in its belief and worship, it forbids associating God with that which is not God. Now if this condemnation first targets the idols, it has a much greater range: it strikes anyone who turns from God and becomes attached exclusively to the goods of here-below, or similarly, those who are interested in and relate everything only to themselves. The Qurʾan condemns those who "choose Satan for a patron instead of God" (4:119; 7:30). Now, Satan is precisely the demon who detaches humanity from God and attaches it to the world and its works. Thus it is written concerning the Qurayshi, enemies of the Prophet (8:48): "And when Satan made their deeds seem fair [or adorned] to them and said: No one of mankind can conquer you this day. . . ."

It is true that the verb *zayyana* (adorn, decorate, embellish) often has God as its subject in the same context: for example (27:4): "Lo! as for those who believe not in the Hereafter, We have made their works fair-seeming unto them so that they are all astray." Yet the same verb also has idols as its subject: "It is thus that to the eyes of many associators [polytheists], what they associate [the false gods] have adorned the death of children."

One touches here on a theological problem: that of the creation of human acts by God. It is certain that Satan can act only when the Lord permits. As for false gods, it is self-evident that they do not act at all. According to most Muslim thinkers, the first efficient cause of all these errors could only be the Creator, who is the only true agent. But we will leave aside these speculations, even though they are grafted onto the qurʾanic text.

Moreover in several verses the verb in question is employed in the impersonal passive: *zuyyina*: an adornment has been made, it has been adorned. Thus one reads (2:212): "Beautified is the life of the world for those who disbelieve," or again, (3:14): "Beautified for mankind is love of the joys (that come) from women and offspring, and stored-up heaps of gold and silver, and horses branded (with their mark), and cattle and land. That is comfort of the life of the world. God! With Him is a more excellent abode" (*ḥusn al-maʿād*). Consequently the Qurʾan, in the name of divine unicity, denounces fetishistic attachments to that which is not God.

The Bible and the Gospels warn the rich who place their trust in material resources. It is written in Proverbs (10:15): "The wealth of the rich [*ʿāšîr*] is their stronghold," and in the Psalms (52:9): "So much for someone who would not place his reliance in God, but relied on his own great wealth, and made himself strong by crime." The Qurʾan recognizes that fortune is a gift of God: " . . . He it is Who enriches and contents" (53:48). Goods so acquired should serve to help the poor and the suffering. But it is foolish for people to think of themselves as rich; it is said of Abū Lahab, one of the uncles of Muhammad who was a bitter enemy of Islam: "His wealth and gains will not exempt him. He will be plunged in flaming fire" (111:2–3).

But above all it is written (3:181): "Verily God heard the saying of those who said: 'God, forsooth, is poor, and we are rich [*aghniyāʾ*, plural of *ghanī*]! . . . We shall say: Taste ye the punishment of burning!'" Yet when one discovers that the root *GhNY* in its first form *ghaniya* and in its tenth *istaghanā* means "to be rich enough to be able to do without" or "not to have need of," the verse acquires a fresh significance: God is the only one who can do without everything that is not God. But as creatures, humans beings need the Creator (*Khāliq*) who grants that they exist and who, being Himself the One who is Subsistent of himself (*Qayyūm*, 2:255; 3:2; 20:111), grants them existence and provides for all their needs (*Rāziq*).

It is thus an illusion for people to believe that they can do without God: essentially a person is poor, whatever one's ephemeral wealth may be, for people always have need of the *Khāliq* and of the *Rāziq*. In the same spirit as Deuteronomy, the Qurʾan denounces, in a lapidary formula, the presumptuousness of the rich: "Nay, but verily man is rebellious that he thinks himself independent [rich enough to be self-sufficient]!" (96:6–7). In contrast, "God is Independent of (all) creatures"[1] (3:97), which is quite unlike His creatures: "O mankind! You are the poor in your relation to God. And God! He is the Absolute, the Owner of Praise." (35:15). God does not even need the faithful: "If you are thankless [or act unfaithfully] yet God is Independent of you" (39:7). God does not need people. God has created through a decree of pure will (*mashīʾa*). Even though it is written (51:56): "I created the jinn and humankind only that they might worship Me," God has no traffic with their adoration. The worship of God is not the *raison d'être* of creation; it is the *raison d'être* of creatures.

So why has God created? Muslim theologians and philosophers will focus on this question: out of pure disinterested love, or goodness, say the mystics; out of pure liberality (*jūd*), says Avicenna; because He willed it, respond most of the doctors of Islam. But that is a problem the message implicitly poses without explicitly treating it. We will leave it aside for now, therefore. We simply note that despite the differences in tone deriving from their religious contexts, the three messages here propose to believers an analogous if not identical subject of meditation.

In fact, in the prophesy of Isaiah (43:7), God announces that He will gather His people from the east and the west, "everyone who bears my name, whom I have created for my glory, whom I have formed, whom I have made." Dhorme explains in a footnote that "the people of Israel were created to manifest the glory of the LORD and that is their *raison d'être*." One can interpret this text just like the corresponding qur'anic verse: God does not need to manifest His glory, and this manifestation is not the *raison d'être* of His creation; it is the *raison d'être* of His creatures. Likewise, God does not need sacrifices, although the Law commands them. The worship of God is a good for humanity not for God. "'What are your endless sacrifices to me?' says the LORD" (Isaiah 1:11). "What do I care about incense imported from Sheba, or fragrant cane from a distant country?" (Jeremiah 6:20). "If I am hungry I shall not tell you, since the world and all it holds is mine" (Psalm 50:12). This means, according to Dhorme, that "God does not need men." To the letter, these texts strongly resemble those of the Qur'an. The differences will be more apparent to theologians than to contemplatives.

DOES GOD NEED HUMAN BEINGS?

As for Christianity, while it insists upon the abomination of the cult of mammon and teaches that true riches are found in the kingdom of God, it does not seem to go so far as to conceive of a God who, while the source of all goods, would be so "rich" in Himself that He would not need human beings. But it is necessary to know what we understand as need. Without any doubt, the monotheistic conception presumes, in all three messages, that God is perfectly independent of all that is not God and that He gains nothing by creating the universe, angels, or human beings.

But then one encounters the same question again: under these metaphysical conditions, why did God create? Why does God take an interest in creatures? And in particular, why does God take an interest in humanity? What value does God's work have in His eyes? The human being is nothingness before the divine Being. But then why do they exist? Why does God speak to them, why does God guide them to Himself? The absence of need is not an absence of interest nor is God disinterested in creatures simply because God cannot derive any profit from them. If the blood of oxen and of goats does not serve God at all, He nonetheless awaits a response from human beings: "Let thanksgiving be your sacrifice to God" (Psalm 50:14).

Here one should recall the words of the scribe to Jesus (Mark 12:32–34): "Well spoken, Master; what you have said is true, that *he is one and there is no other* [cf. Deuteronomy 4:35 and 6:4–5). *To love him with all your heart, with all your understanding and strength*, and to *love your neighbor as yourself*, this is far more important than any burnt offering or sacrifice." Then Jesus says to him: "You are not far from the kingdom of God." And in his first epistle (2:5), Saint Peter speaks of a "holy priesthood" in a "spiritual house [or temple]" destined to "offer spiritual sacrifices made acceptable to God through Jesus Christ." Does God need spiritual sacrifices? No more than any others. But they are acceptable (*euprosdektous*), literally: they are accepted with kindness. These sacrifices are those of the heart. There are then useless offerings which are nonetheless pleasing to God, received and accepted by Him.

The same idea recurs in the Bible. Thus Samuel says: "Is the LORD pleased [*ha-ḥēpeṣ la-YHWH*] by burnt offerings and sacrifices or by obedience to the LORD's voice?" (1 Samuel 15:22). Such is the sense of the words of David at the end of the first book of Chronicles (29:16–18): "LORD our God, all this wealth, which we have provided to build a house for your holy name, has come from you and all belongs to you. Knowing, my God, how you examine our motives and how you delight [*tirṣeh*, from *rāṣâ*] in integrity, with integrity of motive I have willingly given all this. . . ." One finds the same verb *rāṣâ* in a context that leaves no doubt about its meaning, in the prophecy of Isaiah (42:1): "Here is my servant whom I uphold, my chosen one in whom my soul delights [*rāṣtâ napšî*]."

The presence of this verb permits us to align the Qur'an with this set of texts. In fact, the Arabic verb *raḍiya*—from the same semitic origin as *rāṣâ*, with the meaning of being satisfied with someone or something, of accepting or taking pleasure in—is frequently employed in the Book of Islam. So too the substantives from the same root, *riḍā* and *riḍwān*, which signify pleasure, satisfaction, contentment in. . . . So it is said

(48:18): "God was well pleased with the believers when they swore allegiance unto you beneath the tree." This happened at Ḥudaybiyya, when Muhammad had without success sent a series of messengers to Mecca to gain permission to make the pilgrimage; these Companions swore their fidelity to him, when he was sitting beneath a tree. (We will return to the importance accorded in the meditation of the Muslim mystics to those verses which contain this verb and these nouns.)

In Islam, sacrifices play a role even more reduced than in biblical Judaism. Aside from the immolation of a victim following a vow, one can only cite the ritual of the feast of sacrifice (*ʿid al-aḍḥā*) or the Great Feast (*al-ʿīd al-kabīr*), which takes place on the tenth day of the month of pilgrimage. This is an obligatory and traditional practice (*sunna*) for every Muslim. But since the Qurʾan never speaks of it, it should come as no surprise that God does not reveal there that He takes no pleasure in this *sunna.* Does one find, however, in Muslim revelation, the idea of a spiritual sacrifice? Yes, but under a different name. At the level of worship, such a sacrifice is implied through prayer and almsgiving, which demand humility and detachment; at the level of the spiritual life, it is found in *fanāʾ* (abolition of consciousness of self) and in *tawakkul* (total abandon to God).

THE RELIGIOUS EXPERIENCE OF JEWS AND MUSLIMS

The fundamental experiences that Jews and Muslims have lived are at first sight diametrically opposed. For Jews, God is the One who led them out of Egypt, who promised them a land, who helped them to conquer it. Then their unfaithfulness brings about their chastisement: they are beaten and led into captivity; but God pardons and liberates them. On the other hand, the first followers and companions of the Prophet must go into exile in order to preserve their faith: this is the *hijra* or pilgrimage; they must struggle in order to defend the faith against the attacks of pagans: this is the *jihād* (which is translated as holy war, but which means precisely "the struggle"; it is said: *al jihād fī sabīl Allāh*: the struggle in the way of God).

The first believers who made the *hijra*, the *muhājirūn*, abandoned everything—their houses, their goods, their families—in order to follow the Prophet; those who fought, the *mujāhidūn*, risked their lives, paid their own expenses in order to arm themselves, and all this for God (*liʾllāh*). Of course they had the help of their Lord throughout all their labors, but they began by placing everything in the hands of God, because they had answered His call. What God asks of people is a simple unconditional yes. According to the Qurʾan, this is what happened at the moment of a transhistorical pact, what Louis Massignon calls "*the preeternal covenant*," or the *mīthāq* in Arabic. It is written (7:172): "And (remember) when your Lord brought forth from the Children of Adam, from their reins, their seed, and made them testify of themselves, (saying): Am I not your Lord? They said: Yea, verily. We testify."

As we have already seen, for Jews, God is the Savior first of all, and for Muslims, He is the Lord. The LORD says to His people, through the voice of the prophet Isaiah (41:9 and 10): "You are my servant, I have chosen you, I have not rejected you." God takes the initiative to save: "I give you strength, truly I help you, truly I hold you firm with my saving right hand." People are simply asked not to hinder the saving action of God on their behalf. Obedience to the Law means recognizing the love of God for humankind, felt and tested through His love for His people: "Since I regard you as precious [*yāqartā*], since you are honoured and I love you [*ʾăhabtîkâ*] . . ." (43:4). One finds, then, extremely forceful expressions (43:1): "Do not be afraid, for I have redeemed you." The verb *gāʾal* simultaneously means to deliver, to emancipate and to ransom.

It is true that the idea of ransom relates to historical facts, in its immediate sense: "I have given Egypt for your ransom [*kōper*] . . . I therefore give people in exchange for you, and nations in return for your life" (*ibid.*, 43:3, 4). Historically this means that "the LORD hands over these countries to Persian conquest in exchange for the liberation of Israel" (Dhorme). But it was easy to give this idea a spiritual meaning, with its own spiritual value. The Bible already effects this spiritualization, in the sense that it announces salvation for all nations. The redemption of the exiles of Israel carries new implications. These exiles of Israel are no longer the sons of Abraham, Isaac, and Jacob who were led into captivity; these are the peoples who were enemies of Israel, who cut themselves off from him and who must be gathered together from their dispersion, in order to reintegrate them within the chosen people. "No foreigner adhering to the LORD should say, 'The LORD will utterly exclude me from his people.' . . . As for foreigners who adhere to the LORD to serve him, to love the LORD's name . . . , these I shall lead to my holy mountain and make them joyful in my house of prayer. Their burnt offerings and sacrifices will be accepted on my altar, for my house will be called a house of prayer for all peoples. The LORD God who gathers the exiles of Israel declares: There are others I shall gather besides those already gathered" (56:3–8).

As they become universal, the notions of salvation, redemption, and a salvific gathering begin to be detached from historical particularism and thereby imply an interiorization. One can cite in this regard the prophecy of Zephaniah (3:9–10): "Yes, then I shall purge the lips of the peoples, so that all may invoke the name of the LORD and serve him shoulder to shoulder. From beyond the rivers of Ethiopia, my supplicants will bring me tribute." Redemption is universal and linked to the purification of lips, symbolizing that the thoughts of the heart are purified. Christianity will develop this notion, notably through its doctrine of redemption.

SPIRITUALITY OF THE DESERT IN THE BIBLE

The religious experience of salvation by the people of Israel prompted the Jews to develop a meditation on the desert, for God had helped Moses in crossing such wildernesses. In and through these trials, that faith and confidence in God awaken, though not without pain. The examples are numerous, especially in the Book of Exodus: "Moses led Israel away from the Sea of Reeds, and they entered the desert of Shur. They then travelled through the desert for three days without finding water" (Exodus 15:22). The people murmur against Moses, who prays to the LORD and whose prayer is granted. One reads a little farther on (16:2): "The whole community of Israelites began complaining about Moses and Aaron in the desert." Then Moses says to Aaron (16:9–10): "Say to the whole community of Israelites, 'Approach the LORD's presence. . . .'" And the text continues: "As Aaron was speaking . . . they turned towards the desert, and there the glory of the LORD appeared in the cloud."

In the desert God manifests himself; and when, angered by His unfaithful people, He withdraws, everything reverts to desert; it is as if God's creative work has retraced its steps. One reads in the Book of Jeremiah (4:22–26): "This is because my people are stupid. . . . I looked to the earth—it was a formless waste [*tōhû wā-bōhû*; cf. Genesis 1:2]; to the heavens, and their light was gone [*ʾōr*; cf. Genesis 1:3]. . . . I looked—the fruitful land was a desert, and all its towns in ruins before the LORD, before his burning anger." The prophets recall the importance of the desert and rebuke those who forget it. Thus Jeremiah (2:6): "They never said, 'Where is the LORD . . . who led us through the desert, through a land of plains and ravines, through a land of drought, of shadow dark as death, a land through which no one passes and where no human being lives?'"

We will see developing in Judaism a spirituality of the desert, which some of the first Christians, the Desert Fathers, will rediscover. Little by little the desert will become a symbol. The Gospel evokes it through the forty-day fast Jesus made in the desert where he was tempted by Satan. And concerning John the Baptist, the Gospel quotes the famous words of Isaiah (40:3): "A voice cries, 'Prepare in the desert a way for the LORD. Make a straight highway for our God across the wastelands.'" The Greek text of the Gospels (Matthew 3:3; Mark 1:3; Luke 3:4; John 1:23) renders the Hebrew exactly by scrupulously following the order of words; the New Jerusalem Bible renders it properly, thus avoiding the misleading rendition of some translations: "A voice cries in the desert."

IMAGES OF COMMERCE IN THE QUR'AN

The fundamental Muslim experience is of an entirely different order. To be sure, during the *hijra*, the Prophet and his Companions had to cross a desert. But it is not in the desert that God reveals himself. Mount Ḥirāʾ, where Muhammad retreated and where he first received his message, is hardly comparable to Mount Sinai, from this point of view. The revelation to Muhammad comes abruptly from on high: "In the name of thy Lord" (96:1). No allusion to the prior life of the man upon whom it falls, to his religious anguishes, to his meditations, to his experiences. A vertical and abrupt revelation!

And who is this Lord? Unlike the Lord of the Bible, He has not led a people. Rather, He creates and instructs people in the truths they do not know: "Read: And your Lord is the Most Bounteous, Who teaches by the pen, teaches man that which he knew not" (96:3–5). Doubtless, God will later recall all the favors He has heaped on humanity, in particular on the children of Israel, and then on the Muslims themselves. But this is nothing more than a reminder (*dhikr*). The essential lies elsewhere. God manifests himself first of all in His transcendence, which the Qurʾan constantly evokes through the words *subḥānaʾllāh*, Glory to God! *taʿālā*, for He is high! *ʿazza wa jalla*, for He is powerful and great! After these, He is praised for His benefits: *al-ḥamdu liʾllāh*, Praise to God!

The experience of God is from the beginning that of a distant Lord, inaccessible through any steps forward on the path of life. On the contrary one must break with this life which slips away within time here-below (*al-ḥayāt al-dunyā*; among many other verses, cf. 2:85) and which is opposed to the life of the hereafter (*al-ākhira*). Thus one reads (2:86): "Such are those who buy the life of the world at the price of the Hereafter. Their punishment will not be lightened." In the same fashion one reads of those who have purchased error (*ḍalal*) at the price of God's guidance (*hudā*, 2:16 and 175), or unfaithfulness (*kufr*) for the price of faith (*īmān*, 3:177).

This commercial vocabulary bears noting. It is certainly addressed, in the first place, to the great caravaneers and merchants of Mecca, who are attached to the goods of this world. But curiously, the same language is applied to God Himself (9:111): "Lo! God has bought from the believers their lives and their wealth because the Garden will be theirs: they shall fight in the way of God and shall slay and be slain. . . . Rejoice then in your bargain [*bay*ᶜ] that you have made. . . ." Thus the *muhājirūn* and the *mujāhidūn* are, in an etymological sense, the mercenaries of God. They have left everything for Him; if divine help is valuable to them for victories in combat and the gain of booty, this is not what counts, for that does not comprise their wages. Such things do not fulfill the hope of true believers. "Lo! those who read the Scripture of God, and establish worship, and spend [in alms] of that which We have bestowed on them secretly and openly, they look forward to imperishable gain [*tijāra*]. That He will repay them their wages and increase them of His grace" (35:29–30). Later we read this verse (61:10–11): "O all who believe! Shall I show you a commerce that will save you [*tijāra tunjīkum*] from a painful doom? You should all believe in God and His messenger, and should strive for the cause of God with your wealth and your lives."

God does not save by redeeming ("buying back"), but He buys: through the bargain He concludes with humanity He promises salvation. The only condition is to give everything first to God, and then to the poor; one must strip oneself of possessions, because before God, who alone is "rich," no other wealth exists than His own and that which He gives. Such is the truth that prayer and almsgiving recall. The Most-High appears, once more, as the Supreme Exception, the distant God. But once the heart has recognized this frightening distance, it soon experiences within itself the presence of the Creator in the very act of His Creation. God says (50:16): "We verily created a man and We know what his soul whispers to him, and We are nearer to him than his jugular vein."

DIALECTIC OF NEARNESS AND DISTANCE, OF SEARCHING AND FINDING

Muslim experience moves from the remoteness to the proximity of God; Jewish experience moves in the opposite direction, and the LORD must remind His people that He is also a distant God: "Am I a God when near . . . and not a God when far away?" (Jeremiah 23:23). One finds here the kernel of an existential dialectic of nearness and distance that will play an important role among the mystics. God is distant through His universal presence to the immensity of the world, so it is in God's proximity to the heart that one discovers the experience of His distant transcendence: "Seek out the LORD while he is still to be found [*bĕ-himmāṣĕᶜô*], call to him while he is still near [*bi-hyôtô qārôb*]," says Isaiah (55:6).

Another dialectic to which we will return is linked with the first, that of searching and finding. If humanity is incapable of entering into the search for God, God nonetheless finds humanity. It is written concerning the Prophet (93:6–8): "Did He not find you an orphan and protect (you)? Did He not find you wandering and direct (you)? Did He not find you destitute and enrich (you)?" As we will see, Muslim mystics easily culled from the Qurʾan and meditated on this idea of a prevenient action of God. Thus, when people turn toward God through repentance, they find God turned toward them. If, after an error, sinners were to ask pardon of God, "they would find God turned" (toward them) and merciful (*la-wajadūʾ Llah tawwāban raḥīman*), as it says in sūrah 4:64. God reveals even more clearly (9:118): "Then turned He unto them [*tāba ᶜalayhīm*] in mercy that they (too) might turn [*li-yatūbū*] (repentant unto Him). Lo! God! He is the Relenting [*al-Tawwāb*, the One who turns], the Merciful."

In the prophets of Israel one is not surprised to discover utterances that are identical in spirit and in letter, for they employ the verb *šûb*, *yāšûb*, which means to come back, to return, from the same root as the Arab *tāba*, *yatūbu*, a doublet of *thāba*, *yathūbu*, which also has the sense of return. Jeremiah reports this word of the LORD (15:19): "If you repent [*tāšûb*], I shall restore you to plead before me." And Zechariah wrote: "The LORD Sabaoth says this: Return to me . . . and I will return to you" (*šûbû ʾēlay wĕ-ʾāšûb ʾălêkem*). The two acts are presented as simultaneous, but obviously it is God who puts everything into action. The prevenient action of God is plainly indicated in this passage from Isaiah

(65:24) where God says: "Thus, before they call I shall answer, before they stop speaking I shall have heard." But still more clear and more extraordinary are the words where God reveals himself in the transcendence of His absolute initiative (Isaiah 65:1): "I have let myself be approached by those who did not consult me, I have let myself be found by those who did not seek me. I said, 'Here I am, here I am! to a nation that did not invoke my name." For its part, the Qur᾽an never ceases to repeat that "God guides whom He will" (2:213; 10:26); that God "will relent [*yatūbu*] toward whom He will" (9:27). Several Muslim theologians have thought that prayer could not modify God's decree, but rather that God had decreed in advance that He would answer the prayers He asks humanity to address to Him.

The Bible and the Qur᾽an, setting out from different religious experiences, in the end converge. Divine assistance is a sign for His people as the prophets themselves are signs. Isaiah writes (8:18): "Look, [we] shall become signs [*᾽ōtôt*] and portents [*môpĕtîm*] in Israel on behalf of the LORD Sabaoth;" but the same idea is in the Qur᾽an: everything is a sign of God to those who can see; the prophets are equally signs (*āyāt*) and a "mercy" (*raḥma*). In the sūrah *Mary*, God says of Jesus (19:21): "We may make of him a revelation for mankind and a mercy from Us." And it is precisely as signs, that they must be understood.

THE HEART

According to the Bible, the infidelities of the Children of Israel resulted from a lack of comprehension. They discovered God in His blessings but in their success they forget him. It is not enough to encounter Him in the desert; one must keep Him within oneself in prosperity. It is not enough to receive the Law at Sinai; it must be engraved on the heart. That is why God reveals to Jeremiah (24:7): "I shall give them a heart to acknowledge that I am the LORD. They will be my people and I shall be their God, for they will return to me [*yāšubû*] with all their heart." So it is the heart that matters. Thus the Psalmist asks God to create in him a pure heart (Psalm 51:12), and the prophet Jeremiah (4:4) transmits the word of the Lord: "Circumcise yourselves for the LORD, apply circumcision to your hearts." There is nothing worse than an obstinate heart, than an errant and hardened heart (Jeremiah 18:12; Isaiah 44:20).

The prophets clearly distinguish the exterior Law and the interiorized law. The first cannot guarantee salvation. How does the ruin of human beings come about? "The LORD says, 'This is because they have forsaken my Law which I gave them and have not listened to my voice or followed it, but have followed their own stubborn hearts'" (Jeremiah 9:12–13). Isaiah uses a very suggestive image: the Law, in the eyes of those who adopt it from the outside, resembles a rule of discipline that an authoritarian master applies to children. "Therefore the word of the LORD will be to them, 'Precept upon precept, precept upon precept, line upon line, line upon line, here a little, there a little;' in order that they may go, and fall backward, and be broken, and snared, and taken" (Isaiah 28:13).[2] This conception of a law felt to be purely exterior, which leads to perdition, makes one think of the conception that Paul denounces.

On the other hand, the interiorized law has the power to save, for it returns humanity to God: "Within them I shall plant my Law, writing it on their hearts. Then I shall be their God and they will be my people" (Jeremiah 31:33). This interiorization of the Law leads to values that are formed, almost to the letter, in the Christian message: "Is that the sort of fast that pleases me, a day when a person inflicts pain on himself? Hanging your head like a reed, spreading out sackcloth and ashes? Is that what you call fasting, a day acceptable to the LORD? . . . Is it not sharing your food with the hungry, and sheltering the homeless poor; if you see someone lacking clothes . . . ?" (Isaiah 58:5,7).

In the same spirit Christ gives a similar teaching; he denounces the hypocrisy of those who only fast externally (Matthew 6:16–17); one must choose an interior fast that appears only to "your Father who is in secret [*tō patri sou tō en tō krypsaiō*] and your father who sees in secret, will reward you."[3] The *krypsaion* signifies that which is concealed or taken from view; the adverb *krypsa* means: secretly, in a hiding place. God is present in the depth of the heart. But purity of heart is needed: hence the importance of the sixth Beatitude: "Blessed are the pure in heart [*katharoi tē kardia*]: they shall see God" (Matthew 5:8). Concerning the parable of the sower, Saint Luke (8:15) reports the explanation that Jesus gives: " . . . this is a people with a noble and generous heart [*en kardia kalē kai agathē*] who have heard the word and take it to themselves and yield a harvest through perseverance." The expression recalls the *kalokagathia* of the Greek moralists which designates the beauty of moral conduct in a well-born man. Jesus is himself "gentle and humble in heart" (Matthew 11:29); his words inflame the heart of the disciples of Emmaeus: "Did not our hearts burn within us as he talked to us on the road and explained the scriptures to us?" (Luke 24:32).

Saint Paul writes that "It is by believing with the heart that you are justified" (Romans 10:10) and that "the love of God has been poured into our hearts by the Holy Spirit which has been given to us" (*ibid.* 5:5); he prays for the faithful of Ephesus, he tells them, so that God may "give you a spirit of wisdom and perception of what is revealed, to bring you to full knowledge of him, [and may] enlighten the eyes of your mind so that you can see what hope his call holds for you" (Ephesians 1:17–18).

In all these quotations we are only seeking to underscore the importance of the heart, without being detained by the underlying dogmas. It is not that we underestimate their fundamental value. But the dogmatic beliefs diverge. In contrast, one discovers through meditating on the three messages that the primordial role the heart plays provides a point of convergence. We are glad to have found one.

Certainly we must not hide the fact that, here again, certain dissonances will be heard. However, as we will see, they will tend to disappear. For Jews and Christians, the heart is the place of love: "You must love the LORD your God will all your heart [*bĕ-kol lĕbabkā*], with all your soul, with all your strength," Deuteronomy (6:5) teaches; "from there you start searching once more for the LORD your God, and if you search for him honestly and sincerely, you will find him" (*ibid.* 4:29). The Gospels pick up on this commandment of love and place it in the foreground, before all others, for "God is love" (1 John 4:16). But Islam, at least in the way it is conceived by a number of important Muslims who are essentially legalists, diminishes the value of love to the point where it disappears. Only the mystics notice and give it importance.

In any event, the Qur'an forcefully stresses the heart (*qalb*) and the "bosom" (*ṣadr*) as well as on the "secret" (*sirr*). We must limit ourselves to a few quotations chosen among numerous verses. Thus God says to Muhammad (94:1): "Have we not caused your bosom to dilate [open widely]?" This dilation is not a favor reserved for the Prophet; it is written (6:126): "And whomsoever it is God's will to guide, He expands his bosom unto the Surrender [*liʾl-islām*: so that he may perform the act of "submission"]." This person then "follows a light from His Lord" (39:22). Moses had already asked the Lord to open his breast (20:25). Evoking the Day of Judgment, Abraham speaks (26:89–90) of pious men who fear God (*al-muttaqīn*; cf. *al-taqwā*: piety and fear of God), who come to Him with a "whole heart" (*bi-qalb salīm* cf. 37:84), for the infidels, the impious, the hypocrites have a disease in their hearts (*fī qulūbihim maraḍ*, cf. 2:10 among many other verses). It is the memory of God that gives peace to their hearts (13:28). "He it is Who sent down peace of reassurance [*sakīna*, cf. the Hebrew *šĕkînâ*] into the hearts of the believers" (48:4). Paradise is promised to those "who fear the Merciful One in secret [*biʾl-ghayb*, a term which here has the meaning of *sirr*] and who bring a contrite heart [*qalb munīb*]."[4] The verse (16:106) evokes others in which the heart is at peace within (or through) faith (*qalbuhu muṭmaʾinn biʾl-īmān*), for "whosoever believes in God, He guides his heart" (64:11).

We will limit ourselves to these few examples, but not without recalling that in the Qurʾan as in the Bible, the heart can be perverted, and the breast can be "opened wide to infidelity" (16:106). Then God places a seal on them (7:101). In every case, God probes hearts and "comes in between the man and his own heart" (8:24).

The theme of the secret (*sirr*) also appears in the qurʾanic revelation. Yet this term does not immediately seem to designate the most profound reality of the heart. Above all it applies to the secret actions that people keep hidden, in contrast to those that they do publicly (*ʿalāniyya*). More generally, it applies to all feelings and thoughts that one does not disclose, but which God knows. In the vocabulary of the mystics *sirr* will take on an ontological meaning in order to designate the most radical and most authentic reality of the human being. Its meaning will then converge with that of the Christian Greek form, *krypsaion*.

Thus the biblical message was addressed to people who were in a "situation" existentially different from that of the first Muslims. It launched the piety and reflection of Jews onto a way leading them to conceive of God as Savior, and first of all as the Savior of His people. Then, from that vantage point, it leads to the conception of God as universal Lord and all-powerful Creator. Islam, on the other hand, launches its faithful on a path that moves inversely: initially, God is the Lord in His absolute transcendence, the One who speaks in His eternity, who dominates human history from on high. Only then He is discovered to be the gentle and merciful Savior, so that His abrupt and inflexible will of decree (*mashīʾa*) becomes for believers a will of kindness (*irāda*).

Now, in both Arabic and Hebrew, the idea of will encompasses that of love. It was normal that the two ways meet, not in their historical and external journey, but in their journey within the believers' meditation on the message they have received. They meet at that place in human reality which everyone calls the heart. The meditation on the desert and on the Law which was given them in the desert leads the Jews to discover the heart. The meditation of the *hijra* and of the *jihād* leads Muslims to the same discovery! For them in fact the *hijra* and the *jihād* are signs of the absence of all hypocrisy (*nifāq*) and of the authenticity of faith. As for Christians, who directly inherit the Jewish experience, they immediately situate themselves at the level of the heart. The heart is therefore the center towards which the three messages converge, whatever their dogmatic contrasts might be, and the three messages themselves point the way.

Now it is precisely in the heart that the spiritual experience and adventure of mystics from the three monotheisms are rooted. This is why we will focus on them. Each of the three messages carries a mystical reading and above all a mystical understanding. In its own way, each lends itself to these. Therefore, it is not a matter of reducing them to the same denominator, any more than of relativizing them according to external historical factors. The message that the Jewish mystics live is entirely their own; the message that Christian mystics live is entirely their own; the message that Muslim mystics live is entirely their own. But it happens that each group of mystics, through living their own values, can truly open themselves to the values of the other two and that an indisputable communion can be created and radiate at the level of religious experience, which the heart alone can decipher.

EXPERIENCE AND TRUTH

Elsewhere, there is divergence. Who is God in Himself? Those who worship Him will know God in all truth only in the other life. What is this other life? It must be lived to be known. The same holds true for questions about the nature and destiny of humanity. On these different points concerning the first and ultimate Truth, each of the three messages gives teachings that barely concur. Attempting to reconcile them would be a pointless exercise: either they are all false or else only one is true.

But what then mean the agreements and analogies that the mystics present? Must we tell ourselves that only mysticism counts, precisely because the concurrences we have discovered lie here? Or that any truth that makes claims for itself by opposing error is of no interest and should not be taken seriously, precisely because it opposes another claim? Some will tend toward this line of thought. Like Pilate they ask, "What is Truth?" But if there is no truth, these famous concurrences are themselves pointless. How could they, in their specificity, interest us? Would they have only an anthropological significance? Certain kinds of people (the mystics) are simply like that; that's all. There are other kinds of people and one simply classifies them. But the objective and classifying mind is also a certain kind of mind. Does it classify itself? And then what would that classification be worth? One then falls into a full-blown relativism. Or it does not classify itself and so situates itself—in the name of an anthropology that is said to be scientific—above all those others which it has filed away on index cards. But by what right? Does the science of a given era have an absolute worth?

One is justified in thinking that a truth of the matter exists, even if no human being can fully hope to embrace and penetrate it. Because there is truth, the mystical concurrences issuing from contrasting and mutually exclusive messages have a meaning. But what is this truth? Do any of the formulas of the messages themselves provide it? Yes and no.

Yes, because the three revelations literally transmit to us a certain amount of faith content that demands assent, but which, from one monotheism to another, exclude each other reciprocally. Each of the faithful will therefore believe that the truth of his or her religion is *the* truth.

No, because none of these messages ordains that it be held to the letter, that one must stockpile a set of fixed dogmas to be learned and defended as a system and amounting to knowledge-capital. Certainly the theologians who solidify the revealed *given* into rigid dogmatic formulas are useful—even indispensable—to believers in each confession. The human being has been given intelligence and cannot be content with an unexamined faith. We must *know* that which we believe, and why we believe it: we must understand of our faith. But that is finally not our religious and spiritual vocation. Above all we must live our faith, and living our faith implies a path to follow. The mystics have marked out the paths of that life which, while not identical, are parallel and meet at infinity in God. That is an indisputable fact, which moreover we will verify.

HELL

Does one then say that only one of the paths leads to God, since there is only one Truth? This point of view has been argued and has a certain logic on its side. But logic is not life and life often accomplishes what would seem logically impossible or at least highly improbable. How therefore are we concretely to pose the question? The three messages invite human beings to move toward God, the only God. Jews, Christians, Muslims respond to the call and set out. Here we are then, all journeying upon the earth throughout our earthly existence. Should each group of believers, in the name of the truth of their religion, declare that the two other groups cannot reach God because they are in error, that they will be damned and cast into hell?

This has been argued on all sides, especially among Christians and Muslims, who have clearer texts on Gehenna than do Jews. Such condemnation, it seems, has completely disappeared from Christian thinking in our day, and the famous formula "Outside the Church there is no salvation" is no longer interpreted with its former rigor. What a blow to Christ the redeemer, the Good Shepherd, if so many of his sheep meet their end in eternal fire!

Do Muslims still believe that Jews and Christians will be thrown into Gehenna? This conviction does live on among some of them. Several qurʾanic verses can justify it, but on this point there is no explicit declaration, so everything depends on interpretation. One or two texts favorable to Christians stand out, in particular the verse (5:82) that declares them to be through friendship the closest of believers. But elsewhere it is said that those who profess their doctrine are infidels (5:17,72)—and infidels are bound for hell. The Jews are cursed on several occasions (5:13,64), and they are presented as the worst enemies of the believers (5:82). In fact, the People of the Book who find grace are those who have not erased from their scriptures the announcement of Muhammad or who have not concealed it, so that at the coming of the Prophet, they recognized and followed. But the others? "Those unto whom We have given the Scripture, who read it with the right reading, those believe in it. And who so disbelieves in it, those are they who are the losers [*al-khasirūn*]" (2:121). Who are these losers? According to the commentators, they are the Jews who practice their Law and the hypocrites who only act like sincere believers but who have drawn from their works neither good nor reward. Nevertheless, these texts allow for diverse exegeses. Therefore, it belongs to Muslims to say what they think about them today.

In the Bible, *sheol* is only the place of the dead; the notion of hell does not appear. There is the recurrent issue of the wrath of the LORD (for example in Isaiah 30:27). But above all, fire from heaven consumes rebel nations on earth. The idea of eternal punishment is perhaps not totally absent. Thus one reads in Psalm 140:11: "May the slanderer find no rest anywhere, may evil hunt down violent men implacably." It is not always sure that such verses refer to hell. Consequently the Bible never prompts the Jews to consign non-Jews to an eternal chastisement; punishment of the impious occurs here-below.

As for the attitude of Christianity vis-à-vis the Jews, it is clearly defined by Saint Paul (Romans 11:28–29): "[A]s regards those who are God's choice, they are still well beloved for the sake of their ancestors. There is no change of mind on God's part about the gifts he has made or his choice." Christian persecutions of the Jews have no scriptural justification whatsoever.

Thus, even if one risks encountering some reticence from the legalist and literalist sector of Islam, one can acknowledge that the faithful of the three monotheistic religions could concur in believing that all their brothers and sisters are called to a single-minded life of the heart, to a journey toward God according to three routes marked out by the stages defined by the sacred texts to which each is loyal. We will note the resemblances as Jewish, Christian, and Muslim mystics describe these stages.

MYSTICS AND THE MESSAGE

So we set out to discover how the mystics receive their messages. Generally speaking, they do so in the same way as do other Jews, Christians, and Muslims. But in reading the messages, they have their own very particular way. They do not seek to extract dogmatic truths from their readings and still less to define them in theological formulae. At the most they take care to assure that the descriptions they give of their experiences do not contradict the *credo* of their faith. Now, it happens that their meditation, which directs and illumines their life, focuses on those texts which we have found to contain analogies from one message to the other. They do not make theology into something either speculative or apologetic; they do not compare, they do not refute, they do not care about understanding their scriptures historically, they do not explain their elaboration and development. They do meditate closely on certain words and sentences. Such words are certainly filled are with the collective religious experience of the first believers and successive generations, but they are also animated by a personal breath of inspiration that revitalizes those words for the mystics without thereby reducing the meaning they have for everyone.

Thus, in regard to the spiritual life of people belonging to a monotheistic religion here-below, the different mysticisms discover and reveal values so close to one another that one can easily consider them as manifesting a single spirit. Consequently, in our divided world, mystical thought, inspired by monotheism, expresses the unity of a God toward whom humanity tends, and allows us to see in the three Messengers the bearers of a single message, inasmuch as it calls all people to seek and find this God, the only true God within the depths of their heart.

Concerning dogmatic truth as the fundamental given of revelation, it doubtless exists or else everything would collapse. It is certainly active in the life of believers, and even of unbelievers. It is probably at work without their knowing it, at least for the vast majority. Everything will be clear in the beyond, with that knowledge by which—to borrow an expression from Ibn ʿArabī—humanity will no longer journey toward God (*al-safar ilā ʾllāh*), but will journey in God (*al-safar fī ʾllāh*).

Did Saint Paul not write (1 Corinthians 13:12): "Now we see only reflections in a mirror, mere riddles [*eu ainigmati*], but then we shall be seeing face to face. Now, I can know only imperfectly; but then I shall know just as fully as I am myself known."

3

UNDERSTANDING FAITH, THE LIFE OF FAITH

The heart is, as it were, a focal center toward which converge the three monotheistic messages, as believers who are in love with spirituality have received them. The texts beckon believers toward the heart. The mystics, by speaking the language of the heart, have testified to this convergence: they describe how their faith in each case, whether Jew, Christian, or Muslim, is lived within a concrete religious experience.

But we must pursue this path of the mystics prudently and circumspectly. If the interiorization of dogmas in the heart reveals an intentional unity on the horizon, a unity which the different *credos* themselves suggest at the outset, we must repeat that this does not authorize us to think that all beliefs which separate and divide are superficial and trivial. By continually recalling the existence of these essential differences, we are not trying to satisfy speculative theologians and believers or religious authorities who are closely identified with their speculative and dogmatic thought. We only want to show that by setting out from these very differences the mystics have arrived at certain convergences on the spiritual plane.

The mystics are the first to warn us against too hasty an approach. They do this by making reference to their respective scriptural texts, often borrowing terms and expressions from those texts that they find charged with particularly rich values. Equally, however, they warn us by remaining grounded in ideas inspired by doctrine and by adhering to those doctrines as simple believers.

THE INADEQUACY OF MYSTICAL LANGUAGE: ITS REFERENCES TO DOGMA

If we sense a paradox in the language of the mystics, it is this: they wish to describe, indeed to communicate, an incommunicable experience. Even among the mystics themselves, it is difficult, if not impossible, for them to be sure that they have lived these very mystical states. This is all the more reason, then, that they despair of ever managing to engage their lay readers, though they be believers, in the spiritual universe that is theirs.

The language of the mystics is allusive, figurative, symbolic, but always inadequate. It suggests; it calls us to reflect, to meditate; it opens up ways of seeing; it never exactly captures its object. Can we even think of it as having an object, when it plunges into the deepest subjectivity? Mystical language does not even manage to convince us that this subjectivity has a reality and that it does not lead to vain imaginings, to hollow reveries, indeed to fantasies that are more or less morbid. No mystic has ever transmitted to anyone else exactly what his or her experience has been. At best the mystic can suggest it, but only to others who are already capable of sensing, and in this way understanding, what the mystic suggests. Now who are the people most often capable of this? They are precisely those who know and—more particularly, those who share—the foundational faith of the mystic. Consequently, they are those who possess a doctrinal understanding of that faith.

The reality that the mystics wish to describe, if reality there is, resides at the limit of their discourse, a limit toward which their understanding can tend without ever reaching it. In fact, when we read a mystical writing, the mystery that it has excited may touch, move, and attract us. But it is our understanding that seeks to comprehend. We can think of ourselves as illuminated, but we do not know whether this illumination is real or illusory. Often, we only transpose what has touched us into a setting that is our own, without being sure that this transposition does not falsify what the mystic sought to transmit. It comes to us like the impression that symbolic poetry can produce in us. One should not confuse the chatter that can develop around a text and the veritable message of this text, however indecipherable it may be.

Now, in the case that concerns us, it is certain that human thought is unable to embrace God; at best it can succeed in "touching" Him, as Descartes put it. Does the experience of the mystics go farther? A question without a definitive response. One either believes or does not believe what they describe about their states. But what is certain is that ordinary people, if they believe them, will only believe through the faith that is their own and through the doctrines of the religion they profess. Consequently, the statements of the mystics have no value for anyone who is not the object of special graces, except in relation to the content of their religious belief. We clearly see, then, that mystical events make sense or offer something to humanity in general only to the extent that doctrine relates and confirms them.

One could even go so far as to say that the mystics themselves can be sure that they have not fallen into illusions of their imagination or of the devil only if they orient themselves to doctrinal truths that are theologically certain. Thus, Saint Teresa of Avila made a practice of consulting with her theologian, not to submit herself blindly to him, but rather to submit her experiences to him. She wrote, in her autobiography (chapter 10): "what is bad will come from me, and your Reverence will strike it out."[1] And later, whether addressing herself either to F. Ibañez or to F. Garcia de Toledo, who had pressed her for an account of the favors that the Lord had granted her in prayer, she added: "And thus what amounts to more than simply giving an account of my life, your Reverence may judge . . . as to its conformity with the truths of our holy Catholic faith. And if it should not be in conformity with them, your Reverence may burn it immediately, for I would submit to it being burned. And I shall speak of what is taking place in me so that when it is conformed to this faith, it may bring some profit to your Reverence; and if it is not, you will free my soul from illusion so that the devil may not be gaining where it seems to me that I am gaining."[2] Doubtless the concern about remaining within orthodox faith is particularly strong among Roman Catholic mystics. It is no less true that all mystics refer constantly, and more or less explicitly, to the authority of revealed texts that serve as the basis of their meditation. Consequently, they never neglect the doctrinal point of view. We will find other confirmations.

The sacred texts warn, furthermore, against the desire to see God. On this point, the Bible and the Qurʾan are in agreement, despite differences of expression. We might think of the famous passage of Exodus (33:18–23) in which Moses asks to see the Glory (*kābôd*) of God. God replies: "I shall make all my goodness pass before you, and before you I shall pronounce the name of the LORD; and I am gracious to those to whom I am gracious and I take pity on those on whom I take pity." And God continues: "But my face you cannot see, for no human being can see me and survive. . . . Here is a place [*māqôm*] near me. You will stand on the rock, and when my glory passes by, I shall put you in a cleft of the rock and shield you with my hand until I have gone past. Then I shall take my hand away and you will see my back; but my face will not be seen."

The same idea is found in the Qur'an (7:143): "And when Moses came to Our appointed tryst and his Lord had spoken unto him, he said: My Lord! Show me (Your self), that I may gaze upon You. He said: You will not see Me, but gaze upon the mountain! If it stand still in its place, then you will see Me. And when his Lord revealed (His) glory to the mountain He sent it crashing down. And Moses fell down senseless."

This same question was also disputed among the theologians of Islam—whether the guests of paradise will see God and, if so, in what sense one can speak of sight; will it be with the eyes of the resurrected body or with the heart? Be that as it may, the doctors agree in recognizing that the human person, within the framework of life here-below, could not enjoy such a vision.

In what, then, could the contemplation of the mystics consist? What of Himself does God unveil to them, without annihilating them through this revelation? Or should we think, as do certain Indian mystics who have been able on this point to exercise a certain influence, that upon approaching the Absolute being, a creature totally loses itself in the Absolute? This way of seeing would connect in some sense with the idea held by certain philosophers. They argue that the human intellect, at the level of a perfect intellection of intelligibles, is absorbed by the one Intellect and stripped of its individuality.

How are we to know what becomes of the mystic, given that the final experience of the ecstatic is ineffable and incommunicable? On the other hand, if one cannot accompany a mystic all the way to the end of the mystical journey, it is still possible to follow along a part of the path, the length of the stages that plot his or her itinerary. The descriptions that the mystic makes of the journey, often projected through images, speak to the imagination and provide a gateway to thought. Moreover, the God of the mystics is not only the One who reveals himself at the final phase of their ascension. The God of the mystics is in a certain way present at each step along the Way. In each of the stages that He gives them to enjoy, God shines through. One can, then, understand what they are saying without experiencing it and can conjure up some idea of this God who, by intention, is both the God of all believers, and the God who favors chosen souls by approaching them in a unique way.

The one God is the unique goal toward which all the monotheistic mystics strive. In this sense, the end is the same for everyone. Still, the mode through which God presents Himself to them in each of the three revelations will inevitably influence the expression they use to clothe their experience of God. Yet to the degree that the mystics are people of prayer rather than of speculation, it is undeniable that their prayer and worship are addressed to the same God, for there is no other God besides this God. It matters little, then, that the words of these prayers, the gestures that accompany them, the times and seasons in which they are spoken, differ among the mystics. The praise, the glorification of the one God, are singular. One can just as well say: *halalû El* in Hebrew, *al-ḥamdu liʾllāh* or *subḥānaʾllāh* in Arabic, *doxa en hypsistois Theō* in Greek, *gloria in excelsis Deo*, in Latin. One always directs these words toward the same God.

But if those who pray rise on the wings of their prayer, do they succeed in discovering with their prayer a God identical to the One whom all other men and women of prayer discover, through the paths which their respective faiths offer? In other words, if prayer is to be something more than a vague civic prayer at the Acropolis, must it not bear the marks of doctrinal influence? This question leads to others: Does one need the revealed messages in order to worship the one God? If philosophers come to believe in this God through a rational approach and judge it reasonable to address God by turning their meditation toward Him, would they be in exactly the same situation as believers—as those Jews, Christians, or Muslims with spiritual needs? But if, with Pascal, one wishes to maintain a total differentiation between the God of Abraham, Isaac, and Jacob on one hand, and the god of the philosophers on the other, then the proper character of each message must make itself felt even in the technique, indeed, even in the nature of prayer. It seems therefore that no way exists for eluding the differences.

INTENTIONALITY OF THE MYSTICAL APPROACHES

But perhaps we have ignored an important distinction. When we claimed that the three messages address the heart and that the life of the heart belongs to the mystics in the three religions, we assumed that we would find an intentional unity of the three revelations within their experiences. At the same time we recognized that this experience is incommunicable. Therefore we cannot look there for the unity we are pursuing. Is it possible to grasp it elsewhere?

It would seem so. In fact, the messages that are problematic because of their diversity no longer interest those who have reached the goal of their spiritual ascent. Therefore, in relation to our inquiry, the conclusion of this ascent does not interest us. Whether it is ineffable or incommunicable is of little significance to us here. The messages only have meaning relative to the path they point out as a way toward God. Now the paths are not absolutely identical simply because they end up at the same term. So what must interest us is their orientation, rather than the term toward which they orient us; it is their very intentionality that counts. And if we direct our attention to this point, it will no longer be the messages themselves in their contrasting formulations that will come to the forefront; it will be the manner in which they are received and lived by those who receive them. That may perhaps reveal a certain convergence, or more precisely, parallels may emerge or analogies open up.

Paradoxically, we will have to recognize that it is not the doctrine of divine unicity that truly directs the approach of the mystics of the three religions. Islam, most of all, insists upon the doctrine that it calls *tawḥīd*—proclamation of the existence of the one God according to the formula: there is nothing divine except God. But to say that God is one says nothing about what God is and consequently is to turn one's back upon the primordial question of the relations that in fact exist and that rightfully should be established between humanity and God. We can, it is true, construct an entire philosophy of the One under the inspiration of the thought of Plotinus and by drawing from it the kind of mysticism often called speculative. If we go no further, it is quite difficult to escape the conclusion that for humanity the One is identical to nothingness [or no-thing-ness], because we can say nothing about it except that it is. This dialectic of the One dates back to the *Parmenides* of Plato. In this sense, all thinkers who want to achieve by themselves an understanding of their faith in God, whether they be philosophers, speculative theologians, or mystics, are forced to confess that they can only reach the essential unity of God through the path of negation, the *via negativa*, called in Arabic *tanzīh*. It consists in denying of God anything which for us belongs to being. In the final analysis therefore, God is nothing that we might call being or that we know as being.

THE HIDDEN GOD

If one may discern neo-Platonic influences here, influences to which we will return, it is no less true that these reflections are inspired by meditation on the texts of Isaiah concerning the hidden God, *Deus ab-*

sconditus: "Truly you are a God who conceals himself, God of Israel, Saviour!" (45:15). In the history of Jewish kabbalah, the idea slowly emerged through meditation on this verse that the being of God is absolutely indeterminate, insofar as it is "without limit," or is *ʾên-sôp*. Thus several mystical thinkers, such as Nahmanides, have presented the it as absolute nothingness, that is, not the nothingness of the philosophers, but the absolute inasmuch as it reduces all delimitation, all definition, to nothingness.

Gershom G. Scholem has written on this subject: "As soon as the kabbalists grasped the fundamental difference . . . between the hidden God, subsequently to be called by them *ʾên-sôp*, and the attributes or sefiroth [= *sĕpîrôt*: names, measures, limits] by which he manifested himself and through which he acts, they immediately emphasized the thesis that there can be no *kawwānôt* [intentions] addressed directly to *ʾên-sôp*. The nature of the hidden God excludes any such possibility. If we could meet him in *kawwānâ* he would no longer be that hidden God, whose concealment and transcendence cannot be sufficiently emphasized."[3] A little further on, in speaking of the kabbalist mysticism of Isaac the Blind and his disciples (twelfth/thirteenth centuries), Scholem continues: "We may assume, . . . that the pure Thought of God can also be called Nothing. This is not only because it is not determined by any definite content, but because in it the human thought that strives to advance toward it in meditation ceases to be, or as Isaac's disciples put it, 'comes to nothing.'"[4] One can hardly ignore the neo-Platonic influence in these speculations.

One will find an exact parallel to this kind of consideration in Muslim reflection. A qurʾanic verse (57:3) offers the equivalent of *Deus absconditus*: "He is . . . the Outward [Manifest, *al-Ẓāhir*] and the Inward [Hidden, *al-Bāṭin*]." This verse has been the object of numerous meditations, in particular among the esoteric mystics, who are in fact called *al-Bāṭiniyya.*

One of the most famous, whose influence has been the most extensive, is Ibn al-ʿArabī of Murcia (twelfth–thirteenth century). He constructed his system on the dialectic between *ẓāhir* and *bāṭin*, of being and of its manifestation. He designates the hidden essence of God with the word *aḥadiyya*, which one can translate as "monadic unity" and which he applies to the first verse of sūrah 112: "Say He is God, the One [*Aḥad*]!" In contrast to the word *wāḥid*, which according to Ibn ʿArabī, serves to qualify as being "one" every being considered in its unity, the word *aḥad* designates absolute unity: it is the monad of neo-Platonists that is beyond any number. This *aḥadiyya* is ineffable and inaccessible; it stands out by negating all that is not it, that is to say, from all beings given within the universe, and it conveys the sense of the formula of the profession of faith: there is nothing divine except God. Accordingly, this formula is the justification for the *via negativa.*

But Ibn al-ʿArabī further refines the concept and arrives, so to speak, at a negation in the second degree concerning the essence of God. In effect, he writes that God is He who negates the negation of anyone who follows the way of negation. Doubtless someone will say that the negation of a negation is an affirmation, and that is certainly the case here. Nevertheless, it is through this redoubled negation that God affirms himself to human beings. Thus the divine *aḥadiyya* does not hear the prayer that is addressed to it; prayer does not reach it. It is the divine "lordship" that receives prayers and grants them. The word for lordship (*rubūbiyya*) comes from the word *Rabb*, or Lord, which recurs very often in the Qurʾan. God, inaccessible in Himself, is manifested as Lord. Now the One who is manifest, is manifest to some one; the Lord is always the Lord of someone; Ibn al-ʿArabī writes that the *Rabb* is always *Rabb* of a *marbūb*, in other words, of a being for whom He is the Lord. Relation is thus introduced in the midst of the Absolute.

We find the same idea expressed in reference to the names of God: they have two faces: one is turned toward the Essence that they manifest by naming it, the other is turned toward the creature for whom they name it. It is therefore not the absolute Unity of the Essence that interests a human being, even the greatest mystic. It is instead the Lord and His names. In fact, it is as the Knowing and Omniscient One that God knows us; it is as the All-Powerful that He creates us; it is as the Living One that He gives us life here-below and Life here-after. These names express what is inexpressible in the divine Essence. But they are also like sponsors for the beings they call into existence.

In sum, the fundamental problem for this type of mystic is to show how the unknown God reveals Himself as the Creator and King who governs the world, seated on His Throne, by leading human beings to their full realization. Within Judaism, such also was the problem of the mysticism of the *Merkaba*, centered upon meditation of the vision of Ezekiel and the mystical figure of divinity in the symbol of one "with the appearance of a human being" (1:26; *dĕmût kĕma ʾēh ʾādām*), for it is written: "The sight was like the glory of the LORD" (1:28; *hûʾ marʾēh dĕmût kĕbôd-YHWH*). It is God who is manifest in His Glory—under this appearance and this resemblance—that these mystics seek to understand. One finds the same concern in different expressions of the kabbalah.

In Christianity, one must cite Meister Eckhart. He is equally taken with Isaiah's idea of the hidden God and with the teaching of Pseudo-Dionysius the Areopagite, which is strongly tinged with neoplatonism and describes the soul's ascension toward God through the way of negation, until it reaches the "cloud of unknowing" and is progressively illuminated by "the radiance of the divine cloud." This leads Dionysius to speak of God as a "pure nothingness." In like vein, Meister Eckhart writes in his sermon *Renovamini spiritu mentis vestrae*: " . . . if I say God is a being, that is not true: He is a transcendent being, and a superessential nothingness."[5] Evidently, one is not to understand God as a non-being, as though God did not exist, but must instead distinguish the act of being or existing [*être*] (*esse* in Latin) from what contemporary philosophy calls "a being" [*un étant*] (*ens* in Latin). Now what we can know are "beings," and being for us is the being of "beings." But if God is not a being in our sense, God's way of being—the being of a non-being—is inaccessible to us. (This distinction is explained perfectly by Saint Thomas Aquinas.) It follows that our knowledge of God can only be that which results from revelation. For the Christian Meister Eckhart, the revealed God is the triune God and the creator God.

Apart from the doctrine of the Trinity, as important as it is within Christian mysticism, we note that the three spiritualities within the three monotheisms are based less on the oneness of the one God than on the creator God, and more generally on the God who reveals, on the God who speaks, because it is through His Word that He creates and reveals. Certainly any understanding of faith has great difficulty comprehending the transition from the unitary and absolutely transcendent Essence to the Creator who speaks through the prophets to creatures. We can observe signs of this difficulty in the generally keen sense of it that Jewish, Christian, and Muslim mystics have all had.

Islam, especially, has forcefully insisted on the doctrine of divine unicity, or *tawḥīd*; therefore we have seen that those who meditate on it most deeply, such as Ibn al-ʿArabī, end up justifying their mystic quest not in the name of the *Aḥadiyya* but in the name of the *Rubūbiyya*. The Qurʾan, in its most literal sense, teaches ceaselessly that God is one, that God has no partners, nor any thing similar to him. Nevertheless, according to tradition, the first verse that was revealed to Muhammad is: "Read:

in the name of your Lord who creates" (96:1: *Iqraʾ biʾsmi Rabbikaʾ lladhī khalaqa*). It is worth noting that this is the Lord who manifests Himself first, and does so as Creator. A commentator on the Qurʾan, Fakhr al-Dīn al-Rāzī, has distinguished two formulas of invocation; the way they are employed at the beginning of certain sūrahs is not arbitrary. The first is *subḥānaʾllāh* (glory to God), and the second is *al-ḥamdu liʾllāh* (praise to God). Their contexts show that glorification is directed toward God in God's own self, in His pure transcendence, beyond any perfection achieved (*fawq al-tamām*), just as praise is directed toward the creator God, who causes His creatures to subsist and fills them with all good things. The Qurʾan limits itself to juxtaposing these two aspects of God, just as Isaiah juxtaposes the hidden God and the God of Israel, the savior God. Mystical theology will attempt, for better or for worse, to explain the passage from one to the other.

Christian thinkers perhaps have the easier task, by reason of their belief in the Trinity. This is apparent in what Meister Eckhart writes in his *Commentary on the Book of Genesis*: "In the one and the same time in which he was God and in which he begot his coeternal Son as God equal to himself in all things, he also created the world. 'God speaks once and for all' [*kî bĕʾaḥat yĕdabber ʾēl*] (Job 33:14). He speaks in begetting the Son because the Son is the Word; he [also] speaks in creating creatures. . . ."[6] Meister Eckhart certainly interprets the text of Job freely. But it is comprehensible that, in eternity, there could never be two temporally distinct divine words, one which generates the Word, the other which creates creatures. It is this unity of the divine Word that explains the sense in which Meister Eckhart has been able to say that God generates His Word in the created human soul, in this "ground" (*grund*) that he calls the "spark of the soul" (*fünkelin der seele*).

The Essence of God is hidden from us just as our own essential reality is hidden from us. Those who are attached to their own bodies, to their temporal existence, to the multiplicity of their perceptions and their thoughts, fall into sin, which means that they become a nothingness for God. By way of compensation, when they have reduced all these veils to nothing—in other words, recognized the nothingness of all that they had taken for being—they understand in the interior silence of their soul the Word that is intimately united to them. The hidden God who had been a pure nothingness to their senses and their vain intellection reveals Himself in His Word in the ground of their soul, at the same time that He reveals it to itself. One can say that God is nothingness for those who wish to grasp Him, while He gives Himself as the supreme Being to those who allow themselves to be seized by Him.

Using a different language, Saint John of the Cross teaches the same doctrine when he speaks of the *nada*, the nothing. In *The Thorns of the Spirit* (colloquy VI),[7] the bridegroom says to the bride: "One can also consider . . . teaching how to think of nothing for just long enough for the soul to strip itself of all knowing and all personal will. It has nothingness as its object, for during this instant, it has nothing of its own, having entirely left itself, and it has nothing of mine because it still does not know my will; it can only await this will and renounce its personal operation in order to receive my action. As soon as the soul is there, I immediately draw it to myself, I transform it, I unite it to myself for as long as I please. . . . In fact, just as I have drawn all things from nothingness, so it is when the soul has no thought nor will except that I work all perfection in it." The bridegroom is Christ; the bride, the soul, responds: "I wish, Lord, that you always find me within this nothing, since it brings such advantages for the soul." God is only a nothingness for a being who cannot conceive of Being. Only within the nothingness of unknowing can God reveal Himself to the soul.

For Christians, this revelation is the fact of the Word of God, who is a person and who, in being made human, has, through the mouth of Christ, spoken the language of humanity. These doctrines undeniably confer on Christian mysticism a very particular character, and to deny or even blur that character is not at issue. One might think, as we put it, that Christians could respond more easily to the problem of passing from the hidden God to the God who speaks, who creates, and who saves. But the goal of our inquiry does not lie in ranking the value of the different mystical theologies. We are, rather, looking for analogies.

But if the Word of God is, for Christianity, hypostasized in the Person of the Son, generated from all eternity and not created, we must recognize that the idea of a divine Word is present in Judaism and in Islam. We note not only that God speaks, since there is revelation, but that moreover His Word is received and thought of as eternal. For Jewish mystics, there exists a supreme Torah beyond the written Torah and the spoken Torah. It is the primordial Word of God or *Tôrâ qĕdûmâ*, eternal or pre-eternal, that is identified with Wisdom (*ḥokmâ*). For most Muslim theologians, except for the Muʿtazilites, the Qurʾan is the eternal and uncreated Word of God. Now it is interesting to note that, in their controversy, the Muʿtazilites who uphold the doctrine of the created Qurʾan, accuse their adversaries of making the divine word a reality co-eternal with God and similar to the uncreated Word of Christian theology.

Undoubtedly, between the Qurʾan which is a book, and the Son of God who is a person, there is only a distant analogy—we would have to say a simple analogy of function. One could say the same about the Torah. Even so, Muslim hermeneutics, in interpreting certain qurʾanic terms, has given the Book an interpretation that no longer retains anything material; thus, Ibn al-ʿArabī sees the first intellect in the Pen which writes and through which God teaches (cf. sūrah 96:4) and the eternal soul in the well-kept Tablet (*al-Lawḥ al-maḥfūẓ*, 85:22) on which the eternal Qurʾan is preserved. This exegesis is comparable to the one that ultimately makes of the Torah the creative wisdom of God.

THE GOD WHO SPEAKS

We see therefore that an understanding of monotheistic faith cannot help but see itself as a learned ignorance within the negativity of unknowing. But the doctrine of the one God, absolutely transcendent and inaccessible, nevertheless has an immediate influence on how the mystical way is conceived. While the purely speculative theologian is confined within the way of negation and can rely only on manifestations that are themselves mysteries of the hidden and unknown God, the mystic empties self, quiets the faculties, is convinced of their total ineptitude, and in this nothingness, rich with silence, hears God speak. And this God who speaks to the mystic is the same One who speaks in His revelation. So it is normal therefore for the mystics to rediscover—in their very depths, within the silent language of God—an infinitely amplified echo of the words that the written texts confine to letters. In their experience, the mystics enjoy the authentic life of these words, their light, their spirit.

Now if these words are bearers of doctrine for the sake of understanding, they are, above all, for anyone who has understood the fallibility of their understanding, bearers of spiritual values. These values are only accessible to the heart. Are we to say then that there is an opposition between the heart and the understanding, that mysticism transcends systematic theology to the point of eliminating all its significance?

Certainly not. Each mystic begins with texts laced with doctrinal notions. The mystic meditates on them and they set him on the path. But, as someone goes along and advances on this path, the texts from which the mystic began and the doctrines that they entail receive a particular light, a light that shines forth from life experience in a way quite different from the light generated by thought. Shall we then say that in the three monotheisms a discovery, a mystical unveiling, would be able to clarify different or even contrary doctrines, in such a way that they become closer and finally coincide? We may respond affirmatively so long as mysticism is not an illusion. But that could only involve a limit toward which spiritual persons tend without ever reaching it. Even if they achieve the deepest and most authentic experiences, we have seen that they can only attempt to communicate them by choosing a language, one that is always inadequate even when it is drawn from sacred texts.

Therefore we will never know whether the three monotheisms actually converge at the level of the mystics' experiences. But we are right in thinking so if we consider, not the term of their ascension, but the paths they follow, insofar as we have detected, in the orientation of these paths, a certain movement of convergence. Even if we must ultimately content ourselves with a simple parallelism, this very affirmation is already encouraging.

THE LAW

The idea of one God not only called for a mysticism based on negative theology, it also has called for a religious ethic centered on the Law. On this point, one can detect a profound similarity of mentalities between Jewish and Muslim legalists. Undoubtedly the Law given through Muhammad differs in many details from the Law of Moses. But it shows much the same spirit, much the same scruple for obeying the commandments of God exactly. One could make many comparisons between certain discussions on points of law between the Talmud and the tracts of Islamic jurisprudence.

It seems that speculative theology, which formulates doctrine, becomes secondary for this kind of mind. This is particularly evident in Islam. Theology (*kalām*) was introduced into Muslim thought due to historical circumstances—upon contact with Jews and Christians, in order to respond to controversy and the need to defend the faith—and was able to utilize numerous qurʾanic texts. However, one can affirm that it has no place in the fundamental intention of Islam. Several of its most important theologians, such as Abūʾl-Ḥasan al-Ashʿari, in the third/ninth century, and Ghazāli, in the fifth/eleventh century, explain that they turned to theology only because they were forced to do so in order to cure believers of the disease of doubt and the seductions of error. For them the ideal would be not to need *kalām*, as was the case with the Companions of the Prophet and the first rightly guided caliphs, the *Rāshidūn*. After all, an organism in good health has no need of medicine.

There is an Arabic term that signifies knowing in general, the word *fiqh*. But the term has come exclusively to designate juridical knowledge. This semantic evolution is symptomatic. So understanding the message comes down essentially to the comprehension of texts that define the *aḥkām*, that is, the legal opinions that touch upon different human actions. Consequently, legalistic Islam does not seek to know who God is, since God is absolutely transcendent; it is enough for it to know what God commands, and in its eyes the only value is obedience (*ṭāʿa*). It has no concern for understanding how this transcendence fits together with the fact of revelation. In this it is profoundly different from mystical questioning. God speaks and God's word is an order; to this order one must comply. Beyond that, there is no room for inquiry; there is nothing to expect besides the realization of promises and threats in the other life—in paradise or in hell.

For many rabbis, observance of the Law is the fundamental question. There is no need to belabor the point. As for Christianity, despite the teaching of Saint Paul concerning the Law, it too has not failed to give great importance to the commandments of God, to which are added the commandments of the Church. There is therefore a very strong and undeniable tendency in the three monotheistic religions to develop into a juridical system.

The three messages present God with a certain number of attributes: He is Omniscient; He is All-Powerful; He is "seeing" and "understanding." To legalists this means that there is no appealing His commandment. It means that one cannot escape punishment, because He knows all and He understands all. It means that one cannot refuse it and still escape His power. But He is gentle and merciful; He forgives. Thus, it is always possible to repent of one's errors, of one's stubbornness. Certainly then, there is a kind of Judaism, a kind of Christianity (especially in the Jansenist form), and a kind of Islam, that agree about the place they assign to the teaching of the fear of God—not the reverential fear known to the mystics and linked to love, but a veritable dread that the Qurʾan does not hesitate to call by its Arabic name: *khawf.*

Let us note, however, that the cult of supreme force through terror is not unique to the monotheisms, and perhaps even they have inherited it from ancient idolatry. We should not forget what Lucretius said of religion "which reared its head from the heights of the heavenly regions and threatened mortals with its horrible face."

> Quae caput a caeli regionibus ostendebat, horribili super aspectu
> mortalibus instans. (I, 64–65)

Thus one is right in thinking that this way of receiving the messages is far from authentic, if only because it reduces religion to a narrow morality of fearful obligation. In fact, the Bible, the Gospels and the Epistles, and the Qurʾan contain something quite different. We can therefore accord only minimal value to this purely moralistic and legalistic understanding of faith, even if it expresses a real convergence of religious mentalities.

THEOLOGIES AND RELIGIOUS SPECULATIONS

Finally, the idea of one God has equally inspired theologies, more or less Gnostic theosophies, and, indeed, philosophies. If there are differences between them, they arise not from the monotheistic messages but from the differing casts of mind among those whom they inspire. Some are based on rigidly logical reason; others prefer the flexibility of a dialectic; still others allow themselves to express their creative imagination. The opposition becomes extreme if one compares gnostic systems with so-called exoteric systems.

Gnosis emerges in every era and grafts itself onto all religions, be they "pagan" or issued from a revelation of one God. There is therefore a Hellenistic gnosis, a Jewish gnosis, a Judeo-Christian gnosis, a Christian gnosis, an Islamic gnosis. The work of Henry Corbin gives some idea of this and shows that Gnostic tendencies persist even in our day, their expression never having ceased throughout the ages. Corbin believes that it is at the level of these gnoses where ecumenism might be realized. This is hardly likely, for it is precisely the nature of esoteric systems to reject as exoteric, purely and simply, whatever relates to the characteristic doctrines of each religion. They substitute for them, they do not include them. The hermeneutic to which these systems submit doctrinal texts is comparable to digestion: it transforms the substances which nourish it into an entirely different substance, just as the flesh of herbivores differs from the plants they consume.

No Jews can recognize themselves in so-called Jewish gnosis; nor do Christians in so-called Christian gnosis; nor Muslims in so-called Muslim gnosis. The only common idea is that of a single principle, the One, absolutely transcendent, unknowable and ineffable, who is manifested through a series of intermediaries, angels or aeons, or whatever name is given to them, until it reaches us. Upon this very simple—indeed, simplistic—schema, are grafted a multitude of strange and fantastic images, of sagas and mishaps, that occur within a pre-eternal *aevum*, in a metahistory, as Corbin puts it. One may find the finest examples in the Chaldean Oracles, in the gnoses of Basilides and Valentinus, and above all in Manichaean gnosis. Hence one cannot for a single instant argue that the gnostic vision has constituted, for monotheistic believers, an understanding of their faith.

In contrast, speculative theology and philosophy, its servant, which are centered on the idea of one God, for example in the treatises that Latin theologians entitle *De Deo Uno*, do constitute an effort to arrive at an understanding of the faith in the three religions. One will find, by comparing works such as those of Avicenna and Averroës, Maimonides and Saint Thomas, a real kinship of thought, based as it is on a common problematic. Moreover, we know much about the intellectual relationships between these great thinkers of the Middle Ages. There is no point in arguing the fact. But their common project concerns, above all, a rational elaboration for which faith is more an object of reflection than a lived reality. Certainly such works are marked, here and there, in a more or less profound fashion, by a living faith. But this faith, where it exists as faith, extends far beyond those works. Consequently, the kinship, and even at times the agreement, between speculative theologians and philosophers is not enough to satisfy us. Their understanding of faith remains quite conceptual and so lets those values which reason has difficulty discerning fall by the wayside.

As a result, if the understanding of monotheistic faith runs up against such great difficulties, if it runs aground not only in attempting to penetrate Being (meaning the way God exists) but further, in grasping faith itself in its essence at the center of the soul, we again find ourselves in the presence of the only possible issue. We must look at the life of faith among those living believers who are the mystics and for the entire length of their journey. We will pause no longer over the revelation of the one hidden God and seek the savior God and the teaching of salvation that He reveals within the messages.

TWO TYPES OF MYSTICS

But having reached this point, we must make a distinction between the mystics of the three monotheistic religions. Some, who qualify as esoteric, are interested in structuring a mystical universe within which their spirit expands and their mystical experience is inscribed. This is the universe of God's manifestations, and it is made of a certain number of hypostasized divine attributes. In Jewish mysticism, for example, there is the Glory of God, His Wisdom (which we have already encountered), and His gracious Love (*ḥesed*). With Ibn al-ʿArabī, there are the names (*asmāʾ*) and the attributes (*ṣifāt*). The image of the Throne (*kissēʾ*, Ezekiel 1:26; *ʿarsh*, Qurʾan 7:54 and *passim*; *kursī*, Qurʾan 2:255) becomes a cosmological entity. Gershom Scholem speaks of texts that report "the peregrinations of the ecstatic through [the celestial regions of the Merkabah]: the seven heavens and the seven palaces or temples . . . through which the Merkabah mystic travels before he arrives at the throne of God."[8] These temples (*hêkālôt*) are similar to the *hayākil* (plural of *haykal*) in the Islamic sense where, says Louis Massignon concerning Ḥallāj, they are the "temples of the eternal city of souls."

Without pursuing this any further, simply note that this esoteric mysticism remains at the level of gnosis and that its devotees have generally been suspect in the eyes of their fellow believers. Nevertheless, this type of thought should not be ignored. For insofar as it works to extract from sacred texts the spiritual values that they contain, it can be related to the second type of mysticism which is our primary concern.

In fact, there are other mystics who have been total strangers to esoteric mysticism. In Christianity and Islam they are numerous. They are rarer within Judaism, where the spirit of kabbalah, very marked by a neoplatonism with gnostic tendencies, was not unique to the thirteenth century where it was strikingly manifest; rather, as Scholem writes, it was nourished by a heritage that has its roots "in the profound religious ferment of the first generations."[9] Consequently Jewish mysticism, taken as a whole, is situated somewhat apart from that which will now interest us among Christians and Muslims. Yet we will not for this reason leave it aside, because the values of pure spirituality that it carries within it are instructive.

Be that as it may, non-esoteric Christian mystics have drawn abundantly from the Bible and the contribution of Judaism among them is considerable. Meditation on the Psalms and the prophets, and especially on the Song of Songs, is the food of their spiritual life. One cannot deny, of course, that the interpretation of these texts is quite different among Jews and among Christians. One sees this above all in relation to the Song of Songs: for Jews the *šîr haš-šîrîm* supports a gnostic vision. For example, Scholem points out that in the Book of *Bahir*, "the bride in the Song of Songs is interpreted as 'field' (*śādeh*), and also as the 'vessel' (*šiddâ*) in whom higher forces flow." (It is necessary to know that, in Hebraic writing, which is neither punctuated nor vocalized, these two words appear to be identical.) Furthermore, a feminine element is introduced, from this angle, into the work of creation. We are a long way from the interpretation of Saint John of the Cross in his *Spiritual Canticle*, and one thinks of the gnostic writings of Basilides and Valentinus, among others. Whatever the contrasts may be, this love poem has been the occasion for all to reflect on the relationships between God and His creation, His people, and in the last analysis, the human soul.

As we have seen, Judaism and Islam have emphasized the revealed Law. Generally speaking, mystics of these two religions, esoteric or not, have remained faithful to the Law. The symbolic meaning of a rite must not usurp the practice of that rite. The case of circumcision offers a marvelous illustration of this point. We know that God said to Abraham (Genesis 17:11): "You must circumcise the flesh of your foreskin, and that will be the sign of the covenant between myself and you." Now, in other passages of the Bible what is at stake is circumcision of the heart. Thus we read in Deuteronomy (10:15–16): "yet it was on your ancestors, for love of them, that the LORD set his heart to love them. . . . Circumcise your heart and be obstinate no longer." Leviticus (26:41–42) takes up the same idea, this time relating it to the Covenant: "Then their uncircumcised hearts will grow humble. . . . I shall remember my covenant with Jacob. . . ." Ezekiel (44:7 and 9) speaks of the sons of strangers, "uncircumcised in heart and body," which assumes a distinction between the two circumcisions. Jeremiah, for his part, places the accent on circumcision of the heart (4:4): "Circumcise yourselves for the LORD, apply circumcision to your hearts." Finally, we cite this magnificent verse from Deuteronomy (30:6): "The LORD your God will circumcise your heart and the heart of your descendants, so that you will love the LORD your God with all your heart and soul, and so you will live."

However necessary circumcision of the heart may be for salvation, it is clear that it does not eliminate circumcision of the flesh, which is the sign of the Covenant. Going further still, circumcision of the flesh is not a mere symbol whose sole value would be to announce circumcision of heart in a figurative way. It is and remains the sign of Covenant. But the

Covenant is the expression of the love of God, who gives life, and this love is linked to circumcision of the heart, which therefore finds itself on another level of meaning. If we now consider what Philo of Alexandria says, we will see that although he is famous for his allegorical commentaries on the Holy Laws, he does not interpret circumcision of the flesh through circumcision of the heart. This is very revealing.

Philo begins by praising the practice of *peritomē* in its material and physical sense, then he adds: "To these [explanations that tradition has handed down to us] I would add that I consider circumcision to be a symbol of two things most necessary to our well-being. One is the excision of pleasures which bewitch the mind. . . . The other reason is that a man should know himself and banish from the soul the grievous malady of conceit."[10] Therefore, circumcision in the flesh is the sign of this double ascesis, while circumcision of the heart, which is linked to love, belongs to an entirely different order.

Some may say, it is true, that circumcision is not necessary in order to dedicate oneself to the struggle against pleasures and presumption. God can directly so order through His commandments. Moreover, God does just that in the Law. Presumption is condemned (Deuteronomy 1:43): "So I told you, but you would not listen, and you rebelled against the voice of the LORD; presumptuously [*wat-tāzidû*] you marched into the highlands." But just as a promise carries more weight when it is signed and sealed, so too the promise to obey God's orders carries more weight when it receives the seal of circumcision. This mark on the body constantly reminds the faithful Jew of his obligation to renounce pleasures and presumption. No reason exists then for abandoning the sign once one has understood its meaning, for human beings need the constant presence of material signs to remind them of their promises.

Jewish mysticism respects the materiality of the Law all the more because in Judaism, Law is a mark of God's love for His people. In return, obedience to the commandments is an expression of Israel's love for its God. Georges Vajda has emphasized forcefully this in his work on the love of God in Jewish theology of the Middle Ages: "To love and fear God is not, in the perspective of rabbinical Judaism, simply a pious counsel, but *miṣwāh*, in other words, an order or positive precept." Love and fear of God are "integral parts of the Law of Moses" (*L'amour de Dieu* . . . , p. 10). In fact, it is written: "For I, the LORD your God, am a jealous God . . . I act with faithful love towards thousands of those who love me and keep my commandments" (Exodus 20:5–6). The same teaching appears to the letter in Deuteronomy (5:10).

Commenting on the verse (1:2) of the Song of Songs—"Let him kiss me with the kisses of his mouth"—the Targum sees there an allusion to the gift of the written Law and the oral Law, for, at Sinai, God spoke face-to-face with Israel, "just like a man who gives a kiss to his companion, out of the great love with which He has loved us." A frequent theme, in Jewish thought, is the distinction between obedience through love and obedience through fear. The second is sufficient, the first is superior. Bahya b. Paquda contrasts the pure love based on the divine essence with a love that still mixes fear and hope and *a fortiori* with a disposition of soul that knows only fear and hope and that concerns itself only with the divine attributes of action through which the Lord rewards and punishes.

The verse (13:5) of Deuteronomy marks a significant progression: "The LORD your God is the one whom you must follow, him you must fear, his commandments you must keep, his voice you must obey, him you must serve, to him you must hold fast [*tidbāqûn*]." This holding fast is what constitutes the highest degree of obedience. The verb *dābaq* means "to reach" and "to be joined to." From this comes the term *dĕbeqût* that in mysticism means communion with God. Bahya insists on this point. He is not alone; one could also cite the name of Abraham b. Ezra.

In Islam, the Law is so important that most Muslim thinkers believe that there is no revelation except that of a Law. The Qurʾan does not present it as linked to God's love for His creatures. Respect for divine transcendence by Muslims comes from numerous verses which affirm that God does what He wills. He commands, He repeals and replaces one Law with another, without any motive other than His arbitrary and sovereign will. What He commands is good because He commands it; what He promulgates in order to repeal is better than what he has abrogated, because He abrogates it. Even more than in the case of the Mosaic Law, one can and must speak here of a *sic volo, sic jubeo.*

Given that its origin is absolutely transcendent, the Muslim Law is purely extrinsic to human beings. Its prescriptions do not uproot the disease which is in the human heart and which the Qurʾan speaks of repeatedly, for example in verse 2:10. What matters is obedience to the Law, whatever its content, because God has decreed that those who obey Him are saved. "And We delivered those who believed and used to keep their duty to God" (41:18). It is not faith and fear that save, but God, wherever this faith and this fear are found. In a word, what is within a human being, and what comes from a human being, is totally devoid of virtue.

Such a point of view is not opposed to all mysticism—far from it. The great spiritual writers know that it is always God who takes the initiative, that it is always God who acts efficaciously, and that everything comes from God without any merit on the part of God's creatures. In Christianity, this conviction culminates in the idea of grace, of prevenient grace, of a free gift. Under another formulation, and with other overtones, it is equally present in Muslim spirituality. Still, it remains no less true that the Islamic conception of the Law is reduced to a set of *aḥkām* that determines what is prescribed, prohibited, counselled, discouraged or allowed, and before which there is nothing to do but accomplish it without questioning. That is why Muslim mystics have sought to interiorize their Law, and have done so by emphasizing certain qur'anic terms such as pious fear (*taqwā*), patience in trials (*ṣabr*), abandonment to God (*tawakkul*), consent given to divine decrees (*riḍwān*), to name the most important. These are responses that the submissive soul makes and that come to designate the mystic states (*aḥwāl*).

The verses that speak of love and the act of loving, whether on the part of God or on the part of humanity, are to be received with their deep and proper meaning. It is written in the Qur'an (51:56): "I created the jinn and humankind only that they might worship me" (*illā li-yaʿbudūnī*). If we compare this verse to the one cited earlier from Deuteronomy (13:5), we note that it stops at the order to serve God, whereas God insists that his people both serve Him and hold fast to Him: " . . . him you must serve [*'ōtô taʿabōdû*, from the same root as the Arabic *yaʿbudūnī*], to him you must hold fast." The qur'anic verse does not rise as high as *dĕbeqût*, communion with God. But the mystics complete the thought simply by replacing it with the love that other verses mention and by giving this love its full weight.

Despite this interiorization, Muslim spirituality does not nullify the Law, and on this point it therefore agrees with the spiritual thinkers of Judaism. Rare are the Sufis who, after the example of Bisṭāmī, in the third/ninth century, have believed that by progressing along the way one could dispense with all material observance. If the Law ceases to be an end in itself, as legalistic minds would have it be, it continues as an indispensable guide of conduct (*hudā*). This term is qur'anic and designates the Qur'an. But it is worth noting that as a guide it concerns the journey and no longer possesses any meaning once one reaches its goal.

In Arabic it is necessary to distinguish, explains Fakhr al-Dīn al-Rāzī, the act of leading along the path (*hudā*) and the act of being led to its term (*ihtidā'*). One must, through the Law, go beyond the Law, through *sharīʿa*, to go on the Way (*ṭariqa*), all the way to Reality (*ḥaqīqa*), in other words, to reach (*ittiṣāl*, the act of rejoining, equivalent to *děbeqût*) the creator God who gives each being the being which belongs to it, the one whom Islam designates under the name of *al-Ḥaqq*. In this way one reaches a contemplative knowledge (*maᶜrifa*) through unveiling (*mukāshafa*). This progression is especially characteristic of the non-esoteric mystics.

As for the esoteric mystics, they believe material observance of laws serves to testify to the presence of God among beings who, taken in themselves and for themselves, would cause the image of the One who is the source and support of all existence to be forgotten. Thus, Ibn al-ᶜArabī, famous for the audacity of his symbolic hermeneutics, is linked to ẓāhirite law, which understands literally all the prescriptions of the Law. He praises as perfect heirs of the Prophet "those who give themselves to God through the Law of His Messenger, until God opens them, in their heart and in their understanding, to the revelation of that which He caused to descend on His Messenger" (*Futūḥāt*, I, ch. 45).

We can see then that the practice of the Law is a means to give oneself entirely to God, while waiting for God to send a light to illuminate the heart and understanding. Ibn al-ᶜArabī also speaks of "preparation" (*istiᶜdād*). The Law in fact prepares for illumination in two ways. First, it teaches the ways to break with creatures, so as to purify oneself of the blameworthy thoughts that creatures inspire. Then it develops praiseworthy thoughts that allow one to return to creatures in order to call them to God. Practicing the Law thus unifies two contrary realities: a retreat from the world and a presence to the world. It prepares one, in the life here-below, to understand the double aspect of the divine Names in which each person can discover the patterns of the divine image that everyone carries within.

In fact, every name of God is the indivisible unity of two reciprocal names: a "name of retreat" (*ism al-tanzīh*) turned toward the Essence that it names, and a "name of assimilation" (*ism al-tashbīh*) turned toward those "traces" or manifestations that it calls forth. From this it follows that the Law is the expression of this dialectic at the level of life in this world and that the Law itself is the last manifestation of the divine. Conversely, the names, at the highest level except for the ineffable Essence, express this dialectic in its ontological meaning. There could therefore be no question of abandoning the Law, which forms an integral part of the structure of the world itself. As a result, and without denying the many differences of varying importance not only between Jewish and

Muslim mystics but among diverse schools of spirituality (whether gnostic or not) situated within the same monotheistic religion, one may rightly conclude that among them all, observance of the Law is one form of the life of faith.

We have still not grasped the particularly mystical form of this life. Nevertheless, in using the hierarchy of stages that we found in Deuteronomy, we can foresee that the movement of a life empowered by the Law toward the mystical life is the journey from service of God toward communion with God. This holds equally for Muslim mystics, insofar as they introduce love at the summit of their ladder. The proof of this is that they come to distinguish between obedience through love and obedience through fear (or as they say more strongly still, through dread: *khawf*). Fakhr al-Dīn al-Rāzī, in his commentary on verse 2:166, as well as Ghazālī in the chapter on love in his book on the revival of the religious sciences, reports a curious *ḥadīth* which focuses on Jesus.

It goes like this: Jesus happens to pass by three people with thin and pale bodies. He asks them what has brought them to this point. They respond that they were afraid of hell. Jesus says to them: "This is a justice to reassure those who are afraid." Continuing on, Jesus later encounters three other figures who are even weaker and paler. "What has put you in the state that I see?" Jesus asks. They reply, "It comes from the desire for paradise." Jesus tells them: "This is a justice imposed by God to fulfill your aspirations." Further still he happens to come upon a final group of three men, at the extreme limit of pallor and weakness. Jesus asks them, "What has brought you to this degree of exhaustion?" They respond: "We love God." Then Jesus tells them: "You will be the ones near to God (*al-muqarrabūn*) at the Day of the Resurrection."

The account is interesting first because it draws in Jesus, the prophet son of Mary, who respects Islam and in whom the Sufis willingly see the messenger of divine love. Furthermore, it employs a particular and noteworthy language: in fact, weakness and extreme pallor are, among non-religious poets of chaste love, marks of the purest form of love—called *ᶜudhrī*-love in Arabic because according to legend it originated in the tribe of *ᶜUdhra*. This love is not only a perfect stranger to all carnal passion, but goes so far as to kill the body: the loving *ᶜudhrī* is devoted to death. We sense how much mysticism makes of these ideas and this vocabulary. Particularly in Iran the heroes of this love have become heroes of mystical love for God. In a certain sense, this poetry has played, in Islam, the role that the Song of Songs has played in Judaism and

Christianity. (The Qurʾan retains no trace of that biblical poem.) But above all, we find in this *ḥadīth* an important word: the ones near (*al-muqarrabūn*) to God. In the sacred Book of Islam, this word sometimes designates the angels, sometimes the Messiah, and sometimes those human beings who are entirely purified. We may mention a few verses from the Qurʾan: "And you will be three kinds: (First) those on the right hand; what of those on the right hand? And (then) those on the left hand; what of those on the left hand? And the foremost (*al-Sābiqūn*) in the race, the foremost in the race: Those are they who will be brought near" (56:7–11).

Fakhr al-Dīn al-Rāzī offers a remarkable commentary on these verses. We know that, according to Muslim belief, human actions are written down by angels and on the Day of Resurrection every person will have to present his book that holds an account (*ḥisāb*) of his good and evil acts, to have them weighed. Given this belief, Rāzī first notes that human beings have a right hand and a left that oppose one another and that they also have a front and a back. This is the basis for the Qurʾan's division of the race. But instead of dividing humanity into four groups, the Qurʾan retains only three.

The first, composed of people on the right, present the book of their actions with the right hand. They qualify for "the most noble" side because it is the strongest, and they are the object of honors. These then are the believers whose good actions outweigh their evil ones; their obedience to the Law outweighs their disobedience. Thus they enter into paradise where they enjoy all its promised delights. The second group is made up of the people of the left who hold their books in the left hand and who will be objects of contempt. The number of their evil actions outweighs the number of their good ones. They will suffer the fire of hell. But since they are believers nonetheless, they will emerge from hell. As for the *muqarrubūn*, these are the people who are not held to any accounting: "They go ahead of all creation. They have no account to render either in the right hand, or in the left." They are at the highest level, above the people of the right. We are given to understand, then, that while they have observed the Law perfectly, they have gone beyond it, so much so that they are dispensed from having to present the book of their acts. Now, what is beyond legal observance is obedience through love.

This then is how Rāzī explains the order in which God enumerates the three groups: God could have followed an ascending or descending order. In fact, God speaks first of the people of the right and then the people of the left; they go together due to the fact that they do not have enough love for God to avoid disobedience; in their case, God must stimulate desire and fear. Those who go before them, who win the prize of nearness to God, need no such motives to obey. They have only reached this stage through an "attraction" (*jadhb*) that emanates from God, an attraction that proceeds from His mercy and which, by itself, is worth more than any worship, more than a lifetime of service (*ʿibāda*). This attraction certainly seems to play the role of communion or of "holding fast" that Deuteronomy situates higher than the service to God.

Finally Rāzī remarks that God does not speak at all of those people who are behind him, who are far inferior even to those who comprise the people of the left hand. "God does not turn towards them," writes Rāzī, "by reason of the violence of His wrath against them." These are the infidels who have not recognized the unicity of God and who will reside eternally in hell. They have only believed in themselves (here-below) and for God they might as well be non-existent. As for the three other groups, Rāzī thinks that the Qurʾan refers to them again in verse 35:32: "But of them are some who wrong themselves and of them are some who are lukewarm, and of them are some who outstrip (others) through good deeds, by God's leave."

So then, the idea that human beings can gain paradise by observing the Law through faith and hope—but that perfection consists in obeying it through love—is just as present in Islam as it is in Judaism. It is certainly likely that a thinker such as Bahya b. Paquda, who lived in Spain among the Muslims and who wrote in Arabic, was subject to a certain influence by those around him. But we have seen that what he wrote is in perfect conformity with the texts of the Torah, and that is what is essential to us.

What are we to say now about the Christian perspective? Materially it retains only the Decalogue. To this one must add the commandments of the church, yet these cannot be placed on the same plane as the Law of Moses. One could interpret the doctrine of Saint Paul as a pure and simple rejection of this Law, but that would be a mistake. One reads, in the Epistle to the Romans: "God's saving justice was witnessed by the Law and the Prophets, but now has been revealed altogether apart from Law: God's saving justice given through faith in Jesus Christ to all who believe" (3:21–22). And later: "Are we saying that the Law has been made pointless by faith? Out of the question; we are placing the Law on its true footing" (3:31).

What Saint Paul criticizes is the belief that the works of the Law justify by themselves and call for reward as though it were a "salary" or "something due." Justification is a pure grace of God founded on His love. Christ, when asked which is the greatest commandment, responds by citing Deuteronomy (6:4,5): "This is the first: *Listen, Israel, the Lord our God is the one, only Lord, and you must love the Lord your God with all your heart, with all your soul,* with all your mind *and with all your strength*" (Mark 12:29–30). And he adds: "The second is this: *You must love your neighbor as yourself*" (12:31). That is why, in the eyes of Christians, what "fulfills" the Law of Moses is the Law of love, founded in the Law of liberty of which Saint James speaks (1:25): "But anyone who looks steadily at the perfect law of freedom and keeps to it [*parameinas*]—not listening and forgetting, but putting it into practice—will be blessed in every undertaking."

This Law of liberty (*nomos tēs eleutherias*) seems to correspond exactly to what holding fast to God demands, namely, the communion of which Deuteronomy speaks and which surpasses simple service. One thinks of what Saint John reports from Christ, in his Gospel (15:15): "I shall no longer call you servants [*doulous*], because a servant does not know his master's business; I call you friends [*philous*], because I have made known to you everything I have learnt from my Father." The Law of liberty liberates from slavery, which is reduced to those things one does only through fear and desire. Moreover, the slave-servant always threatens to betray the master and become unfaithful. It is a *leitmotif* throughout the Bible.

"Who so blind as my servant [*ʿabdî*], so deaf as the messenger I send?" (Isaiah 42:19a). God has given a "great and glorious" Law, but his servant, Israel, has turned away from it. And God complains: "Who is so blind as he who has been restored?" [*mĕšullâm*, in other words, returned to God from exile] (42:19b).[11] The root of this word also implies the idea of a friendship at peace.[12] And in fact, it is divine love that straightens out the distracted servant; the true servant is the one whom God loves and who, thus sustained, serves God through love. "Here is my servant whom I uphold, my chosen one in whom my soul delights" (Isaiah 42:1). And it is certain that God frees this servant from all captivity, from all slavery and from all fear, when He says to the servant: "Do not be afraid, for I have redeemed you; I have called you by your name, you are mine" (43:1), and later: "Since I regard you as precious, . . . you are honored and I love you" (43:4). One can easily move from liberation out of exile to the spiritual liberation it symbolizes.

The idea expressed by Saint James then conforms perfectly to the spirit of Judaism as expressed by the prophet Isaiah. The only difference—and for Christians it is considerable—is that the Law of liberty is founded on faith in the Christ who liberates. Saint Paul is very clear on this point: "Christ set us free, so that we should remain free. Stand firm, then, and do not let yourselves be fastened again to the yoke of slavery" (Galatians 5:1).

FAITH AND WORKS

The issue of faith and works has been the object of grave theological discussions within all three religions. Judaism has made a distinction between *ṣaddîq*—the just and faithful one who, in the rabbinical tradition, observes the commandments and above all the prohibitions that multiply in each generation of the oral Torah—and the *ḥāsid*—the devout and contemplative person who defines the Law (*ʾĕmûnâ*) through communion with God (*dĕbeqût*). In Christianity, the quarrels of the Reformation are well known.

Muslim thought is equally divided over this problem: are works an integral part of faith? The Murjite sect says no: in the presence of faith, disobedience can do no harm, just as obedience is without profit where there is unbelief. A subgroup of Murjites, the Yūnusiyya, disciples of Yūnus b. ʿAwn, teaches that "faith is in the heart and on the tongue, it consists of the knowledge of God, in the love (*maḥabba*) that one bears Him, in the humility that one has in one's heart before Him, and in the recognition by one's tongue that He is one and that there is no other like Him." Faith results when all these elements come together. This sect does clarify that "action carried out by the bodily members" (*al-ʿamal biʾl-jawāriḥ*) does not constitute faith. In contrast, one can cite the Kharijites, who hold that every grave error (*habīra*) amounts to unbelief and that it will be the object of eternal punishment. The Muʿtazilites have attempted to maintain a mediating doctrine by introducing an intermediate state between faith and unbelief, that of people who believe in one God and who still do works of *fāsiq* (those which depart from divine precepts): it is the principle of "the station between two stations" (*al-manzila bayn al-mazilatayn*). Certainly this schematic opening hardly exhausts all the nuances that Muslim theologians have introduced into their discussion of this problem. It is enough, however, to show that the relation between faith and works is presented in Islam in terms that are very close to those of Jewish and Christian theology.

There is no denying that this same problem exists at the base of all mystical reflection, but here its theoretical interest is not really central. Nor does it lie in the practical utility of knowing who is a believer and who is not. Every religious society can be led, in certain times and circumstances, to distinguish sharply between the faithful and the impious, and each requires a criterion. The three monotheistic religions have known condemnations, with more or less serious consequences. The mystics, moreover, have often been victims of such condemnations. But they have not themselves been interested in these two aspects of the question.

HYPOCRISY AND ACTION

In order to understand the issue of faith and works, we must begin by examining what has happened within Christianity.

It is well known that if the thesis of Saint Paul and the thesis of Saint James are read literally, they seem diametrically opposed. In the Epistle to the Romans (4:10 and 13) Saint Paul says of Abraham that "*his faith was reckoned to him as uprightness. . . .* For the promise to Abraham and his descendants that he should inherit the world was not through the Law, but through the uprightness of faith (*dia dikoiosynēs pisteōs*)." Conversely Saint James writes (2:21–23): "Was not Abraham our father justified by his deed, because he *offered his son Isaac on the altar*? So you can see that his faith was working together with his deeds: his faith became perfect by what he did. In this way the scripture was fulfilled: *Abraham put his faith in God, and this was considered as making him upright*." By relying on Saint James himself, theologians have explained quite well that a faith without works is a dead faith: "As a body without a spirit is dead, so is faith without deeds" (2:26; *ē pistis chōris ergōn nekra estin*). Consequently, there is no more contradiction.

If we bring together these two texts that seem to be opposed, we come to the idea that humanity is not justified through the works of the Law, but through a faith that is only true and living insofar as it inspires works. The profound thought of Saint Paul is that practicing the works of the Law carries the serious risk of leading those who practice them to imagine that they are saved through their own merit, of taking pride in the exactitude with which they practice its precepts.

This is the root vice that Jesus denounces in the parable of the Pharisee and the publican: "The Pharisee stood there and said this prayer to himself, 'I thank you, God, that I am not grasping, unjust, adulterous like everyone else, and particularly that I am not like this tax collector here. I fast twice a week; I pay tithes on all I get'" (Luke 18:11–12). This is not—let us note well—a condemnation of the party of the Pharisees, whose zeal Jesus admired; what he attacks is "pharisaism" the behavior of some Pharisees, but not their doctrine, which we propose to call "phariseeism." He says: "The scribes and the Pharisees occupy the chair of Moses. You must therefore do and observe what they tell you; but do not be guided by what they do, since they do not practice what they preach" (Matthew 23:2–3). That is why they are called hypocrites.

The Greek word *hypokritēs* denotes an actor or comedian who wears a mask. The hypocrite is the person who plays a role, who puts on a spectacle. That is why Jesus repeatedly warns against this evil: "Be careful not to parade your uprightness in public to attract attention [*pros to theathēnai autois*. . . . So when you give alms, do not have it trumpeted before you; this is what the hypocrites do in the synagogues and in the streets to win human admiration. . . . And when you pray, do not imitate the hypocrites: they love to say their prayers standing up in the synagogues and at the street corners for people to see them [*opōs phanōsin tois anthrōpois*]" (Matthew 6:1–2,5). So then, the great danger in action is that the "actors" are always tempted to put on a spectacle for others and for themselves. When we put the accent on action, it leads us to forget that, for the substance of the spiritual life, the initiative comes from God. That is why subordinating works to faith in God is indispensable. We do this by cultivating total humility with God's help (Christians say: by God's grace).

Works should be oriented toward God through right intention. Jews call this intention *kawwānâ*. Martin Buber, in his book on Hasidism, dedicated an important passage to it, concerning the teaching of Baᶜal Shem Tov: "*Kavana* is the mystery of a soul directed to a goal [*Ziel*]. Kavana is not will. It does not think of transplanting an image into the world of actual things. . . . Kavana does not mean purpose [*Zweck*] but goal. But there are no *goals*, only the *goal* . . . : redemption."[13] Nothing illustrates better how one should not become attached to the materiality of a work or to its visible aspect, which one would want everyone to see in order to draw acclaim.

We find these same ideas expressed in the thought of an earlier and thus very different thinker, Juda b. Samuel Halévi. To him, writes Georges Vajda in the work cited above, "Authentic communion between the human person and God cannot exist through the intermediary of Israel's faith, apart from the practices imposed by revelation."[14] Consequently, observance of the Law, though essential, is valuable only through faith and in the act of faith. Moreover, this is a faith that transcends individuals and raises them above themselves. It does not look to merits and rewards, but to the love of God. Juda Halévi writes in the *Kuzari*: "You should rejoice in the Law itself, out of love for the lawgiver. Consider the distinction by which you have been the object by having received this Law; think of yourself as guest of the lawgiver, invited to His table and profiting from His kindly welcome, and be thankful for it both in your heart of hearts and publicly." To observe the Law is not to increase one's personal value; it is to participate in an order according to which God through His love has organized the people of Israel, in the desert, after the image of the order of the created universe.

From this point of view, we can say analogically that Christ is for Christians what mystical Israel is for Jews. If there is a great difference at the level of doctrinal reality, it diminishes considerably at the level of lived spiritual reality. In Israel and through Israel God shows His Love; through and with Israel, Jews respond to God's love by observing the Law that God sent out of love for Israel, by sending it Abraham, Isaac, Jacob, Moses. Likewise, through Christ and in Christ God shows love to His creatures, for all has been created for Christ who recapitulates all creation, since at the end of time, all things will be recapitulated in him (Ephesians 1:10: *anakephalaiōsasthai ta panta en tō Cristō*); it is also through Christ, in him and with him, that Christians glorify God. We clearly see here how doctrinal conflicts can give way to profound analogies on the plane of lived experience.

If Jesus denounced the hypocrisy of Pharisees who were scrupulously attached to the letter of the Law, the prophets did the same. In Isaiah (29:13–14) it is the Lord who denounces the conduct of God's people who, He says, "approach me only in words, honour me only with lip-service, while their hearts are far from me," for "reverence for me, as far as they are concerned, is nothing but human commandment" (*miṣwat ʾănôšîm mĕlummādâ*; 29:13–14). The end of this verse is very important. We have seen that *kawwānâ* should not be the product of human will. In fact, observance of the Law demands a perfect stripping of self and a total humility, lest pride slip in and destroy the value of observing the Law. Consequently, the teachings of Judaism, just like those of Christianity, demand of both that the practice of works not engender any ostentation, any self-satisfaction, if it is to maintain its meaning and its authentic spiritual impact.

Among Christian thinkers following the apostolic age, it would be necessary to cite at length Saint Augustine and the numerous commentaries he made on the verses of Paul and James we mentioned above. For him, "to be under the Law" presumes that one has the power to justify oneself by observing it, and within this presumption lies evil, while the Law itself is good. It makes the reality of sin clear to people and, to the degree that it is unable to liberate them, it must make them understand their weakness when unaided by grace. Yet Augustine believes that the Jews of the ancient covenant, who practiced their Law in their heart, were justified by grace without knowing it. What stands out here is the testimony of a great doctor in favor of the idea that it is possible, as we have suggested, to dissociate, up to a certain point, the reality of doctrinal truths and the reality of lived values.

Jews, of course, will not accept this explanation, but they could draw the same conclusion about Christians by maintaining that those among them who are justified will be so thanks to their union—at least their implicit union—with Israel. This is what one can legitimately draw from the verses of Isaiah where he says that God will bring together the "foreigners [*bĕnê han-nēkār*] who adhere to the LORD to serve him, to love the LORD's name" with those who observe the Sabbath, on His holy mountain. "[F]or my house will be called a house of prayer for all peoples [*lĕkol hā-ʿammîn*]. The LORD God who gathers the exiles of Israel declares: There are others I shall gather besides those already gathered" (Isaiah 56:8). The expression *ben-nēkar* designates the foreigner, in the sense of the pagan or non-Jew. In his prophecy Isaiah juxtaposes the return from exile and the gathering of God's people on one hand, and the return and reassembly of the nations on the other hand. He goes even farther, it seems, and suggests that the two series of events are linked.

Consequently, on this point at least, the kabbalah of Luria and his disciples in the fourteenth century certainly seems to be in line with this ancient tradition. Gershom Scholem writes in this regard: "Galut [exile] and redemption are not historical manifestations peculiar to Israel, but manifestations of all being . . . and though the redemption of Israel in the national and secular sense remained a very real ideal [that is never repudiated], it was widened and deepened by making it the symbol of the redemption of the whole world, the restoration of the universe to the state it was to have attained when the Creator planned its creation."[15] For Christians, the whole world will be saved through the Messiah, who is Jesus. For Jews, the whole world will be saved through Israel: "The Messiah here becomes the entire people of Israel rather than an individual Redeemer: the people of Israel as a whole prepares itself to amend the primal flaw."[16] In any case, for the great spiritual writers of these two kindred religions, what counts as essential in both cases is the life of the heart and love.

VAINGLORY AND SELF-OSTENTATION

But let us return to Saint Augustine. He too denounces the quest for vainglory through the practice of works. Note the remarks he makes in the treatise on the Sermon on the Mount: "How senseless, therefore, are they who look for God with bodily eyes, since He is seen by the heart, as elsewhere it is written: 'And seek Him in simplicity of heart' [Wisdom 1:1]. For this is a clean [or pure] heart, one that is a simple heart; and as the light of this world cannot be seen save with sound eyes, so God cannot be seen unless that is sound by which He can be seen."[17]

Later, Augustine makes this important observation: "Once we have cleansed this eye [of the heart] in good part, it is difficult to prevent particles of dirt from finding their way in unnoticed—from the things that usually go with our good actions, as, for instance, human praise. If it is true that not to live well leads to ruin; but to live well and yet not wish to be praised—what is this but to be an enemy of human ways, which surely are the more to be pitied the less the good lives of men meet with approval. Therefore, if the people with whom you live do not praise you for your right living, they are at fault; but if they do praise you, you are in danger—unless you are so single-hearted and pure that what you do as you should you do not do because of men's praise, and that you give credit to those who praise what is right because they delight in good, rather than to yourself, because you would live uprightly even if no one praised you; and that you realize that praise accorded you redounds to the benefit of those who praise you if they honor not you for your good life, but God, whose most holy temple everyone is who leads a good life; so that what David said is fulfilled: 'In the Lord shall my soul be praised; let the meek hear and rejoice' [Psalm 34:3]. . . . The heart of simplicity, that is, the clean heart, belongs only to him who lives beyond human praise and in his right living looks only to Him and strives to please only Him who alone reads the conscience. And whatever proceeds from the purity of such a conscience is praise-deserving in proportion to its lack of desire for human praise."[18] Saint Augustine denounces only the quest for the good opinion of others. But it goes without saying that the good opinion one can have of oneself is no less dangerous.

Saint Teresa of Avila recounts, in the *Foundations*, the story of a sick nun for whom a priest came each day to celebrate mass and give her communion. When the illness dragged on, the ecclesiastic, "a great servant of God" according to the saint, believed that he should no longer give her communion this way, every day at home. Having heard mass without receiving communion, the sister flew into a violent rage. She died that same day. "Hence I came to understand," writes Saint Teresa, "the harm done by following our own will in no matter what; and especially in so important a matter. . . . This good soul had the opportunity to humble herself very much, and perhaps she would have thereby merited more than by receiving communion." And Saint Teresa concludes: "Believe me, it is clear that a love of God (I do not mean that it is really love but that in our opinion it is) that so stirs the passions that one ends up offending the Lord, or so alters the peace of the enamored soul that no attention is paid to reason, is in fact self-seeking."[19]

Using another language, one that contrasts "spiritual willpower" with "sensible willpower," Saint John of the Cross teaches the same doctrine. Note the words he places in the mouth of the bridegroom (*Thorns of the Spirit*, colloquy V):[20] "Note that desire, love, joy, sadness, spiritual fear and hatred of evil or love of good produce peace and repose in your soul, just as all the sentiments coming from passion and the sensible appetite give birth to trouble and agitation. Is it possible that you are not content with spiritual love, spiritual fear and spiritual joy, but that you still want sensible desire, love and joy for good, and likewise sensible sadness, hatred and horror for evil?" The difficulty is to do good out of spiritual love for God, to turn from evil out of spiritual love for God, and not to do either out of a sensibility that relates everything to oneself.

Shall we inquire of a German mystic? Here is what Johannes Tauler says in a sermon (no. 40) on the passage, "Have one soul at prayer" (1 Peter 3:8):[21] "When Saint Peter says that we should be single-minded, he means that we should cling to God as our sole and supreme good, that at the moment of prayer we must fix our soul's gaze firmly and unswervingly on Him, and adhere to God with patience and love. . . . The same is true of an inward, regenerate person; his enjoyment is all inward. With the light of reason he swiftly surveys his exterior faculties and instructs them in their activity; but inwardly he is immersed and drawn into God, joyfully adhering to Him. And in this state he remains unhindered by his activity [or works]."[22]

This text clearly evokes the Jewish doctrine of *dĕbeqût* and the text from Deuteronomy on service to God and communion or holding fast to God. In his work on the books of the Hasidism, Martin Buber translates the thought of Baᶜal Shem Tov in terms that agree exactly with what Tauler says: "When [man] collects himself and becomes one [*sich sammelt und vereint*], he draws near to the oneness of God—he serves his Lord. This is avoda [*ᶜabōdâ*, service]. . . . Similarly, there are two kinds of love for God: the love through the teaching and prayer and the fulfillment of the commandments—this love ought properly to be consummated in silence and not in public, in order that it may not tempt one to glory and pride—and the love in the time in which one mixes with the creatures, when one speaks and hears, gives and takes with them, and yet in the secret of one's heart one cleaves to God and does not cease to think of Him. And this [second kind of love] is a higher rung than that [first kind of love]."[23]

Muslim mysticism, in its non-gnostic form, offers exactly the same type of meditation. Qushayrī (986–1064), in his *Risāla*, furnishes us with its elements. Human reality entails three levels.

First, there is a superficial level, that of the soul, which we may call consciousness of self. For the Arab word *nafs* (soul) normally serves to express the reflexive (in order to say "to be killed" one employs the phrase "to kill the soul"). The time of the soul (*zamān*) is a continuous duration (*mudda*) that allows for effort (*ijtihād*) and that develops. So it is that a person can observe the commandments by making an effort of obedience on one hand and resistance to all that pulls toward rebellion on the other. This level of the soul belongs to the Law (*sharīᶜa*). Here the conscious will can operate, but the consciousness involved in an effort of will is ambiguous. In fact, it is indispensable if one is to exert oneself to observe the Law. But on the other hand, it is conscious of itself, and all self-consciousness implies, as Sartre rightly observed, some bad faith. Making an effort for something to be is indistinguishable from making an effort for it to be visible. Those who make an effort to practice justice perform acts that appear just without their necessarily being so. And for this reason it is necessary both to follow the path of action and not to stop there.

The Arabic language has a verb form that carries with it the idea of demonstrating a quality, most often by surpassing others. Thus there is *karuma* (first form: to be generous); *kārama* (third form: to vie with generosity); *takārama* (sixth form: to show oneself generous). Consequently, the effort to apply the Law implies a self-consciousness through which one sees oneself act and in which one takes pleasure. So it is that those who act, even in doing good, develop a tendency to admire themselves, to glorify themselves, to make a spectacle of themselves before both themselves and others.

Every believer who observes the Law more or less risks playing to the gallery then — that is, risks becoming a hypocrite in the etymological sense of the word. In the language of the mystics, this kind of hypocrisy bears the name of *riʾāʾ*, from the root *raʾā*, which has the meaning of "to see." It involves precisely the act of making oneself seen or of seeing oneself. Those who let themselves fall into the trap of *riʾāʾ* are inexorably turned away from God. Thus it is indispensable to wipe away self-consciousness by struggling against the soul (*mujāhadat-al-nafs*); what the mystics call *fanāʾ*, which we must not take to be the annihilation of self but the suppression of that self-consciousness which involves self-love (*ʿujb*) and affectation (*taṣannuʿ*).

The problem is therefore to escape from *riʾāʾ* in order to arrive at sincerity (*ikhlāṣ*), which consists in discovering the authenticity of one's being. This is practically impossible for human beings unless they obtain help from God. For sincerity is always outside any consciousness one may have of it. The mystic Abū Yaʿqūb al-Sūsī said: "When they have sincerity before their eyes, within their sincerity, their sincerity needs sincerity." Qushayrī gives to *ikhlāṣ* a definition that recalls what Martin Buber said of *ḥāsîd* in the passage cited above: "Sincerity consists in taking God alone as goal [*qaṣd* = *Ziel* in German] in the act of obedience, and in willing, by obeying Him, to draw closer to Him." One should not seek anything besides this drawing close, and that excludes "affectation before some creature, acquisition of some title of honor among men, or love of praise proceeding from a created being."

Al-Daqqāq, a Moroccan Sufi of the twelfth century, distinguishes two kinds of sincerity: one which he calls *ikhlāṣ* "which consists in guarding against the consideration accorded by creatures," and *ṣidq*, which can be translated as "interior truth" and that consists in "purifying oneself of the attention given to the soul." He adds that the sincere person (*mukhliṣ*) is someone with no hypocritical ostentation (*riʾāʾ*), and that the true person (*ṣādiq*) is the one in whom there is no self-infatuation (*iʿjāb*; cf. *ʿujb*: self-love).

The second level is that of the heart (*qalb*). In the heart, continuous time is no longer. Instead, there are discontinuous moments (*awqāt*). Thus, personal effort no longer exists; everything is a gift of God in these privileged moments. Consciousness of self has disappeared; the person is entirely turned toward God and one's entire life is for God's sake (*liʿllāh*). Here is the place where human love for God resides. At this stage the faithful believer is the "lover" (*murīd*) and God the "beloved" (*murād*). But since in reality all initiative proceeds from God, and since human love for God is necessarily given by God in the heart, the person soon discovers a third level.

On the third level, the level of an intimate secret (*sirr*), one discovers that in fact it is God who loves, and that it is the human being who is loved. Then the mystic experiences the action of God at the deepest core of the self, through divine touches called *tawāriq*, which are outside the states of the heart (*aḥwāl*) and are purely instantaneous, without any duration at all. This is the experience of God's action at the source of being. Works become, at this level, the works of God in the person, who then fulfills that word of the Qurʾan which affirms that God is nearer to us than our jugular vein (50:16).

Thus, because the life of faith implies a life at the level of works, whatever one's idea of divine Law may be, one notes that on this issue of works, their place in the quest for God, their importance and their dangers—the spiritual writers of the three monotheistic religions have had similar doctrines and analogous experiences. For all of them, the problem is the following: to obey God and do good without erecting the screen of actions in which one takes pleasure, until it comes between God and the human agent.

The situation is logically inextricable. It is necessary to sustain a middle course that at first glance seems untenable, a course between action that concentrates on the conscious subjects of action and cuts off their relationship with God, and non-action that leads to quietism. And quietism is a great temptation for many mystics. The solution is to consider and eventually become intimately convinced that the sole value of an action resides in the fact that it is willed by God and that in executing it the faithful are united with God's will. It seems therefore that the first degree of union after works and obedience to the Law consists in this union of will.

GOD'S WILL AND HUMAN WILL

Explaining the nature or even the simple existence of an *ad extra* will in God involves a difficult theological problem. Why and how would

God will that there be something outside of Himself? Such a will can be eternal, and if not, how does it appear? What is its relation with divine wisdom? Is it purely arbitrary, does it conform to wisdom, or is it identified with wisdom? Within the three theologies of the three monotheisms, whether speculative or mystical, diverse and conflicting theories have been formulated. We cannot consider them because they are outside our objective. But we cannot allow ourselves to suppose that there is unanimous agreement here; contrary to what one would expect, questions of a speculative order where reason is at work raise the greatest and most serious divergences.

But theology can lead us far from spiritual experience, even when it concerns so-called mystic theology, and most especially when it turns toward esotericism and is nourished, not on the Word of God, but on quite human systems of gnosis and on neoplatonic doctrines (as is often the case, we have said, for most medieval Jewish writings linked to the kabbalah). The mystical soul bases itself on divine teaching; it only knows the Way that God has revealed. Further still, it confesses that it is God who causes the soul to know and asks for this help in its prayers: "Direct me in your ways, O LORD, and teach me your paths. . . . Integrity and generosity are marks of the LORD, for he brings sinners back to the path. Judiciously he guides the humble, instructing the poor in his way [*darkô*]" (Psalm 25:4,8,9). We may also cite these verses: "Let dawn bring news of your faithful love, for I place my trust in you. . . . Teach me to do your will, for you are my God" (Psalm 143:8,10). "Teach me, LORD, your ways, that I may not stray from your loyalty [*ba-ʾămitekā*]; let my heart's one aim [*yaḥēd*] be to fear your name" (Psalm 86:11). The biblical texts then are very clear. To do the will of God, to follow His ways and thus to be united to Him in fear (here, reverential fear formed out of love, respect and humility) — this is what we must ask in prayer.

Concerning medieval Jewish mysticism, we should keep in mind what Gershom Scholem writes on the kabbalah from the center in Gerona: The creature's return to God "is accomplished in the elevation of the *kawwānâ*, in the introversion of the will that, instead of spending itself in multiplicity, 'collects' and concentrates itself and, purifying itself of all selfishness, attaches itself to the will of God, that is, joins the 'lower will' to the 'higher will.' The commandments and their fulfillment are the vehicles of this movement of return to God."[24]

Clearly, one must allow for God's initiative and this is precisely what one asks in prayer. Otherwise there is no greater danger, both for oneself and for others than the danger of attempting to do God's will through a decision of one's own will. It can likewise happen, as Scholem points out, that "The mystical conformity of the will is visibly transformed into a magical one." On this point the author reports what Rabbi Gamaliel, son of Juda Hanasi, said: "Make His will as your will in order that He make your will as His will. Abolish your will before His will, in order that He abolish the will of others before your will."[25]

In Christian revelation, Christ's prayer on the Mount of Olives is well known: "Nevertheless, let your will be done, not mine" (Luke 22:42). And it is said in the Our Father "Your will be done on earth as it is in heaven." Christian mystics have meditated deeply on these words. We will limit ourselves to quoting Saint Teresa of Avila.

Saint Teresa remarks that there are souls who are not exercised "in denying their own will." That is why "they think they don't fear the world anymore but instead fear God." In fact they remain sensitive to things of the world, even in matters concerning the glory of God, and at the least occasion, "their concern for their own honor revives."[26] In the next chapter, commenting on the verse from the Song of Songs (1:2): "Let him kiss me with the kisses of his mouth," Saint Teresa has the Bridegroom say: "O holy bride, let us turn to what you ask for: that holy peace which makes the soul, while remaining itself completely secure and tranquil, venture out to war against all worldly kinds of peace. Oh, how happy will be the lot of one who obtains this favor since it is a union with the will of God; such a union that there is no division between Him and the soul, but one same will. It is a union not based on words or desires alone, but a union proved by deeds."[27] It is necessary then that the works God commands express this unity of human and divine wills.

In Islam, the same idea, drawn from qurʾanic texts, is equally central to the mystics. An extremely important word is *riḍā* (or *riḍwān*) which means consent to or enjoyment of something or someone. This term is, let us recall, from the same semitic root as the Hebrew *rāṣāh* (to want, to take pleasure in, to accept), from which comes the word *rāṣôn* in Psalm 143, where it has the sense of will.

The Qurʾan uses this root frequently. "God taking pleasure [*raḍiyaʾ llāhu ʿanhum*] in them and they in Him. That is the great triumph" (5:119). "God has pleasure in them and they have pleasure in Him. This is (in store) for him who fears his Lord" (98:8). "Through it [the Book], God guides those who follow His pleasure [*riḍwān*] on paths of salvation." We end these qurʾanic quotations with the beautiful verse

89:27–28: "But ah, you soul at peace! Return unto your Lord, content in His good pleasure [*rāḍiyatan marḍiyya*]!"

We see that this consent, this pleasure, is reciprocal, and that it designates well the union of human will and divine will in *riḍwān*. The question arises whether *riḍā* is a mystic station (*maqāma*) that humans can reach through their efforts and whether it is therefore an acquisition (*iktisāb*), or whether instead it concerns a mystic state (*ḥāl*), in other words a pure gift of God bestowed on the heart. The Sufis of Khurāsān hold the first thesis, those of Iraq hold the second. Qushayrī tries to reconcile the two points of view by saying that "the beginning of *riḍā* is acquired by man and constitutes a station, while its term is one of the states (*aḥwāl*) and is not acquired."

This solution is satisfactory, for it is clear that the faithful can make an effort to fulfill God's will and give one's consent to it. But such an effort risks involving pride and taking pleasure in self; in a word, such an intention must be purified, something that can truly be realized only through God's action. Abū ʿAlī al-Daqqāq said: "*Riḍā* consists in the fact that one does not revolt against the ruling [*ḥukm*] and the decree [*qaḍāʾ*] of God. . . . Know that humans can hardly give their consent to God, and then only after God consents to them." It is said (in a *ḥadīth*) that Moses says, "My God, show me an act such that, when I have fulfilled it, You will give me Your consent thanks to it." God replies to him: "You cannot do such an act." Then Moses prostrates himself upon the ground in all humility. When God says to him: "O son of ʿImrān. My consent is in the consent that you give to My decree."

Consequently, no human act is capable of obtaining God's consent as such. The precondition is that a person accept the divine decree, the one, al-Daqqāq explains, "by which he has received the order to consent," that is to say, the one that touches and engages him. In fact, the decree that emanates from the absolute will of God, the *mashīʾa*, is itself so transcendent that humanity would not be able to know it. Consequently, one cannot be asked to consent to it. If we imagine a man who rebels against the will of God and who thinks that his rebellion is an effect of divine decree, we can insist that he is not allowed to consent to such a decree whose existence he supposes without knowing it. In a general fashion, he is not allowed to accept being unfaithful under the pretext that God wills it.

Another error, close to the preceding, consists in being more attached to the evils one suffers than to the goods one enjoys, by thinking that the former come closer to God's will. This is purely human evaluation that overestimates the values of ascesis and that is the very inverse of pure *riḍā*. A comment of Abū Dharr, a Companion of the Prophet, famous for his ascetic life, was reported to Ḥusayn, son of the caliph ʿAlī. Abū Dharr had said: "For me, poverty is more pleasant than wealth, and sickness is more pleasant than health." Ḥusayn responded: "May God have mercy on Abū Dharr! As for me, this is what I say: Those who have trust in the goodness of the choices God has made for them desire nothing other than what God has chosen for them."

It is necessary in fact to keep the doctrine of *riḍā* from turning into quietism. Some Muslim mystics have not been able to avoid the danger. Thus Abū Sulaymān al-Dārānī said: "*Riḍā* consists of not asking God for paradise and not seeking God's help against hell." And, still more clearly: "If God sent me into hell, I would give that my consent." We may note that quietism remains a virtual tendency among all mystics. Perhaps it has distant roots in Buddhism. It has existed in Christianity; recall the Alumbrados, Miguel de Molinos and Madame Guyon. The Catholic Church has condemned it. In Islam, it has remained marginal.

Abū Bakr b. Ṭāhir defined *riḍā* in these terms: "It is the act of expelling from one's heart every aversion until nothing remains except joy [*faraḥ*] and contentment [*surūr*]." But one must still avoid taking pleasure in this joy. Ibn al-Khafif said that *riḍā* is the repose [*sukūn*] of the heart that trusts itself to divine decrees, and the consent of the heart to God's good pleasure. But one must not seek to consent in order to enjoy this repose: the goal is consent itself, for that consent is itself repose in God's will, and it would be a mistake to think of it as the means for reaching such repose. Qushayrī in fact remarks: "When a man seeks to enjoy his *riḍā* and finds the quietude [*rāḥā*] of *riḍā* in his heart, he is in a state that like a veil hides from him the view of what he should be seeing." And he cites the testimony of dʾal-Wāsiṭṭī: "You who find acts of obedience sweet, beware, for they are then a lethal poison." In a word, *riḍā* consists of taking pleasure in the will of God and in God's decree, but not taking pleasure in one's own pleasure.

Concerning the soul at peace, consenting and consented to [by God], of which the Qurʾan speaks, it is also present in the experience of Jewish and Christian mystics. Bahya b. Paquda speaks of it as a soul prepared to receive the love of God. But perhaps there is a trace of Muslim influence in him. He writes in the *Introduction aux devoirs des coeurs*: "Abandon, by its essence, is what gives peace to the heart." Abandonment is born of submission to God. Now "the submission that is born from the Torah's warning can be by heavenly intention, but it is equally possible that it is exercised within an impious will to attract the praise and honor of men." If human beings have the power to accomplish the worship that the Torah imposes, since it suffices to so will and to be ready, on the other hand "the submission of praise and jubilation is only accomplished within a person through the power and help of the Lord." And Bahya cites Psalm 119, for example verses 35–37: "Guide me in the way of your commandments, for my delight [*ḥāpāṣtî*] is there. Bend my heart to your instructions, not to selfish gain. Avert my eyes from pointless images [or vanity; *šāwʾ*], by your word give me life." We also find verse 165: "Great peace [*šālôm rāb*] for those who love your Law; no stumbling-blocks for them!"

Saint Teresa of Avila expresses insights of comparable worth in several passages of her works. She writes for example in *The Interior Castle*: "[O]ne cannot arrive at the delightful union if the union coming from being resigned to God's will is not very certain. Oh how desirable is this union with God's will! Happy the soul that has reached it. Such a soul will live tranquilly in this life, and in the next as well. Nothing in earthly events afflicts it unless it finds itself in some danger of losing God or sees that He is offended: neither sickness, nor poverty, nor death. . . ."[28]

CONCLUSION

So even while the monotheistic understanding of faith must come to grips with the speculative demands of the philosophical theology of the One and the Absolute, the life of this faith is not at all troubled by such problems. Certainly belief in One God does not say who this God is, because in fact to speak of what is one and absolutely one is to recognize that God is not at all what we call a being. It is in this sense that God is *no-thing*. But this nothingness of God, in the meditation of the mystics, is a constant call to detachment from all that is not God—detachment from creatures, but further and above all, detachment from oneself, from what one desires, from what one does.

In sum, a certain ascesis, what Christian spiritual writers designate under the name of the purgative way, occurs on the level of what is lived out, as a parallel to the *via negativa* on the level of speculation.

But the negative way leads nowhere, except to the confession that God is inaccessible and ineffable. Does the ascetical way lead to some thing, or rather, does it discover some one? Does the way that follows the purgative life make an illuminative life accessible, and beyond that, a unitive life? The evidence is clear for the mystics who have experienced the love of God and with it the will to unite their will to God's will. To love God, does that mean loving a dream? To do God's will, is that not simply to submit to destiny?

There is, in Islam, a significant *ḥadīth* of the prophet: "Do not insult destiny [*dahr*], for God is *dahr*." The meaning, it is said, is that all the blows of destiny which strike one have God as their agent; consequently, to insult destiny is to insult God. But it is faith that substitutes God for destiny in this way. There exists, moreover, a variant on this *ḥadīth* that says: "for *dahr* is God." This is more satisfying for a believer, given that reducing God to destiny is something entirely different from reducing destiny to God.

Ultimately that is the whole question. But it is a speculative question that mystics find totally pointless, because they speak in the name of an experience engendered by faith in a God who is no doubt one, but who also speaks; faith in a Word which gives birth to faith and nourishes it. Fundamentally, it is not so much the content of the message with all its dogmatic and theological extensions, but the very fact of the message that matters and serves as motivation for the journey toward God.

It is clear that the God of Islam, who repeals the Law of Moses and who relativizes the Covenant with Israel, could not be the God of the Jews; neither can this be the God of Christians, because He reveals the error that constitutes and must constitute for every Muslim the belief in the Trinity and in the Incarnation, without which there is no Christianity. On this plane, the three monotheisms cannot but mutually exclude one another. But the Jew believes that God speaks in the Bible; the Christian believes that God, through His Word made flesh, speaks in the Gospels; the Muslim believes that God speaks in the Qurʾan, indeed, that the Qurʾan is His own eternal Word.

For mystics of the three religions, this Word announces God's love for humanity, God's mercy, God's pardon of failings, God's salvific will; it guarantees God's assistance on the Way, the Way that this Word reveals and that allows the faithful to respond through their own love to the Love that proceeds from God. Under these conditions, one would expect to find, in each description of this Way, profound similarities, analogies, parallelisms, between the declarations of Jewish, Christian, and Muslim mystics. Moreover, they essentially agree in affirming the authentic reality of their experience, the experience of union between their will and God's, thanks to an indispensable divine help, the experience of their love for God being fanned into a flame by the Love of God for them. What characterizes this experience, among all monotheistic mystics, is that it is felt to be given; in other words, it is not produced by any particular activity of their psyche. Rather it is a spiritual revelation which, through an unveiling that breaks with that psychic activity, begins by reducing it to nothing, to a *nada*, in order to invade the soul in its place.

Thus God speaks first of all in His revelation, and this revelation is received by the mystics of the three monotheisms in such a way that it becomes for them the guide that leads them to spiritual, interior revelation, in which the Word that appeals to their heart now penetrates their heart, enlivens it, and lives in them as a Word of love.

4

EXPRESSIONS OF MYSTICAL EXPERIENCE: THE LANGUAGE OF NEOPLATONISM

Our quest for kinship, affinities, parallelisms, or convergences should remain prudent. A foundational remark needs to be made: a great number of differing mystical doctrines exist within one and the same religion. We can find varied and often even opposed conceptions within Judaism, Christianity, and Islam. What then will happen when we move from one religious climate to another?

It is always possible, amid so many variations, that some tendency which appears at the heart of one of the three religions will oppose other tendencies evident in this same religion, but yet at the same time agree with tendencies one can discover elsewhere. For example certain Hasidic values appear among Christian or Muslim mystics, even while they conflict with kabbalah, properly speaking. So the situation is very complicated. There can be no question here of reviewing the ways of conceptualizing proper to all the spiritual families and as well as systems through which they express themselves. We will have to go to the essential.

But what is the essential? Would it not be arbitrary to define it? Certainly. But because we have seen that the monotheistic mystics are unique in asserting that their particular experience of God is authentic, we will continue to focus our effort on examining what they say about their experience, without stopping to scrutinize systematic forms of expression; the latter have no meaning except within mystical theology. Such a theology may very well integrate the communicable characteristics of a particular experience, but it remains a conceptual elaboration, even though produced by the mystic himself. Saint Teresa of Avila was extremely prudent on this point. She wrote, for example, in the eighth chapter of her *Life*: "The good that one who practices prayer possesses has been written of by many saints and holy men. . . . If it were not for this good, even though I have little humility, I should not be so proud as to dare speak about mental prayer. I can speak of what I have experience of."[1]

Again, we may cite a passage from a letter to Don Alvaro de Mendoza, the bishop of Avila, where Saint Teresa rendered, as she had been asked to do, her judgment on how several religious had treated the theme "Seek yourself in Me." Among them were Father Julián of Avila and Father John of the Cross. Note what Saint Teresa says of the first of these: Father Julián de Avila "began well, but ended poorly. . . . They didn't ask him here to explain how the uncreated and the created light are joined but how we seek ourselves in God. Nor did we ask him what a soul feels when it is united with its Creator. And if it is united with Him, how does it have an opinion about whether there is a difference or not? In this union the intellect is, I think, incapable of entering into these disputes. If it were capable, it could easily understand the difference that lies between the Creator and the creature."[2]

Now, these questions about the nature of union with God, which Saint Teresa sets aside, are precisely those questions that mystical theologies attempt to resolve by spawning many different doctrines, indeed conflicting ones. We also find explanations by way of pantheistic monism, or pantheism, or epiphanies of gnostic origin. We will encounter them, for it is impossible to avoid them completely. But these are not the systems that will retain our attention.

What counts in our eyes is the very experience of the mystics, and on this point we will follow the advice of Saint Teresa. Certainly this experience is itself incommunicable. Consequently one will ask what we expect to draw from it. The response is simple: we will consider the language of the mystics. For even if inadequate, it is the mode of expression that ought to furnish useful information. In fact, unless it is oracular, which is not the case among the mystics, the style of someone's language always involves using a shared and living language in a personal way. Languages can be translated one to another, with a close enough approximation that one can compare what they are intended to express.

In that way, we may be able to assess what the existing differences consist of—not only the differences between mystical theologies, but above all between diverse expressions of spiritual experiences. Are these differences only a matter of language, or do they in fact touch upon the reality of what the language of the mystics expresses? That is the question we hope to resolve.

THE ENCOUNTER WITH GREEK CULTURE

Language, considered as lexical technique, always relates to a certain frame of thought. This framework is itself linked to a certain type of culture, indeed, a certain type of civilization. Now, we know that historically, as the three monotheistic worldviews spread throughout the world, they encountered Greek thought along the way. Despite strong reactions from Jews as well as Christians and Muslims, Hellenism very quickly imposed itself and dominated speculative and mystical theology. The translation of the Bible into Greek, especially the Septuagint translation intended for the diaspora of Israel in the Graeco-Roman world, played a large role in this transformation. Greek words, whether written or spoken, transmitted Greek ideas.

The work of Philo of Alexandria is typical: his allegorical commentary on the Law injected into the Bible a philosophical syncretism composed of Platonism, Aristotelianism, and Stoicism. This mixture prefigures the neoplatonism of Plotinus. If Philo had little audience among Jews, he exercised a huge influence on the Greek Church Fathers. But the Jews were equally touched by neoplatonism and by Hellenistic forms of gnosticism. A Jewish gnosticism existed already in the era of Christ and had even more ancient roots. Gershom Scholem writes that "the earliest Jewish mysticism is throne-mysticism." The throne represents what the *plērōma* represents for the Greek gnostics and the hermetics—the brilliant sphere of divinity with its aeons, archaeons, and dominions. But at this ancient stage, notes Scholem, "The Jewish mystic, though guided by motives similar to theirs, nevertheless expresses his vision in terms of his own religious background."[3] Whatever that religion might be, neoplatonic language rapidly imposed itself, and an entire philosophy of emanation, inspired by Plotinus, invaded Jewish thought with its cosmological and symbolic visions.

Even though to a certain extent Christianity had inspired gnostic systems such as those of Cerinthus, Basilides, and Valentinus, the Church used its institutions to struggle vigorously and victoriously against gnostic influences and infiltrations. Certainly there were also rabbis within Judaism who condemned the excesses of kabbalistic doctrines. They could not hinder their development, for these doctrines perhaps responded less to purely spiritual needs than to the questions posed by a minority people exiled in Christian or Muslim countries, suffering from numerous persecutions or at the very least held in an inferior socio-political condition. This people, bearer of the promise made by God to its ancestors, had to struggle to understand its situation within the divine plan and government. The gnostic conception of the world, its origin, its structures and development, allowed them to situate the destiny of the Jewish people within a universal conception of creation.

On this point, one can compare Jewish forms of gnosticism with the Shiʾite forms in Islam, and particularly Ismaili gnosis. In similar fashion, the latter inserted into the texture of the *cosmos* the arrival of a humanity whose legal guides were the imans, but who were in fact under the control of usurpers—the caliphs who had successfully seized power. The evolution of the world was to bring about the return to earth of the hidden iman, who had been taken up to heaven but who was to return at the end of time as the awaited *Mahdī* (*al-Mahdī al-muntaẓir*) in order to make justice reign and inaugurate a messianic era. One can hardly find any place for such conceptions within Christianity. Neither millenarian ideas, nor views of history held by someone like Joachim of Fiore and his disciples were accompanied by a gnostic cosmogony.

We may assume that the forms of gnosticism which were introduced to various degrees in the three monotheistic religions are marginal proliferations, even when they succeeded in assuming the importance of Jewish kabbalah. Nevertheless, if esotericism too often taints the purity of Jewish spirituality by pulling it in the direction of a "theosophy," the living spirit of the Bible breathes throughout so that the conceptual schemes are never deprived of their authentic religious point. That is why, without making them central to our research, we are careful not to ignore them. As to Muslim forms of gnosticism, properly so called, we can leave them aside, even if they exercised an influence on thinkers such as dʾIbn al-ʿArabī, which remains to be proved.

CRITIQUE OF THE GNOSTICS

Our investigation must clearly distinguish neoplatonism from the forms of gnosticism that exploited it. We should not forget that Plotinus himself labeled the ninth treatise of his *Second Ennead* a refutation of the gnostics, particularly those who claimed that the demiurge, creator of the world, is evil and that the created world is equally evil.

Actually, Plotinus attacks a conception that is common to all gnostic systems. In fact, after having recalled that there are three hypostases, the One, Mind, and Soul—no more, no less—he ridicules those who multiplied the number of intelligible beings: "we are not to introduce superfluous distinctions [*epinoias perittas*] which their nature rejects."[4] The gnostics introduce other hypostases, but these are nothing but empty words. They did not remain faithful to ancient Greek tradition, for the Greeks had a clear view and spoke simply (*eidotōn saphōs tōn Hellōnōn kai atyphōs legontōn*): "For, in sum, a part of their [the gnostics'] doctrine comes from Plato; all the novelties through which they seek to establish a philosophy of their own have been picked up outside of the truth. . . . [A]s for the plurality they assert in the Intellectual Realm—the Authentic Existent, the Intellectual-Principle, the Second Creator, and the Soul—all this is taken over from [Plato's] *Timaeus* [39,0], where we read: 'As many Ideal-Forms as the Divine Mind behold dwelling within the Veritably Living Being, so many the Maker resolved should be contained in this All.' Misunderstanding their text, they conceived one Mind passively including within itself all that has being, another mind, a distinct existence, having vision, and a third planning the Universe,—though often they substitute Soul for this planning Mind as the creating Principle—and they think that this third being is the Creator [or Demiurge] according to Plato."[5] This accusation, coming from Plotinus, is weighty. The gnostics, even though they claim to be faithful to Plato, have not understood him.

As to how one is to understand the novelties they have invented, it is difficult to speak positively. Emile Bréhier thinks that these were the contribution of Christianity. But it suffices to quote this historian himself to be convinced that this opinion is entirely inconsistent: "For the rest, what Plotinus criticizes most about them is the thoroughly anti-Hellenistic character of their doctrine; indeed, one could say, their Christian character." On the Hellenistic doctrine of virtue, "he is opposed to a conception of salvation that is mechanical and passive. . . ." Man assumes the right "to disrupt his vision of the world and arbitrarily to introduce into it fantastic powers to meet the needs of his personal salvation. In this there was a lack of intellectual rigor and even moral rigor that deeply troubled Plotinus, like the Christian beliefs that could later strike Spinoza as introducing irrationality and discontinuity into the universe."[6] One would think that the author had ignored the existence in Greece of mystery religions that focused on the problem of salvation and that he had missed the fact that Christian doctrine (not that of so-called Christian gnosticism) did not involve any cosmology. It seems much more reasonable in fact to think that Plotinus had an Apollinarian conception of Greek culture and that he excluded from it everything that might resemble a drama or a Dionysian tragedy. But it is certain that "oriental" elements, particularly those of Iranian origin, had infiltrated into the religious thought of Greece and that they reemerged in Hellenistic forms of gnosticism. Since, on the other hand, certain data from the Bible—those concerning angels and angelology, among other things—are equally marked by influences from the East, it is not surprising that Jewish mysticism could be open to gnostic conceptions.

It was easy to turn angels into hypostases constituting the "council of God" or expressing His powers. We already have an example of this in Philo of Alexandria. The divine Names were hyposticized in the same way, and above all the attributes (*middôt*). G. Scholem writes on this subject: "Each *middah* is a particular spiritual potency. This manner of speaking, which renders the *middoth* autonomous and hypostizes them, is already found in the ancient Aggadah. We occasionally encounter words there that almost seem like Jewish prefigurations of, or parallels to, the gnostic terminology regarding the aeons. . . ." He then enumerates the seven *middôt* that serve before the throne of Glory: "they are: Wisdom, Justice and the Law, Grace and Mercy, Truth and Peace."[7] Wisdom (*hokmâ*) plays a role exactly parallel to the one that *Sophia* plays in the so-called Christian gnosticism. Arithmological speculation on the numbers that are the measures of creation has given birth to the theory of the *sepîrôt* (from a root word that means both letter and number, since numbers are represented by the letters of the Hebrew alphabet): the *sepîrôt*, which number ten, relate to the ten words (*maʾămārôt*) through which the world was created; they are the living forces that order the great divine work. They play the role of *logoi*, which appear in the thought of Philo with an angelic nature, as in Greek gnostic writings. Finally, we mention the *ḥayyôt*, the animals, or more precisely the living Creatures of Ezekiel's vision. The meaning of all these terms has varied through the course of centuries, as well as their relationships, their differences or their identification—so much so that it is impossible to speak of them in general terms without referring to individual systems. But that is not our goal here. We simply want to stress the production of a great number of entities, which were certainly considered created when these speculations began, but that soon emerged as emanations and epiphanies of God—in other words, exactly what Plotinus criticized in the gnostics.

If we may speak of an orthodox Christianity defined by the councils as the faith of the Church, we can be sure that it succeeded in insulating itself from the gnostic invasion so that the great Christian mystics owed nothing to gnosticism. It was not so in Islam. Although Suni Islam fought rigorously against this kind of thought, Shiism offered most fertile ground, and some Sunni mystics, like Ibn al-ʿArabī, fell under its contagion. Nevertheless, as we said, a non-esoteric Muslim mysticism developed upon which we will focus, yet without neglecting other schools. But we believe we are justified, given our purpose, in leaving aside every system which properly speaking belongs to any kind of gnosticism.

THE VALUES OF PLATONISM

We return therefore to neoplatonism and to its source, Platonism, which are serious modes of thought. Platonism was, from whichever direction, easy for religious souls to use and assimilate. After all, its theory of the soul as an incorporeal reality, its theory of purification (*katharsis*), and its theory of ascension toward the Beautiful and the Good, whose image is the sun, could not leave people taken with spirituality untouched.

True, one does note that the sharp dualism for which Plato is blamed—perhaps wrongly—is not in line with biblical conceptions that see the human being as a unity. But this is a question concerning metaphysics and speculative theology more than mysticism, where what counts as essential is the spirituality of the soul. Certainly the doctrine of the resurrection of the body, especially affirmed by Christianity and Islam, cannot accommodate a teaching that would define human beings only by their souls, teaching that it is only the soul, separated from the body, that is saved in paradise or punished in hell. Ghazāli attacked the theory of Avicenna and the Platonic "philosophers" on that point. Still, it is fundamental that the soul be spiritual in some way in order that spirituality be possible for humanity.

Consequently, the distinction between soul and body establishes the asceticism that is found in all the rules of monotheistic mysticism. At the level of moral life one finds a beautiful exposition of it in *The Gorgias* and *The Banquet*, among other dialogues of Plato. On the other hand, the Platonic images of light concur with belief in salvific illumination, of which the Bible, the books of the New Testament, and the Qurʾan all speak. We read in Psalm 4:6: "Let the light of your face shine on us," and later (Psalm 27:1): "The LORD is my light and my salvation." One could give many more biblical citations of this sort. For Christians, Jesus, the Son of God, is the light of the world (John 9:5). Finally, the Qurʾan expresses the same image: "God is the Light of the heavens and the earth" (24:35) and: "Now has come unto you light from God" (5:15).

THE ISSUE OF ASCETICISM

If ascesis is important, in brings with it dangers: above all when it is regulated by ritual commandments, such as the practice of fasting, which subdues the body, and almsgiving, which detaches the giver from the goods of this world. The ancient mysticism of Merkaba and later the book of Bahir teach that, in order to know the name of God, it is necessary to remove oneself from the world and that "those who want to possess life must reject the pleasures of the body." For the kabbalist Isaac, contemplation and asceticism are combined: "Those who renounce their other qualities in order to engage solely in thought, for whom everything depends on thought, and who elevate thought while suppressing the body, in order to give highest place to their soul" are offered as exemplary individuals. Yet ascesis is held within reasonable limits.

The same thing applies to Islam. The Qurʾan counsels against allowing the attractions of the world below to seduce one; against purchasing the pleasures of this life at the price of the after-life. But ascesis is not recommended as an end in itself. A widely accepted idea is that Islam received a Law that holds in balance the duties that the faithful are responsible for as members of the Muslim community and the purely religious duties that define the worship of God. Even a mind as open to mysticism as Ghazālī condemned what he called *tabattul*, in other words the act of dedicating oneself only to the worship of God, particularly by renouncing marriage in order to give oneself exclusively to worship. It was said, according to what he relates in the *Ihyāʾ ʿUlūm-al-Dīn* (XII ch. 1), "that a married man is superior to a celibate just like a combatant in holy war is superior to him who remains safely at home, and that a single act of prostration on the part of a married man has more value than seventy prostrations by a celibate." Thus, asceticism as a total retreat from the life of the world is reproved. This is what the adversaries of mysticism stress.

Ibn al-Jawzī, in the twelfth century, writes in *Talbīs Iblīs* (*On the Confusion that Iblīs Spreads*): "The uneducated think that the glorious Qurʾan and some of the *ḥadīth* censure this world. They also think that salvation requires one to abandon the world, without even knowing the world that is condemned. Then Iblīs breathes confusion on the common man: You will only be saved in the after-life if you abandon the world. Therefore this man leaves it and heads straight for the mountains, distancing himself from the assembly of believers and from human society as well as from knowledge. He becomes like a wild beast and imagines that that is true ascesis (*al-zuhd al-ḥaqīqī*). What else could he think when he hears that someone is wandering here and there like a madman, or of some other that he has retired to the mountains, even though he may have a starving family or a mother who mourns his absence. And even then it happens that he does not know as he should the rudiments of canonical prayer and that the faults he has committed and from which he cannot escape weigh upon him."

Ghazālī, in the passage cited above, reports a remark by Sufyān b. ᶜUyayna: "To have several wives is not one of the goods of this world; in fact ᶜAlī, the most ascetic (*azhad*) of the Comrades of the Prophet, had four wives and seventeen concubines." All the prophets were married; it was said, again according to Ghazālī, that John the Baptist was married; he did not have sexual relations before the marriage, but he took a wife in order to respect religious custom (*sunna*); concerning Jesus, he is to marry when he returns to earth from heaven at the end of time. This opinion, even though it is hardly shared by the majority of interpreters, still reveals a marked tendency in Islam: sexual activity can go hand-in-hand with asceticism.

We touch here upon a problem that Louis Massignon took up and treated at length in his *Essay on the Origins of the Technical Language of Islamic Mysticism*,[8] in relation to the famous *ḥadīth*, "There is no monasticism in Islam" (*lā rahbāniyya fīʾl-Islam*). For Massignon, who wants to defend the thesis that Sufiism is indigenous to Islam, this *ḥadīth* is not authentic, thereby resolving the question. But it remains to be shown that monasticism has its place in Muslim spirituality, not only in fact, but by right. Massignon writes: "In what exactly does *rahbaniyya* consist, for Arab writers? It is to make a vow (*nadhr*) to abstain from sexual relations, and live in a hermitage (*ṣawmaᶜa*). This can go so far as abstaining from eating meat and making forty-day retreats (Firūzabādī, *Qāmūs*); and to wear a hairshirt (*musūḥ*)." He adds that Islam is so little opposed to such ascetic practices "that a temporary vow of chastity is imposed on pilgrims during their sojourn upon the sacred territory of Mecca." We recall the requirement of the Ramadan fast and the practice of expiatory fasts.

Nevertheless, these remarks do not lead to the conclusion that the monastic life is an institution recognized by the Qurʾan. Here is found one of its most obscure verses (57:27), which the commentators understand in contradictory ways. Even though Massignon claims that it is "grammatically impeccable," it can be translated in at least two opposing ways. We will not enter into the complicated details of this philological exegesis, leaving that to the text of Massignon's essay. What matters to us is not whether God prescribed the monastic life for the disciples of Jesus (since the verse concerns them) or whether Christians have invented it. We need only note the reticence of Islam and its thinkers vis-à-vis the ascetic life as Christian monasticism conceives of it.

What is certain is that Muslim mysticism has integrated asceticism within itself. But opinions diverge. Some reduce it to abstaining from what is forbidden by the Law: it is one of God's blessings to have allowed humanity to enjoy those things that are permitted; there is no reason to lay them aside by personal choice and will. Others, to the contrary, hold that ascesis (*zuhd*) is, in relation to things forbidden, an obligation and, among things permitted, a virtue (*faḍīla*). The whole question is to know what is included in the domain of what is allowed, what is lawful (*al-ḥalāl*). Something is deemed lawful, for example, when God declares (5:5): "The food of those who have received the Scripture is lawful for you," in other words, animals butchered by People of the Book. But something that is neither prescribed nor forbidden is also lawful, what Ibn Ḥazm of Cordova calls *mubāḥ*; in this case, God leaves people free to choose, to abstain if they want and to practice an ascesis, or to take advantage of the possibility of not abstaining.

The problem of ascesis, then, is quite nuanced. Generally, the basis for *zuhd* is sought in verse 57:23: "That you grieve not for the sake of that which has escaped you, nor yet exult because of that which has been given." This speaks of holy indifference. Qushayrī, from whom these observations are borrowed, says concerning the censure that the world deserves, that people must not choose to abandon what God permits, by imposing an obligation upon themselves; that they must not seek to have more than they need and that they should limit themselves to preserving the portion granted them. If God gives them fortunes, they must thank Him; if He keeps them on the edge of what is sufficient, they should not seek an increase in goods, for patience in trials (*ṣabr*) is the best course for those in poverty, and thanksgiving (*shukr*) is what is most appropriate for those who possess lawful goods. Now *ṣabr* and *shukr* are already the mystical states of a heart turned toward God. What we see here is that ascesis is not defined as an end in itself.

It seems that ascesis is much more developed within Christianity. Not only are the world and its perversions denounced, but there is praise for chastity and virginity as literally the perfect state for human beings. Certainly many Christian ascetics committed excesses whose dangers, moreover, the Church has denounced. In particular, it has condemned the encratism which condemned marriage as a shameful stain, under the markedly gnostic influence of apocryphal books such as the Acts of John and the Acts of Thomas. But abuse of asceticism has not appeared in the realm of sexuality alone. The fierce determination to reduce bodily powers through iron discipline and through the most painful macerations has never been totally broken.

Now such practices, which testify to a hatred of the body, are absolutely suspect; they put one's physical and mental health in danger—especially one's mental health—and cast only doubt upon the value of any visions that ensue. There in fact is the greatest danger from the point of view of a mystic who wishes to be authentic: such practices lead one to believe that there are recipes and methods one can put to work in order to release ecstasy, while all the great spiritual writers, in the three monotheisms, know that everything comes from the gratuitous favor of God, who alone acts. It is true that the mystics who practice this asceticism do not see in it a sort of magic procedure for gaining access to God. The blessed Henri Suso, as hard as he was upon himself, recommends that beginners, as a first conversion, make a retreat in solitude and silence, to mortify themselves, but to do so with moderation and prudence, while renouncing material things and created beings.

Moderation and prudence are in fact absolutely necessary. Certainly human beings have some power of renunciation, abnegation, or abstinence; people can give themselves the discipline, wear a hairshirt, or flagellate themselves. But the only goal to be attained through all this is to quiet the appeals of the world and the passions within oneself, in order to hear the appeal of God—to create an empty space within, or to realize the "nakedness" of which Tauler speaks, so that God may take up that place. As John of the Cross writes: "As soon as the two rooms of the soul (sensitive and spiritual) are perfectly quieted and secured, as soon as their multitude of powers and appetites is plunged into silence and sleep in relation to all things here-below and all things on high, divine Wisdom is united to the soul. . . ."[9] The purgative and ascetic life, far from creating a disequilibrium in the senses and in spirit, should result in a contribution to their equilibrium and peace. It is not through journeys into madness that God gives Himself. Asceticism must not become a drug.

On this subject, Saint Teresa of Avila is a model of prudence. This is what she writes to Father Gracian: "As for [Sister Isabel de] San Jerónimo, she will have to be made to eat meat for a few days, and to give up prayer. . . . For she has an unsteady imagination which leads her to think she is seeing and hearing the things she meditates on."[10] In a letter to Don Lorenzo de Cepeda, she gives him these counsels of wisdom: "[O]n no account take [the discipline] more often than I say [in my letter] — that is to say, only twice a week. During Lent you may wear the hair-shirt one day every week, on the understanding that, if you find it does you harm, you take it off again: you are so sanguine that I am very much afraid of its effect on you. I cannot agree to your taking the discipline oftener than I have said, as it is bad for the sight. . . ."[11]

One could provide many more quotations of this sort. Therefore, we will only report one more, the critique she addressed to Saint John of the Cross concerning the manner in which he had treated the theme "Seek yourself in Me." She shows how deeply she understood the human condition and distrusted the tendency to advance too quickly toward a high spirituality: "Seeking God would be very costly if we could not do so until we were dead to the world. The Magdalene was not dead to the world when she found [the Savior], nor was the Samaritan woman or the Canaanite woman. . . . God deliver me from people so spiritual that they want to turn everything into perfect contemplation, no matter what."[12] We must factor in the irony that Saint Teresa knew how to put to use, with finesse. Still, in her eyes, the quest for God occurs within the world and it would be reckless to evade it through a forced and misplaced ascesis.

Consequently, the mystics seek a purification of the soul the way Plato conceived of it, for he always emphasized the right proportion, the *metrion*, in all things. It was he who understood the importance of equilibrium, who called it the virtue of justice, not only with regard to others, but also within the soul itself. Through this measure, this moderation, a person can rise to contemplate the Good through illumination. Ascesis is, as the name indicates in Greek, an exercise for the soul, comparable to what gymnastics or medicine does for the body. Now, good doctors prevent their patients from satisfying their tastes and appetites. A program for the soul will be much the same: "As long as it's corrupt, senseless, intemperate, unjust, and impious, we should restrain it from its appetites, and not allow it to do anything else except what will make it better."[13]

Therefore Plato could easily furnish a philosophical and moral vocabulary to express one whole dimension of a religious ideal present in the three monotheisms. His own analysis of human nature certainly helped cast light on conceptions that were latent in the revealed texts because he helped religious meditation to elaborate their meaning within a sharply defined spirituality, while avoiding the historical excesses produced by a quest for total purification from the "stains" of the body. The rules for monastic orders which are especially characteristic of Christianity, with Saint Pachomius and later Saint Benedict, but also exist within Muslim brotherhoods, respond to this need for measure which the Platonic ideal expresses.

NEOPLATONIC PHILOSOPHY

But above all it is neoplatonism, as a non-gnostic philosophical system that brought to the reflection of the mystics much more important elements: a certain vision of the world and of the place of the human soul within the universe and in its relations with the first principle.

Plotinus introduces the system of hypostatic processions: Mind (*nous*) proceeds from the One, and the Soul proceeds from Mind. Obviously this system contradicts the idea of creation that stands at the center of the three monotheistic revelations. This is not the place to examine how Jewish, Christian, and Muslim philosophical theologies have elaborated a conception of creation *ab aeterno* that adequately incorporates the idea of emanation or procession into the conception of creation *ex nihilo* within time. This movement of thought, clearly initiated by Philo of Alexandria, will continue through the *falsafa* of Fārābī and Avicenna, and into Jewish and Christian philosophy of the Middle Ages.

But in relation to mysticism itself, we will draw attention especially to the teaching of Plotinus concerning Mind. It is born out of a kind of superabundance and overflow of the One, which is characterized as *huperplēres*, "full beyond measure" (a term that Avicenna will translate exactly through the expression *fawq al-tamām*: "above completeness"). Mind [*l'Intelligence*] is the perfect unity of intelligibles that reflect on one another: it is as fully identical with the intelligibles as it is with what it knows [*intellige*] in them. Intelligibles, taken in themselves, are not abstract ideas, poorer than the concretely existing realities from which they are drawn, but rather they bear in themselves all the wealth of the lower, sensible world, although in an immaterial manner. Consequently, nothing prevents an idea of the individual as such (*tou kathekaston estin idea*) from existing within the hypostasis of Mind.

Plotinus asks how we are to know "whether I [*egō*, I myself] and every other human being go back to the Intellectual [*anagōgēn epi to noēton*], every (living) thing having origin and principle There [*hekastou ē archē ekei*]."[14] We must underscore the use of the word "I." The context makes clear that this is the soul, no longer the "physical" principle of voluntary movement, as was the case with Aristotle, but a person. What is then at stake here is the individual personality of each person, inscribed in the intelligible. We should also note the term *anagōgē*, which carries the connotations of an ascension. The notion received, both in Jamblique and in Christian vocabulary, the idea of the soul's elevation and, thus, of spirituality. Therefore, the general idea of the human being is not what exists within Mind, but rather the idea of Socrates, for example, with all that made Socrates historically and integrally Socrates—in short, the "me" of Socrates himself (*autosōkratēs*). We see how monotheistic thought can utilize such a conception to its advantage.

Certainly monotheism does not dare to incorporate the entire Plotinian system as such. But the One, transcendent and ineffable, agrees perfectly with the expression of belief in one God, beyond all that is created. Once the God of revelation is introduced into the system by means of this agreement, Mind will be attributed to Him, either as a manifestation of Himself, or as His Word. Through Mind, God knows all beings down to their least detail, to all that concretely constitutes them and relates to them. He does not know them as abstract ideas, therefore, but as individuals themselves. Consequently, God knows each human being in what is irreducibly his or her own and cannot be reduced to anything other than him or herself. So there is established between the creator and the creature a relation that aids greatly in describing a mystical experience that grows into the lived discovery of what one is—in the authentic reality of one's being—within the eternal thought of God.

Plotinus provided yet another teaching of great value. Since "the Cosmos contains the Reason-Principles [*logoi*] not merely of man, but also of all individual living things, so must the Soul."[15] In fact, souls arise from the third hypostasis, which, having proceeded from Mind, returns to it by contemplating it.

Now, within Mind, all is within all. It is therefore normal for individual souls, as they return to the intelligible principle of their individuality, to discover the entire universe in themselves by rediscovering that principle. What constitutes each one's individuality is that one of the *logoi* is more active in it than in the others. But if one reunites with others, all are articulated, so to speak, with one another: one *logos* that had been in the background for one, finds itself in the foreground for another, and so on until totalization is achieved. This is what Emile Bréhier showed when he wrote: "Together the individuals form a tightly-bound system, each revealing some aspect of the intelligible world, and all together revealing it successively in its entirety."[16]

One only needs to replace "intelligible world" with "manifestation" or "word" of God to have a doctrine that has inspired a certain number of monotheistic mystics, at least at the level of expression. In any case, this system clarifies, in philosophical terms, the biblical revelation according to which human beings were created in the likeness and according to the image of God. It is true that some unbending forms of Islam would not allow that God could have an image. The thinkers who object consider the *ḥadīth* that offers its own version of Genesis 1:26 to be inauthentic. But mystics like Ibn al-ʿArabī accept it, and on this point one can compare his vision of God, humanity, and the world with that of the *Zohar* in Judaism. It is also worth noting that the conception of the "human being made in the image" does not necessarily lead to esoteric forms of mysticism.

Psalm 8 offers us an interesting synthesis of two ideas, which it shows to be complementary. On one hand, human beings only have value through the gift of God that allows them to participate in God's glory. We must understand that, according to several exegetes, an allusion is being made here to the creating of human beings according to God's image. On the other hand, as a result of this, God thinks of humanity, meaning human individuals, according to the gift by which they are distinguished. Here is the text (8:4–5): "What are human beings that you spare a thought for them, or the child of Adam that you care for him [*kî-tipqĕdennû*]? Yet you have made him little less than a god, you have crowned him [*tĕʿăṭṭĕrēhû*] with glory and beauty." The idea that God probes (*yibḥan*) the human heart is frequent: "You probe my heart, examine me at night" (Psalm 17:3). Surely then God knows the individual; God inclines toward them and responds to their prayers. And when God turns toward a human being, God sees a reflection of His glory.

The same idea appears in Christian revelation. The accent there falls strongly on the parental providence of God. Concerning the necessities of life, Jesus declares: "Your heavenly Father knows you need them all" (Matthew 6:32). God feeds the birds of the sky: "Are you not worth much more than they are?" God clothes the lilies of the fields which neither sow nor spin; so "will he not much more look after you?" (6:25–31).

Human preeminence is reaffirmed, not just the preeminence of human beings in general, but of each human being whom God knows and cares for. "Why, every hair on your head has been counted. So there is no need to be afraid; you are worth more than many sparrows" (10:30–31).

The Qur'an also teaches that nothing escapes the knowledge of God. "Lo! nothing in the earth or in the heavens is hidden from God" (3:5). God "knows what you hide and what you proclaim" (27:25). It is certain therefore that God knows individuals and individual persons most particularly. Does God not say (4:125): "God (Himself) chose Abraham for friend"? Or later, in addressing Muhammad (93:6): "Did He not find you an orphan and protect (you)?" Obviously the question of knowing what kind of knowledge is at issue was asked of theologians and philosophers. How can God know material beings when it seems that only their meanings can be grasped? How, from the height of His transcendence, can God know future events or contingencies? And since God's knowledge is eternal, how can it reach creatures for whom that means to be born, to develop, and to vanish within time? The qur'anic verses cited above pose the problem without giving the slightest clue as to its solution. One can say the very same thing about biblical and Gospel texts.

THE PROBLEM OF INDIVIDUATION

Since we are speaking of Islam, let us pause for a moment at the theory of Avicenna, which has equivalents in Christian and Jewish philosophical thought. Without going into detail, let us simply recall that Avicenna thinks that individuation (*tashakhkhuṣ*) occurs not only by matter, but also by form. He writes in his *Ishārāt*: "Form is individuated through matter and matter is likewise individuated through form."[17] Is there a vicious circle there? Let us recall that form and matter do not exist apart from one another. This can only mean that in their coexistence they converge to produce an individual (*shakhṣ*). But in this convergence, their roles are different, so that there is no circle.

A commentator on the *Ishārāt*, Naṣīr al-Dīn al-Ṭūsī, explains this clearly. He writes: "Individualization of form is done by a determined matter, insofar as it can receive individuation from this form. But the individuation of matter through form is accomplished by any form insofar as it acts to individuate this matter." The first matter is purely passive and receptive. It can receive any form whatsoever and so finds itself individuated by that form, coming to exist and no longer able to receive any form whatsoever but only a determined form. In other words, by this action it is determined to receive such a form and none other. And when this determined form is received by this determined matter, what ensues is the individuation of the aforesaid form. In this way, matter can exist as this flesh and these bones. It can then receive human form and become the body of Socrates, while complementary-wise, the human form becomes the form of Socrates.

How is God going to know this individual, Socrates? Here, in a general way, is how Avicenna responds to this question in the *Kitāb al-Najāt*: "As to how God knows particular things, this is explained by the fact that when God knows Himself, and knows that He is the first cause of every being, God knows the principles of beings that come forth from Him and what is going to result from these principles. There is nothing at all which does not become in some way necessary from the fact that God is its cause. The interplay of colliding causes is what produces particular realities. Now the first cause (God) knows these causes and their arrangement; necessarily then, God knows that to which they lead. . . . He grasps particular realities insofar as they are universal, in other words, insofar as they have attributes. And if, through these attributes, they are themselves characterized as individuals, it is with respect to an individual time, or an individual mode of being."[18]

This reiterates that God knows individuals by means of a universal set of actions and causal reactions, at the heart of which they receive their own proper qualities, which define the times and the mode of their individual existence. But that does not mean God knows the individual directly and in him or herself; this only tells us the process by which the individual must be born, behave, define itself, and present this and that characteristic.

While Avicenna recognized that the human soul was an "I" (*anā*), regrettably he did not succeed in satisfactorily explaining to the mystics how we are to comprehend the existence of God's intimate and immediate knowledge of this self. Of course God instantly knows the multiplicity of causes that result in the me, so that one may rightly say that God knows me directly. Yet it is clear that mystical experience will gain incomparable depth if God knows this human self in itself, rather than simply knowing it through its causes. Therefore the way Plotinus explains the presence of the intelligible idea of each individual and each me within

Mind suits the requirements of mystical expression far more than does Avicenna's explanation, in spite of all that the illustrious philosopher owes to neoplatonic and Plotinian thought. In fact, even though Avicenna places the accent on form, and therefore on the intelligible element, matter is only involved in the process of individuation insofar as it has already received form as a second matter. The individual remains just as much as ever the result of a complex interaction of material and formal causes.

Now the I cannot allow itself to decompose into such a network of elements: an individual person must be absolutely and simply one in his or her principle. In other words, all that constitutes the person in its manifestations must lead back to a perfect original unity. This is just the inverse of what Avicenna teaches by explaining the individual, and thus the individual me, as the result of a multiplicity of causes. Such is the unity of a multiplicity, a unity that is merely derived and not fundamental.

It is rightly said that the philosophy of Avicenna opens out onto mysticism. But it is an intellectualist mysticism based on contemplation of intelligibles in God. It can accommodate, for better or for worse, the demands of monotheistic revelation, but it is not inspired by them. Avicenna's disciple, Abūʾl-Barakāt al-Baghdādī, came close to Plotinus' position by arguing that each human soul is a species, which gives it a solid ontological foundation. Avempace, while hardly a religiously-oriented thinker, then gave a definition to "the blessed" (*al-suʿadâʾ*) which conformed more to the ideal of mystical experience: those who contemplate not merely intelligibles but the mind of their own intellect. One need only replace intelligibility with the spirituality of the soul, and the intelligible intellect with the spiritual me, in order to have a fine expression of what comprises beatitude for the mystics, at the end of their journey. This expression, we can see, is of entirely Plotinian inspiration.

THE QUESTION OF ASCETICISM AGAIN

So we return to what we have said about ascesis. If the personality of the individual me does not exclude the body, no quest for spirituality ought to imply a total rupture with the body. We might say that to realize the spirituality of the soul in all its purity requires a spiritualization of the body. Consequently, every imprudent form of ascesis is to be rejected. What must be combated in the body is its insubordination to the spirit.

As Philo of Alexandria well understood, ascesis should be the means of reestablishing an equilibrium between body and spirit. The Church Fathers followed him on this point: for them, disequilibrium results from original sin, which has engendered what Saint John calls "concupiscence of the flesh, concupiscence of the eyes and pride of life" (1 John 2:16).[19] One might need to recall here the full teaching of Saint Paul concerning the body (*sōma*) and the flesh (*sarx*). The body expresses the human person as God created it. But the flesh, inhabited by sin (Romans 7:12), enslaves the body so that it becomes the "body of sin" (6:6), just as there is a "flesh of sin" (8:3).

True, the doctrine of original sin has assumed more importance in Christianity, though it took it from the Bible, while Islam rejected this teaching. Nevertheless, the Qurʾan has its own equivalent to the Johannine concept of concupiscence; it does not relate to the flesh, which is a notion that is absent from its vocabulary, but to the soul that enjoins evil (*al-nafs al-ammāra biʾl-sūʾ*, 12:53). Against this soul the mystics take up the battle (*mujāhadat al-nafs*) known as the *great jihād*. In comparison, holy warfare is only the small *jihād*.

We should pause at a rather enigmatic passage in the Qurʾan, which has given rise to various commentaries, of which one is important for our subject. The passage occurs in verses 4 and 5 of sūrah 95: "Surely We created man of the best stature, then We reduced him to the lowest of the low." Among the exegeses reported by the commentator Qurṭubī, we highlight the following one. Ibn al-ʿArabī said: "God has no creature finer than man," which he explains by citing the *ḥadīth* in which "God created Adam in His image," that is, according to His attributes of knowledge, power, life, etc. This being the case, he says: "Once God had characterized man by those attributes by which He had composed him, man exceeds his limits and becomes so self-inflated that he says: I am your Lord the Highest. These are the words that sūrah 79:24 puts into the mouth of Pharaoh. Then God reduced man to the lowest of the low, that is to say, He makes him a being full of filth and impurities. . . ." Human beings have exceeded their limits and swelled with pride: this is what destroys the beautiful equilibrium (*iʿtiddāl*) of primal human stature. One recalls the notion of inordinate pride, that "interior injustice," which the Greeks called *hubris* and which asceticism is supposed to remedy.

The proper equilibrium, according to Muslim mystics, translates into the state of unshakeable certitude (*yaqīn*): the Qurʾan distinguishes between the knowledge of certitude (102:5), the eye (or source, or essence) of certitude (102:7) and the reality of certitude (56:95; 69:51). In fact, for the mystics certitude is first of all a knowledge deposited in the heart that strengthens it and excludes every kind of doubt and hesitation. It is then an intuition that unifies the heart and fixes its constant attention on God. Finally, it is the very presence of God that gives unchanging peace. Through asceticism, one builds on a secure knowledge and does not go astray amid the fickle seductions of the world, nor is one scattered by allowing oneself to become distracted and tossed about this way and that. Then, perfectly centered, those who practice asceticism can return to themselves in that perfect equilibrium that human beings received at the beginning from God's creation.

In the last analysis, then, we see that in practice Muslim and Christian mystics are not as far from one another as their doctrinal difference might lead us to think. For both groups, just as for the kabbalist Isaac the Blind, cited above, the goal to be attained is to unite ascesis to the contemplation of God so that we might rediscover ourselves in Him in the way He desires for us and knows us in the intimate secret of our personal being.

ESOTERIC MYSTICS

Still, Plotinus and above all the neoplatonists who followed him have exercised another kind of influence. Even though he had criticized the gnostics, the mystics whom we have called esoteric mystics are linked to him, especially within Judaism and to a more limited degree within Islam. The esoteric mystics are the ones closest to gnosticism. We will discuss them, therefore, in order to see how and to what extent we can compare them to certain Christian mystics whose expressions sometimes approach theirs. Since we have to chose within an abundance of systems, we will limit ourselves to comparing *The Book of the Zohar* to the thought of Ibn al-ᶜArabī.

Toward the end of the thirteenth century the *seper ha-zōhar* [The Book of Splendor], appeared in Castille. It seems slightly later than the work of Ibn al-ᶜArabī, who died in 1240. But one finds a certain community of thought, even though it is impossible to trace a direct influence. In any case, while such influences are important from the historical perspective, simple parallelisms are much more interesting from the philosophical perspective. Whoever he was, the mind of the author of the *Zohar* was, as Gershom Scholem said, "completely immersed in the world of Kabbalistic thought," yet "the manner in which he deals with the subject bears the imprint of his own personality."[20] His method is modeled on that of the *Midrash.* He seeks to bring out the mystical meaning of scriptural passages. Altogether the readings in the *Zohar,* without constituting a full commentary, form a midrash on the Torah, the Song of Songs, and the Book of Ruth. One can say the same thing about the masterwork of Ibn al-ᶜArabī, *Al-Futūḥāt al-Makkiyya* (The revelations of Mecca), except that here the author reflects and meditates upon the verses of the Qurʾan. Without being a real commentary, it draws conclusions from the qurʾanic texts that are comparable, on the level of esoteric mysticism, to those which the *Zohar* draws from the Bible.

The essence of God is concealed, having neither qualities nor attributes. We have seen that Ibn al-ᶜArabī calls this unicity (*Aḥadiyya*), and the kabbalists call it *ʾên-sōp* (infinity, the endless). This notion reflects the One of Plotinus, which he was unable to define. But God is not just this transcendent absolute, an in-itself separated in perfect isolation. God is also, one may say, a "for-itself." God is manifest, first of all to Himself, then to His creatures through the epiphanies of His essence, which are His names and His attributes.

So far, the *Zohar* and Ibn al-ᶜArabī are in total agreement. Kabbalah enumerates ten attributes, which are real symbols of divine Reality. It designates them with the name of *sepîrôt*. These are "at the same time ten stages through which the divine life pulsates back and forth."[21] But they emanate from the very interior of God: they are "various phases in the manifestation of the Divinity,"[22] in other words, the principal names of God. In their totality, the *sepîrôt* form the great name of God. They are not passive entities, but powers whose dynamism is transmitted throughout creation. "All mundane and created things exist only because something of the power of the *sepîrôt* lives and acts in them."[23]

Scholem is correct in underscoring the difference that exists, on one hand, between the *sepîrôt* and the attributes that speculative theologians describe and, on the other hand, the "hypostases which Plotinus, in his doctrine of emanation, interposed between the Absolute and the phenomenal world."[24] In fact the Plotinian hypostases are limited to two, Mind and Soul. Nevertheless, when he writes that the *sepîrôt* "illuminate each other" and are "far from being static,"[25] he places his finger exactly on the essential characteristics of Ideas, which according to Plotinus, are within Mind, although Plotinus does not limit these Ideas to ten.

But perhaps we do not need to pause too long at the limiting quality of this number; it is determined on the basis of terms that emerge from different verses of the Bible. The first three, for example, are Wisdom, Understanding, and Knowledge, from the Book of Proverbs 3:19–20: "In wisdom [*ḥokmâ*], the LORD laid the earth's foundations, in understanding [*tĕbbûnâ* = *bînâ*], he spread out the heavens. Through his knowledge [*daᶜat*] the depths were cleft open. . . ." The same terms appear in Exodus 31:3: "I have filled him with the spirit of God in wisdom, knowledge and skill," and in 1 Kings 7:14, which concerns the gifts God gives to human beings, gifts whose qualities correspond to God's own attributes. That is why, writes Scholem, the *sepîrôt* "are the creative names which God called into the world, the names which He gave to Himself."[26] It follows that if, in Plotinian thought, every individual being, precisely as a being, has its root in the intelligible world (which is here the world of the *sepîrôt*) we cannot deny the identical inspiration that is strikingly evident in the two conceptions. One conception belongs to the philosopher and the other to the mystical and esoteric author of the *Zohar.* They converge in spite of numerous differences that, on one hand result from purely rational reflection, and on the other result from a religious preoccupation linked to meditation on revealed texts.

The thought of Ibn al-ᶜArabī is very similar to the preceding and is drawn, like it, from both a philosophical source and a living source, that of revelation. God, absolutely One and ineffable, manifests Himself first of all through His names ("the most beautiful names:" *al-asmā al-ḥusnā*, Qurʾan 7:180; 17:110; 20:8); then through His attributes (*al-ṣifāt*); and finally through His actions (*al-afᶜāl*) within creation. The names of God are real beings that beseech the Creator to give them "those things that they name." Each name is a *rāʾis*, an authority who commands and who needs a *marʾūs*, a being to command. This means that the names are like "patrons" who give the measure of creatures by establishing their being and their meaning. Every person is therefore placed under the authority of a name that names him or her.

We will simply point out one important aspect of the teaching of *Zohar* and that of Ibn al-ᶜArabī. In both cases, human beings in their perfection and the fullness of their humanity are manifestations of God. It is this ideal being who here and there is named Adām Qadmōn, the ancestral human being, or *al-Insān al-Kamīl*, the perfect human being, and the title of a work by al-Jilānī, a disciple of Ibn al-ᶜArabī. In fact, human beings are microcosms who reproduce, in their constitution, the universe in miniature. Furthermore, human individuals, endowed with reason clarified through revelation, can find within themselves worth as the image of

God, discover that all other particular beings are partial images like them, gather in their spiritual experience all these images into a single image, and thus progress in the intimate knowledge of God. Ibn al-ʿArabī speaks of three journeys: the journey that departs from God (*ʿan Allāh*) and corresponds to the creation through which created beings are situated in the world of becoming, far from God; then there is the journey toward God (*safar ilāʾllāh*) in which human beings rediscover all the values of the images that fill the universe; finally there is the journey in God (*safar fīʾllāh*), which is endless and in which human beings take part in the infinite manifestation of divine Essence by discovering that God is "with them."

Ibn al-ʿArabī meditated profoundly on this notion of *being-with* (*maʿiyya*, from *maʿa* or with). In Himself, God can only be designated through the third-person pronoun, the pronoun that expresses, according to Arabic grammarians, the one who is absent (*al-ghāʾib*): He (*Huwa*). But insofar as He is with someone, He says I, and the creature, denying all that is not Him, responds: Thou. So God says in the Qurʾan: "There is no God save Him" (2:163 to cite one verse among many). But He also says: "There is no God save Me" (16:2; 20:14; 21:25). Finally, Jonah, from the belly of the fish, cries out: "There is no God but You" (21:87). Thus God designates Himself through all three personal pronouns: I (*anā*); Thou (*anta*) and He (*huwa*). Now God, as I, is I in relation to a you. It is because He says I that we can say Thou to Him and that He speaks by taking us as interlocutors. (Among Arabic grammarians, the interlocutor, the one to whom one speaks, *al-mukhāṭab*, designates the second person). Put differently, it is because God is with us that we are with God, in the journey in Him. But it is also said (3:62): "There is no God but God [Allah]." Therefore the name of Allah has two poles, consisting of the *Huwa* (Him) and the *Anā* (I) — one pole turned toward the Essence, one pole turned toward the creature. Just as God is the greatest name, within which each name reflects all the others, because it unites them all, one can say that in and through it one passes from the journey toward God to the journey in God. (We note here that the name of God plays the role of Plotinian Mind and that the names that it holds in its unity play the role of Ideas mirroring one another.)

We encounter the same sort of speculations in the *Zohar*. Thus Gershom Scholem signals an analogous, if not identical, reflection, on personal pronouns. He writes: "God in the most deeply hidden of His manifestations, when He has as it were just decided to launch upon His work of creation, is called He. God in the complete unfolding of His Being, Grace and Love, in which He becomes capable of being perceived by the 'reason of heart,' and therefore of being expressed, is called 'You.' But God, in His supreme manifestation, where the fullness of His being finds its final expression in the last and most all-embracing of His attributes, is called 'I.' This is the stage of true individuation in which God as a person says 'I' to Himself. This divine Self, this 'I,' according to the theosophical Kabbalists . . . is the *Shekhina*, the presence and immanence of God in the whole of creation. It is the point where man, in attaining the deepest understanding of his own self, becomes aware of the presence of God."[27]

This text is superb. We note that the Hebrew term meaning the presence of God has its Arabic equivalent, *sakīna*, which Jurjāni, in his *Book of Definitions*, defines this way: "It is peace [*ṭumaʾnīna*; cf. *al-nafs al-mutmaʾinna*, the soul at peace, supra] that the heart finds at the moment it descends into the divine mystery [*al-Ghayb*]; it is a light within the heart and it brings rest and peace to those who see it. There lie the principles and the essence of certitude [*ʿayn al-yaqīn*]." The difference is that *sakīna* is a state of the heart resulting from the divine presence (*ḥaḍra* in Arabic), for this term comes from a word that simultaneously means to be at rest and to dwell, while *šĕkînâ* is the very presence of God both in the world and within the human person.

CONVERGENCE OF VOCABULARY AMONG JEWISH AND MUSLIM MYSTICS

It is fascinating to compare term-by-term the vocabularies employed by Jewish and Muslim thinkers who relate to this type of theosophic mysticism. We will do this by beginning with the kabbalah and following the work of Ernst Müller on the teaching of *Zohar*, noting how he presents the ensemble of *sepîrôt*. The first, the Crown (*keter*), is contained at the highest point in the ineffable heights. It exists in continuity with the *ʾên-sôp* and is sometimes considered the same thing. At the opposite extreme is the *malkût*, the human Kingdom, or simply, the Kingdom. Between the two lies a first level of Wisdom and Understanding, which we have already noted. At a second level are Love *ḥesed* or Grandeur (*gĕdullâ*), Justice (*dîn*) or Power (*gĕbûrâ*), Magnificence (*tipʾeret*) or Mercy (*raḥămîm*) in which the harmony of all the *sepîrôt* is realized. At a third level is Constancy or perseverance in being (*neṣaḥ*), and Beauty (*hôd*). At a fourth level lies the Foundation (*yĕsôd*). Sometimes this ensemble is represented with the image of a tree whose seed is in the Crown and which blossoms in the productions of *malkût*. The *šĕkînâ* that dwells in the Kingdom is the sublime foundation of all receptivity to the Spirit and of every reception of the concept of the Spirit.

Müller remarked that the names of Grandeur, Power, Magnificence, Constancy, and Beauty come together in a single verse of the Bible, 1 Chronicles 29:11, "Yours, O LORD, is the greatness, the power, the splendor, length of days and glory." A little later we read: "Yours, O LORD, is the sovereignty" (or kingship, *mamlākâ*), which must not be confused with the Kingdom (the two notions will be clearly distinguished in Islam). The rest of the passage is very interesting, because it speaks of the gift of God that allows creatures to participate in God's attributes: "Wealth and riches come from you. . . . in your hand lie strength and power, and you bestow greatness and might on whomsoever you please."

Finally Müller links the biblical names of these *sepîrôt* with the proper names of God, which are taken from different passages of the Bible. The Crown is related to the name of *Ehyeh* (I-Am; cf. Exodus 3:14: "This is what you are to say to the Israelites, 'I am has sent me to you'"). *Yahweh* is placed in relation with Understanding; *Elohim*, with Magnificence; *Sabaoth* with Constancy and Beauty, which always accompany one another; *Shaddai*, with the Foundation; and *Adonai* (my Lord) with the Kingdom of the human sphere.

Obviously no system exists in Ibn al-ʿArabī that is exactly parallel. Moreover, the different currents of kabbalah do not present tables of *sepîrôt* which are perfectly identical either. Besides, the realities that the names include, even when their roots are parallel or identical, are not always situated in the same way and do not always play identical roles. We noted this with the term *šĕkînâ / sakīna*. One could say as much about Wisdom (*ḥôkmâ / ḥikma*). Wisdom, in Muslim thought, does not have the same importance that it has in Jewish thought. The Qurʾan, in fact, does not contain any verses like those of Jewish wisdom literature. The word *ḥikma* designates a gift that God gives to prophets and whomever he wishes, and it is generally placed on the same level as revealed books and signs (*āyāt*) from God. If the Qurʾan frequently refers to God as Wise (*ḥakim*), it does not expressly say that Wisdom resides with Him. Nevertheless, Ibn al-ʿArabī writes: "God has a Wisdom that he has hidden in my existence and that no eye can see."[28] He speaks of divine Wisdom (*al-ḥikmat al-ilāhiyya*), which is in the world (*fiʾl-ʿālam*), in the movement of the spheres and in all movement, none of which is empty and without purpose. But it is above all within myself that it is hidden, and that I must discover not with the eyes of the body, but through an illumination (*tajallī*) that comes from God. Now in Jewish mysticism, Wisdom is both the primordial Torah and the primordial light, and the issue there is the flash (*zîb*) of *Sophia* which contains all essences that the "flashing light" (*ʾôr bâhir*) causes to shine forth. Yet, for certain kabbalists the *ʾôr bâhir* cannot be the *hokmâ*, but the *bînâ*, and for others it is the *tipʾeret.* However numerous the doctrinal nuances, one can conclude that a certain analogy exists in the two mysticisms between *ḥôkmâ* and *ḥikma.*

Grandeur (*gĕdullâ*) can be compared to *Jalāl*, Majesty. The Qurʾan speaks (55:27 and 78) of the face and the name of the Lord, filled with Majesty and Glory (*dhūʾl-Jalāl waʾl-Ikrām*). Beauty (or Splendor) has its equivalent in the Arabic *Jamāl*). To tell the truth, in the Qurʾan neither this word nor the adjective *jamīl* (beautiful) is applied to God. However the school of Ibn al-ʿArabī relates these two terms, *Jalāl* and *Jamāl.* In his work, *al-Insān al-Kāmil* [The perfect man], Jīlānī writes: "Majesty expresses the essence of God in His manifestation within His names and His attributes such as they are together in Him. Differentiated, Majesty expresses Grandeur [*ʿAẓama*] and Magnitude [*Kibriyāʾ*], Glory [*Majd*] and Elevation [*Sanāʾ*]. All beauty belongs to Majesty; in fact, its full manifestation is called *Jalāl*; all Majesty belongs likewise to Beauty, for through the principles of its manifestation to creatures it is called *Jamāl.* We can say therefore that all Beauty has Majesty, and all Majesty has Beauty. From the Beauty of God, only the Beauty of Majesty or the Majesty of Beauty are manifested to the eyes of creatures. As for Beauty in itself and Majesty in itself, God alone beholds them." Thus, just as in the system that portrays the *sepîrôt* as a tree, the interplay of divine Majesty and Beauty assures the passage of the absolute to creation through the names and attributes. We recall, moreover, that it is said in the Qurʾan (using another root word with the same qurʾanic meaning), that God has the most beautiful names (*al-asmāʾ al-ḥusnā*). It is written, for example (3:14): "With God is the beauty of refuge [*ḥusn al-maʾā*]."[29] Here the word *ḥusn* is nearly synonymous with *jamāl.*

The Hebrew term for power corresponds exactly to the Arabic—*gĕbûrâ* on one hand, *jabarūt* on the other. *Jabarūt* stands in constant relation to *malkût*: it designates what is all-powerful and able to exercise constraint (*qahr*), while the other term designates divine sovereignty (or kingship), which one must relate to the Hebrew *mamlākâ* and not *malkût*, the Kingdom (*Mulk* in Arabic). *Malakūt* appears in the Qurʾan, which speaks of the "dominion [or sovereignty] of the heavens and the earth" (6:76; 7:185) and proclaims (36:82): "Glory be to Him in Whose hand is the dominion over all things!" (cf. 23:88). On the other hand, *jabarūt* appears only in the *ḥadīth*, for example: "Glory to Him who possesses *jabarūt* and *malakūt*!" The ordering of the two terms and their corresponding realities varies according to different systems of thought. For Ibn al-ʿArabī, the *malakūt* is the world of archetypical Ideas (*ʿalām al-mithāl*) and the *jabarūt* is the power that imprints them in the created world, called the Kingdom (*Mulk*). The Qurʾan affirms several times that it is God who owns the Kingdom of the earth and heavens (2:107; 3:189); God is Possessor of the Kingdom (*Mālik al-Mulk*, 3:26). This is why we can affirm that *mulk* holds, in the thought of Ibn ʿArabī, the same place *as the malkût* in the *Zohar*.

Finally the term *raḥămîn* (Mercy) is, in Hebrew, the exact translation of the Arabic *raḥma*. In the language of the Qurʾan, two adjectives, *raḥmān* and *raḥīm*, correspond to this noun. They regularly apply to God and are usually translated into English as merciful and compassionate, approximately. The doctors have often discussed the relation between the two qualities. Ibn al-ʿArabī and his disciples think that God, as *Raḥmān*, gives everyone possible their perfection through the presence of the totality of His attributes, from which existence emanates; they forged the term *raḥmāniyya*, which corresponds rather well to the Hebrew term *tipʾeret*, magnificence. On the other hand, God, as *Raḥīm*, gives spiritual perfections (*maʿnawiyya*), such as knowledge, to people who have faith in God's unicity. Consequently, *raḥmaniyya* is the providence that creates and maintains the harmony and order of the world; *raḥma*, as a qualification of *raḥīm*, is providence relative to human beings, which provides their salvation.

We have left aside the exclusively gnostic aspects of these doctrines. What we have discussed adequately demonstrates that they all seek to show that within God there exists a kind of overflow, which created not only the world and humankind, but also comes down upon them, dwells in the world, and bears a divine light that is reflected there. This is particularly true of human beings, who were created capable of discovering, with the indispensable help of the Lord, that they are the mirror or the image of God. That, precisely, is the basis for mystical experience.

SAINT AUGUSTINE AND SAINT PAUL

As we turn to Christianity, the thought of Saint Augustine stands out vividly, for its influence on Christian mysticism is well known. In a famous passage in the *Confessions* (7.9.13), Augustine addresses God and writes: "It was first your will to show me how you resist the proud and give grace to the humble, and how great is your mercy in showing men the way of humility, for the reason that 'the Word was made flesh, and dwelt among' men [John 1:14]. Therefore, by means of a certain man puffed up with most unnatural pride, you procured for me certain books of the Platonists that had been translated out of Greek into Latin. In them I read, not indeed in these words but much the same thought, enforced by many varied arguments that 'In the beginning was the Word, and the Word was with God, and the Word was God' [John 1:1]."[30] Saint Augustine then quotes the entire opening of the prologue of the Gospel of Saint John, while inserting this reflection: "I read that the soul of man, although it gives testimony of the light, is not itself the light, but the Word, God himself, is 'the true light, which enlightens every man that comes into this world.'" And he ends by saying: "But I did not read there [in the Platonic books] that 'the Word was made flesh, and dwelt among us.'"

This opposition between a philosophical datum, accessible to reason though conforming to the sacred text, and a purely religious datum that can only come from revelation and be received through faith, is repeated a bit later in these terms (*Confessions* 7.9.14): "That before all times and above all times your Only-begotten Son remains unchangeably coeternal with you; and that souls receive 'of his fullness,' so that they may be blessed; and that they are renewed by participation in the wisdom 'remaining in herself,' so as to the wise: these truths are found in those books. But that 'according to the time, he died for the ungodly,' and that 'you spared not your only Son, but delivered him up for us all' is not there."

Obviously Augustine is thinking of the second hypostasis, while interpreting it in a Christian sense. The divine Word is thus placed at the level of Mind in Plotinus, or perhaps of the Logos of Philo. This generation of the only-begotten Son is obviously within God. To say that the Word is the first-born among creatures, does not mean that he is a creature, but simply prior to all others. He is therefore, mutatis mutandis, like the great name of God in Jewish and Muslim theosophies. But Saint

Augustine immediately uproots all the seeds of gnosticism that such a point of view might contain.

Augustine aptly shows why the rational framework that Plotinian thought provides him, even when reworked, remains insufficient and invalid when it comes to the reality of spiritual life. The image of the light, which all forms of platonism share with the three monotheisms, ceases to be a pure symbol intended to sustain the idea of emanation or epiphany. This light becomes a person, the Son of God, the incarnate Word who is the way, the truth and the life. From there, everything is simplified. The names of God, the attributes, the *sepîrôt*, are all concentrated in Christ—who fulfills all their functions, who realizes the divine presence in the world and within human beings. As Saint Paul writes, "I am alive; yet it is no longer I, but Christ living in me" (Galatians 2:20). All the divine epiphanies, more or less reminiscent of gnosticism, are applied to Christ alone, who is "the image of the unseen God" (Colossians 1:15).

As we have seen, some kind of mediation between the divine absolute and the creaturely relative is necessary. But now there is only a single mediator, "for in him were created all things in heaven and on earth, everything visible and everything invisible, thrones, ruling forces, sovereignties, powers—all things were created through him and for him" (1:15). Consequently, the angels are not intermediate orders, as theosophic angelologies suggest; they are creatures subordinated to Christ, like all other creatures. Numerous texts of Saint Paul illustrate this Christocentrism, which is a monocentrism. We will cite two passages where we find several terms, inherited no doubt from the Bible. The *Zohar* would later build its heavenly palaces on these passages, as we have seen, but Paul relates them entirely to the one Christ.

One passage is drawn from Paul's second letter to the Corinthians (4:6): it deals with the glory of Christ, who is the image of God and who shines forth in the Gospel: "It is God who said, 'Let light shine out of darkness,' that has shone into our hearts to enlighten them with the knowledge of God's glory, the glory on the face of Christ." The second comes from the letter to the Ephesians (1:4–5,7–10): "Thus he chose us in Christ before the world was made . . . marking us out for himself beforehand, to be adopted sons through Jesus . . . , in whom we gain our freedom, the forgiveness of sins. Such is the richness of the grace which he has showered on us in all wisdom and insight." Love (*agapē*) and grace (*charis*) recall the Hebrew *hesed*; wisdom (*sophia*) is *ḥokmā*; and knowledge or insight (*phronēsis*) is *bīnā*. But here all these terms come into play only in relation to Christ. Analogies persist, in a certain sense, but the comparable elements are organized in a totally different way. Still, we cannot deny a real kinship of thought.

THE VALUE OF HUMILITY

One crucial idea that does not appear in Plotinus, and that Saint Augustine underscores, is the value—the ontological value, so to speak—of humility. Before God, the human being truly exists only in and through humility. All monotheistic mystics have stressed this essential point. To be sure, we also find conceptions of humility that are purely moral and simply opposed to pride; they risk leading to an undue depreciation of the self that amounts to pride in reverse. Moral values here are subject to this kind of ambiguity. But mystical humility is entirely different.

Martin Buber, in his work on Hasidism, sets forth the interesting teaching of Ba^cal Shem Tov, for whom the act of debasing oneself excessively and forgetting the dignity of the human being is an "impure" form of humility. Those who are truly humble are those who perceive others in the same way they perceive themselves, and who perceive themselves in others. Pride consists in contrasting oneself with others. "But when a man rests in himself as in nothing, he is not limited by any other thing, he is limitless and God pours his glory into him. The humility which is meant here is no willed and practiced virtue. It is nothing but an inner being, feeling, and expressing. Nowhere in it is there a compulsion, nowhere a self-humbling, a self-restraining, a self-resolve. It is indivisible as the glance of a child and simple as a child's speech."[31]

We do not find such a clear-cut declaration in Muslim mysticism. Still, the importance of humility as an existential reality is clearly evident in this *ḥadīth* of the Prophet: "Those who have the weight of a grain of pride in their hearts will not enter into paradise; and those who have the weight of a grain of faith will not enter into hell," with faith presented here as implying humility. Qusharyī reported the opinion according to which "greatness is in humility: those who seek greatness in pride do not find it." Ibrāhim b. Shaybān also said that "nobility is in humility." Yet for Arabs, nobility (*sharaf*) really concerns a person's being and cannot be reduced to a simple virtue.

But, with Christianity and its Christocentrism, the value of humility, as Augustine saw well, stands in strikingly sharp relief. In fact, Christ becomes the living example of humility, as emerges in the teaching of

Saint Paul. "Make your own the mind of Christ Jesus: Who, being in the form of God, did not count equality with God something to be grasped [*harpagmon*]. But he emptied [*ekenōsen*] himself, taking the form of a slave . . ." (Philippians 2:5–7).

What does the exemplary quality of the Incarnation mean in relation to the nature of humility? The divine being of Christ belongs to him by right. Yet he "emptied" himself (this is the proper meaning of the verb *kenō*) of his majesty, in order to humble himself even to taking on human form in order to save human beings. In contrast, for human beings it is an improper form of proprietorship (*harpagmon*) to attach themselves to their being as though it were their own, and glorify themselves as though they were its principle and its master, meriting praise. Human beings belong to God, body and soul, and for their part they must recognize this belonging by "emptying" themselves of this possession, which they tend to cling to unjustly. But, while Christ "empties" himself of divine Majesty in order to make room for the humanity he assumes, human beings must empty themselves of their proud and self-sufficient "me," in order to be assumed by Christ in the adoption of the Father.

The passages cited above from Saint Paul clearly show this. We must add the following verses taken from the letter to the Ephesians, (2:4f.): "But God, being rich in faithful love, through the great love with which he loved us, even when we were dead in our sins, brought us to life with Christ. Because it is by grace that you have been saved . . . by a gift from God. . . . We are God's work of art, created in Christ Jesus. . . ." We are to understand, therefore, that all people find their true being, such as God wills it, in Jesus Christ, just as in some sense the individual in Plotinus discovers the intelligible exemplar of his or her own "me" within Mind. (There is no reason to dwell on the differences that leap to mind and that Saint Augustine has rightly brought to light.)

THE DIALECTIC BETWEEN FULLNESS AND EMPTINESS

We discover in Saint Paul's teaching concerning Christ, however, a sort of existential dialectic between fullness and emptiness. In fact, "God wanted all fullness to be found in him" (Colossians 1:19). What is this fullness (*plērōma*)? At first glance it seems to be the totality of beings that are created in him, through him and for him. This is the interpretation that the context favors: " . . . and through him to reconcile all things to himself" by His Son assuming them. But a little later (2:2–3) we read that

Paul wishes to bind the faithful "together in love and to encourage their resolution until they are rich in the assurance of their complete understanding and have knowledge of the mystery of God in which all the jewels of wisdom and knowledge are hidden." Here it would seem to be a question of the fullness of divine attributes. This second explanation, which does not however rule out the first, is more satisfying. Christ has made himself empty, even while preserving the fullness of divinity. That is why God can effect that *coïncidentia oppositorum* of which the theologians have spoken.

But the action in the foreground is no longer the philosophical problem of the union of the divine person with the human person; for Christian mystics the mystery of Incarnation takes on a meaning with entirely different implications. The Incarnation makes possible the mystical life and it is foundational for the mystical experience. Christ has already effected what he summons human beings to effect for themselves in him. The union that theologians call "hypostatic union" (of the divine nature and the human nature in Christ) is the prototype of all mystical union.

All the spiritual writers, in the three monotheisms, agree in recognizing that human beings cannot achieve such a union through their own efforts and that they cannot mount an assault on the divinity through themselves and their own free decision. Such an enterprise would be sacrilegiously presumptuous. Even in pagan mythology, the Titans who wanted to scale to heaven were struck down by Zeus. The initiative, then, necessarily returns to God. In Christianity, God predestines human beings to be united to God in Christ and through Christ, by virtue of His immense mercy, love, and grace. In Judaism, it is through Israel that love is effected. In Islam, God grants His benefits and His aid to whomever He chooses. But, in all three cases, the God who turns toward humankind through a prevenient step (or a prevenient grace) cannot be totally identified with and reduced to absolute Being, locked up in Himself, the transcendent One of which we have spoken, ineffable and inaccessible. In a word, if God in His perfect transcendence is a nothing (or better, no-thing) for us, and if in our ontological misery we are no-thing for Him, how is a union between God and us thinkable? And what can we expect of an ascesis that confirms us in our nothingness?

The upshot is that humility truly becomes a way of life. It consists not in self-contempt, nor in considering oneself vile (which would insult God), nor in resting in an imaginary nothingness. Human beings are not nothing, for God has created and set them apart among all His creatures, according to what all three revealed scriptures teach. Humility consists in perceiving profoundly that one does not exist in oneself, through and for oneself, but that one is in God, through God and for God.

It is true that outside of God human beings are not. That is precisely why wallowing in the asceticism of nothingness is not what it means to relate to God, but on the contrary, it is to place oneself far from Him. To be humble is therefore to associate one's emptiness with the fullness of God. The mystic lives out this association, so that coming into union with God does not mean ceasing to be a creature. This is how monotheistic mysticism avoids pantheism. For the Christian, as Saint Augustine noted well, this life of humility is founded in the Christ who possesses the fullness of God and who emptied himself of divine majesty in order to take on human nature—thus associating what appears logically incompatible, fullness and emptiness. Be that as it may, all monotheistic mystics are engaged in this dialectic and carry it out in analogically comparable ways.

MYSTICAL "JOURNEYS" TOWARD THE LIGHT

There is being that is the guarantor of each human individual. The cause that makes us what we are is not a set of accidents emerging from matter, to which is added the idea of the human being, as the form under which these accidents come together in an individual who is destined to disappear without a trace. Our most profound self is pre-eternally anchored in the Logos—each system of thought conceiving of that Logos in its own way, while assigning it the same role according to analogies of function.

To rediscover this self in the being that causes it to exist and subsist—this is the goal of the mystical adventure as the three monotheisms conceive of it. According to the Platonic and neoplatonic philosophy that inspires them, the way to follow is an ascending way. Plotinus speaks of the soul's double ascension. The first ascension, similar to Plato's description in *The Symposium* and in *The Phaedrus*, begins with things "from below" (*apo tōn katō*), meaning that this is a journey (*poreia*) from the sensible toward the intelligible; the second concerns those who have already reached the intelligible, "those that have already made their way to the sphere of the Intelligibles, have set as it were a footprint there but must still advance within the realm," and it "lasts until they reach the extreme hold of the place, the Term attained when the topmost peak of the Intellectual realm is won [*ep' akrō tō noētō*]."[32] It is worth noting that the image of a journey toward God and a journey in God, which Ibn al-ʿArabī employs, is already present in Plotinus.

What is the summit toward which one must rise? As was true for Plato, it is the Good: "Therefore we must ascend again towards the Good, the desired of every Soul."[33] The soul then returns to its origin. "Therefore the Soul must be trained—to the habit of remarking, first, all noble pursuits, then the works of beauty produced not by the labor of the arts but by the virtue of men known for their goodness: lastly, you must search the souls of those that have shaped these beautiful forms. But how are you to see into a virtuous Soul and know its loveliness? Withdraw into yourself and look. And if you do not find yourself beautiful yet, act as does the creator of a statue that is to be made beautiful: he cuts away here, he smoothes there, he makes this line lighter, this other purer, until a lovely face has grown upon his work. So do you also: cut away all that is excessive, straighten all that is crooked, bring light to all that is overcast, labor to make all one glow of beauty and never cease chiseling your statue, until there shall shine out on you from it the godlike splendor of virtue, until you shall see the perfect goodness [or: simplicity of heart, *sōphrosynē*] surely established in the stainless shrine. When you know that you have become this perfect work, when you are self-gathered in the purity of your being, nothing now remaining that can shatter that inner unity, nothing from without clinging to the authentic man, when you find yourself wholly true to your essential nature, wholly that only veritable light . . . , when you perceive that you have grown to this, you are now become very vision. . . ."[34]

THE PREVENIENT INITIATIVE OF GOD

This text from Plotinus is of considerable importance. Taken together, he describes the step that the monotheistic mystics will take: they too will speak, if not of an ascension toward the intelligible, at least of an ascension toward God, a journey toward God. They will also speak of the soul's purification through ascesis: the purgative way, according to Christian vocabulary. They will even introduce, as we have seen, the idea of divine Beauty, and clearly the idea of divine splendour and light. Their ideal is to reach a pure gaze contemplating God, without any blemish clouding the spiritual eye.

Still, for all of the mystics, there is a fundamental difference that separates them from Plotinus, in spite of all that they borrow from him, directly or indirectly, in order to express themselves. The difference is that this journey is not conducted through human quest and effort. It is a response to a divine appeal and it is commanded by the aid and grace of God. Here is where the profound mark of all monotheistic faith appears.

The Bible teaches us to recognize God's initiative. Thus it is written (Isaiah 26:12): "Oh Lord, you will grant us peace, having completed all our undertakings for us [*kî gam kol-maᶜăśênû pāᶜaltā lānû*]." And the following curse can be turned against all pure philosophers (Isaiah 5:21): "Woe to those who think themselves wise and believe themselves enlightened."

In Christianity, the affirmation of divine initiative is consistent. The teaching of Saint John is explicit: "This is the revelation of God's love for us, that God sent his only Son into the world that we might have life through him. Love consists in this: it is not we who loved God, but God loved us and sent his Son to expiate our sins" (1 John 4:9–10). Even what seems to be a free and generous gift on the part of a human being remains ineffective and falls short: when Saint Peter tells Christ that he will give his life for him, Jesus replies (John 13:38): "Lay down your life for me? In all truth I tell you, before the cock crows you will have disowned me three times." And Saint James writes (1:17): "All that is good, all that is perfect, is given us from above; it comes down from the Father of all light; with him there is no such thing as alteration, no shadow caused by change." One may profitably compare the words with which Plotinus encourages people to make an effort at purification, with the text of *Veni, Sancte Spiritus*, in the liturgy of Pentecost. Plotinus tells his disciple to "cut away all that is excessive, straighten all that is crooked, bring light to all that is overcast, labor to make all one glow of beauty . . . , until there shall shine out on you from it the godlike splendor of virtue." In contrast, though with similar images, Christians sing this hymn:

Holy Spirit, Lord Divine
Come from heights of heav'n and shine . . .
Come, our heart's unfailing light . . .
Cleanse our soiled hearts of sin,
Arid souls refresh within.

Wounded lives to health restore.
Bend the stubborn heart and will
Melt the frozen, warm the chill.
Guide the wayward home once more.

The juxtaposition of the two texts speaks for itself.

In Islam, we have already seen that mystical states (*aḥwāl*) are considered pure gifts of God, independent of all human effort. If human beings love God, it is because God loves them; if they turn toward God to repent, it is because God first turns toward them; if they remember God, it is because God Himself remembers them first.

There is nothing more striking in this regard than what the great thinker Abū Ḥayyān al-Tawḥīdī wrote in the tenth century in his collection of invocations to God, *al-Ishārāt al-Ilāhiyya*: "Oh my God! Be for us, even if we are not for ourselves." In saying "Be for us [*kun lanā*]," Tawḥīdī repeats as prayer (*duʿāʾ*) the imperative that God employs in order to grant existence to creatures. God created us in order that we might worship Him (cf. Qurʾan 51:56). But we cannot worship God—in other words, be for God by serving God (the verb *ʿabada* means both worship and serve)—unless God be for us first.

In our hands, everything is negative, or turns into negativity: "There is no memory that forgetfulness does not betray; there is no love that frivolity does not squander; there is no being that does not tend constantly to disintegrate; there is no grandeur that does not end in debasement." What human beings bear in themselves is a "weight that drags down" and causes them to descend far from God. Thus Tawḥīdī exclaims: "You are more befitting to us than we to ourselves. When we fear You, our fear of You is mixed with our hope in You. When we are overcome with the despair that is inspired in us by You, receive it in exchange for hope in You! In our movement of turning ourselves toward You, we announce the good news of our arrival before You!"

The *duʿāʾ* is a prayer asking for divine help, and it is inspired entirely by God. Through it, human existence is stabilized, for in it God's beneficial action is intensified. "You have realized the hopes we have for protection in the abode of Your power; You have confirmed our expectation through the favor that You have already granted us, for You are the Generous One (*al-Jawād*); You give without our praying; how much more generous will You be when we pray to You! You are the dispenser of goods, even when we ask You nothing; how much more will You be so when we ask You!" And then comes an entire chain of prayers marking stages in the journey toward God: "O my God! In the same way as You hold us as Your possession, be good to us; and when You have been good to us, emancipate us; and when You have emancipated us, greet us; and when You have greeted us, then be there for us (*kun lanā*); and when you have been there for us, be with us (*kun maᶜanā*); and when you have been with us, then You, You, are the Master of Praise!"

In this quest for true existence and for all the benefits that accompany it, it is God who in fact prepares everything in advance for the human being: in this resides the goodness and justice of God: "He is more benevolent toward you than you are for yourself; He is more a friend to you than you are for yourself; He has more tenderness of heart for you than you have within for yourself. He has wanted [or loved: *arādaka*] you even before you loved Him; He has responded to you even before you invoked Him; it is He who assists you, even before you ask Him for help."

Divine prevenience is also linked to an idea that evokes the Plotinian doctrine of the existence within God of that which is intelligible in each individual. It says in the Qurʾan (33:72): "We offered the trust [of faith; *amāna*] unto the heavens and the earth and the hills, but they shrank from bearing it and were afraid of it. And man assumed it." Tawḥīdī makes the following reflections on this verse: "By God! What a sublime investment! It existed before you, on the part of God, while you were but scattered in the dust and no form had yet united you into a whole; no name had been given you, nothing was known of your individual reality, no one spoke to you, no space enclosed you, no eye could see to describe you, no time passed over you. And you, you were in the world of divine sovereignty [*malakūt*], within the mystery of God, established in His knowledge, stripped and abandoned by everything except His will of decree [*mashīʾa*]. You were formed to know Him, you were visible in the choice of God, capable of responding to His call. You are then blessed, oh man! For it is the eternal Providence of your generous Lord that aided you before you aided yourself, and that aided you by that which your desire could not grasp."

For Tawḥīdī, therefore, the goal of the mystic quest is to find true existence in God. That, moreover, is the goal of all monotheistic mystics. Now, in Arabic, the word "existence" is derived from the verb (*wujūd*), whose three-letter root WJD has as its earliest meaning "to find." To exist is "to be found" (*wujida*). Thus, after exclaiming "That God is sublime in His being-sought and in His being-found! [*ᶜazza maṭlūban wa mawjūdan*]" Tawḥīdī writes: "O my God! Who can seek You, when before every quest You are found [and existing: *mawjūd*]? And how would we find You, when after the quest, you are lost?—not lost for the eye but lost to the eyes; not found through the reason [*ʿaql*], but found through a gift made to the spirit."

In fact, when people take the initiative in seeking God, God slips away from their eyes: it is not that our eyes, after having found God, lose sight of God; it is God who, in our very quest, makes it impossible for us to find Him, for our desire to find Him would not be able to take hold of Him. Therefore, God precedes us; God gives Himself as one found before we seek, and we only seek because God is already found. One cannot help but think of the words that Pascal, in his *Pensées*, places in the mouth of Christ: "Take heart; you would not seek me if you had not found me." Obviously, as a Christian, Pascal was reflecting along the lines of a Christocentric vision, so that the prevenience of God expresses itself in a particularly vivid and tangible manner at the climax of Christ's passion: "I thought of you in my agony, I have shed drops of blood for you." What greater guarantee of a person's existence is there than to know that one has been in the thought of the redeemer at the very hour of redemption?

But we must return to Tawḥīdī for a final quotation: "You are existing [or: one can find You] in every thing, not in the way that things exist which endure and need You to exist, but in the way that You exist, You yourself. No one finds You but You, and the one who finds for You, and the one who finds through You, the one who finds on account of You: the one who finds through You, because our concrete reality exists [is found to be] through You; the one who finds for You, because our acts of finding only exist [are only found to be] in relation to You; the one who finds on account of You, because that through which we find what we find only exists [is only found to be] on account of You and proceeds from You." There is no way to express more forcefully the idea of prevenience and divine initiative.

We also find this idea in the Bible. God says to the prophet Jeremiah (1:5): "Before I formed you in the womb I knew you; before you came to birth I consecrated you." All these citations provide evidence that these different mystical conceptions, within the three monotheisms, share the same spiritual idea, whose expression is inspired by a certain Plotinian philosophy on one hand and, on the other, the particular teachings that give them their diversity.

LIKE KNOWN THROUGH LIKE

We must not neglect either the influence on mystical reflection of an old axiom according to which like cannot be known except by what is like. Here is the form it takes in Plotinus: "Never did eye see the sun unless it had first become sunlike, and never can the Soul have vision of the First Beauty unless itself be beautiful. Therefore, first let each become godlike and each beautiful who cares to see God and Beauty."[35]

Aesthetic consideration of the beauty of creation as it reflects the Beauty of God is not foreign to mystical modes of expression. It follows that the way of religious mysticism and what has been called "speculative mysticism" display a certain parallelism. Furthermore, this speculative mysticism cannot help but be colored, in Plotinus, by religious sentiments, even though the religion in question was pagan. "Even the desire [for Beauty] is to be desired as a Good. To attain it is for those that will take the upward path, who will set all their forces towards it, who will divest themselves of all that we have put on in our descent: so, to those that approach the Holy Celebrations of the Mysteries, there are appointed purifications and the laying aside of the garments worn before, and the entry in nakedness. . . ."[36] Philo had not hesitated to employ the vocabulary of pagan mysteries in order to express certain biblical values. We should not be surprised that Jewish, Christian, and Muslim mystics could use Plotinian language in order to communicate their experience in journeying toward their God.

Another idea appears in the text cited above, one that the mystics honored highly: the soul must be unified in order to be able to move toward God. There is always a screen between our selves and the true reality of our being which should be one, as with every authentic existence, so that we apprehend ourselves by means of multiple affections tugging at us in every direction. Such is *sōphrosynē*, a term we should translate by taking into account an etymology that combines *sōs* and *phryn* and yields the idea of an "intact heart." We have therefore rendered the term as "simplicity of heart," understanding by that the healthy state of a heart that preserves its original purity and innocence, sheltered from every profanation and corruption. Moreover, the ideal of simplicity of heart is linked to that of sincerity, which we mentioned in relation to the *ikhlās* of the Muslim mystics.

But sincerity, for religious thinkers, cannot proceed without humility, if only because the proud think more highly of themselves than they truly are. Now, such humility is totally absent from Greek conceptions. The adjective *tapeinos*, which means "humble" in the sense we noted when commenting on Saint Augustine, appears with this meaning in the Gospels and in Saint Paul. But in non-Christian literature it has an entirely different meaning: it often indicates lowly origin. This is the case in a passage from Plotinus where it is associated with *idiōtēs*, a lowly person, and with *metrios*, a person of modest means. Plotinus explains in this passage that infatuation (*authadeia*) can characterize very ordinary people. Yet this has nothing to do with humility. In the case of Plato, the term [*authadeia*] indicates modesty, in the sense of proportion. It is for example associated with *kekosmenos* (*Laws* IV, 716a4) which means "arranged, well ordered."

Nowhere is the issue one of humility before God, as a mode of being. If, in the tragedies, the gods (or the fates) punish pride, that is because it violates the hierarchical order of the universe. In the tragedy of Aeschylus, Agamemnon, returning victorious from the war with Troy, glorifies himself even while thanking the gods. "We owe faithful gratitude to the gods, if we have drawn vengeance without measure from the rape [of Helen]." There is no humility here. Nevertheless, when Clytemnestra wants him to enter the palace by trampling a purple cloth, he says to her, "It is the gods who should be honored in this way. . . . I want to be honored as a man, not as God." With dignity he claims only this position as a man and this will to hold onto his place cannot help but imply an affirmation of self in the face of the gods. One renders the homage to the gods that is their due, but then one is released from duty, and such freedom is a refined form of pride. Saint Augustine, therefore, had reason to stress humility as a religious value far removed from Greek models.

We have emphasized the idea of unification with oneself. Now, Plotinus (V 9.1) also speaks of an ascension toward the One by specifying that this ascension concerns the One who is truly one (*anagōgē . . . eis hen kai alēthōs hen*), and not what is one only as a unity within multiplicity, even the unity of ideas within Mind. Here we rediscover the observations we made concerning an understanding of faith in a single God thought of as absolutely One. Can we, in contemplation, go beyond Mind (intellectual understanding) where our intelligible self exists [is found]? So far we have spoken of what Christians call the purgative life and the illuminative life. Now we must take up the mystery of the unitive life.

THE UNITIVE LIFE

Plato, in *The Republic*, declares that the Good is beyond essence (*etekeina tēs ousias*), in other words, beyond all intelligibles. Plotinus likewise introduces the Good, of which he speaks in the same terms as the One: It has nothing that can be qualified: " . . . containing nothing, it is The Good by that very absence of content. Thus we rob it of its very being as The Absolute Good if we ascribe anything to it, existence or intellect or goodness." "[C]ontaining nothing, it is alone: it is void of all but itself."[37] Under these conditions, whoever ascends to the point where they unite with the One or with the Good will be unable to speak of their experience. At this level of contemplation, the mystics can only employ a very approximate language that is entirely inadequate and often does them a disservice.

Plotinus himself writes: "We are in agony for a true expression; we are talking of the untellable."[38] In fact, what is involved here is no longer an intellectual or even a spiritual contemplation. As Bréhier writes in his *History of Philosophy*, "we are dealing rather with an ineffable type of contact in which we cannot even speak of a knowing subject and a known object, in which the duality itself vanishes and unification is complete. . . ."[39]

The Plotinian model introduces the mystics who are inspired by it into the realm of the inexpressible. Here we touch upon the problem of ecstasy. The term implies that contemplatives are drawn away from their selves, transported and transposed. But then, what becomes of contemplatives in this ecstasy? Won't they be lost within an Absolute, so that their being can no longer subsist as such? Won't the contemplatives' personal individuality have been a mere illusion? But how can it be illusory if it is guaranteed by an intelligible within Mind? In religious terms, is it that those persons to whom God speaks, whom God has created to lead them to worship Him, are called to self-annihilation in Him? Is it possible that perfection of worship ends in the disappearance of the worshiper and the one worshiped? Must the supreme mystical experience toward which the monotheistic mystics journey be consummated in a sort of *brahman*, which Masson-Oursel characterizes as "neutral forms" and "anonymous forces," or even *nirvana*? Does the truth then lie with Hinduism or Buddhism, which deny the personal God of the three monotheistic revelations? This is a serious question, which we will have to examine. It involves the accusation of pantheism that has been leveled against various Jewish, Christian, or Muslim mystics, yet it is not easy, and perhaps impossible, to resolve it with certainty.

Among Jews, the term *dĕbeqût*, which as we have seen derives from a root word meaning "to reach" or "to be joined to," has come to mean intimate and close communion with God. But whereas for Nahmanides it involves communion with the last of the ten *sepîrôt*, for Ezra b. Salomon it involves communion with nothingness (no-thing-ness). Gershom Scholem writes on the subject that this "is certainly a much higher rank than communion with the Shekhinah, Naught [or Nothingness] being the most hidden recess of divinity which contemplation may behold."[40] But that is clearly meaningless if it refers to absolute nothingness, or indeed to an undifferentiated absolute which for the contemplative is equivalent to nothingness. Moreover, how could we still speak of contemplation? One could not contemplate Nothingness, but one could contemplate a being that can be expressed by no-thing, a being that takes the breath away from anyone contemplating it, and leaves them speechless.

There is another term, *yiḥûd*, unification, though Scholem notes that "it is not always easy to determine what is meant by it."[41] Sometimes it refers to a unified concentration of the mind. Sometimes such concentration focuses on the "root" of the Torah. In the latter case, a human being "does not become God, but he becomes 'united' with Him by the process in which the core of his own being is bound up with the core of all being."[42] But for Baᶜal Shem Tov, *yiḥûd* is accomplished through *dĕbeqût* and "transforms the Ego, or *ani*, into the Naught, or *ain*."[43] Here we have an example of a play on words, which is frequent among Jews as well as among esoteric Muslims. But the problem is to know how much weight to give to such an expression. Under these conditions, Scholem's conclusion, which distinguishes "communion" and "union," seems the most judicious: "In fixing all one's attention on God, thought, sunk in contemplation of the ineffable light, loses its definite content as an intellectual act. By the practice of *devekut* [*dĕbeqût*], thought is transformed into emotion; it is, if I may be permitted to use the expression, de-intellectualized. In other words, the insight which is won by *devekut* has no rational and intellectual content and, being of a most intimate and emotional character, cannot be translated into rational terms."[44] In sum, contemplation, at this level, attains the God of whom Pascal is aware in his heart.

It remains no less true that pantheism still haunts Jewish kabbalah, at least to the extent that the only reasonable way to understand the term requires the idea of everything that exists emanating from God, in contrast to the idea of creation *ex nihilo.* The *Zohar* has been particularly marked by such a pantheism. But we must also recall the teaching of *Tsimtsum* by Isaac Luria, whose profound originality "acted as a counterpoise to the pantheism which some scholars think is implied by the theory of emanation," as Scholem puts it: "Not only is there a residue of divine manifestation in every being, but under the aspect of *Tsimtsum* it also acquires a reality of its own which guards it against the danger of dissolution into the non-individual being of the divine 'all in all.'"[45] In effect, in an earlier, primal "time," God withdraws into Himself through a kind of exile, as though "banishing Himself from His totality into profound seclusion."[46] Through this act of limitation, the primordial space of God's proper creation appears where, in a second "time," God sends the light of His revelation and manifests Himself as God the Creator. Within this "space," each being has its assigned place and can encounter God and contemplate God's light without ceasing to be itself. Here is a dialectic between exile and presence through which God can disclose himself to human beings without annihilating them. This dialectic evokes, *mutatis mutandis*, the dialectic of emptiness and fullness of which we have spoken with reference to Christ.

In Islam, the problem of the final mystical experience clusters around two terms: *ittiṣāl*, which means attachment or conjoining, and *ittiḥād*, which means union. *Ittiṣāl* is defined through a break (*inqiṭāᶜ*) with everything that is not God. But it is not the kind of contact that is possible only between two bodily essences. This *ḥadīth* of the Prophet is cited: "Attachment [*ittiṣāl*] exists to the degree that there is detachment [*infiṣāl*] from creatures." Tahānawī, in his *Dictionary of Technical Terms*, provides us with some interesting definitions. "The lowest degree of attachment is the vision [Arabic: *mushāhada*; Persian: *dīdan*] that people have of their Lord through the eye of the heart, from however far away. The Sufis call this vision from afar being present before God [*muḥāḍara*, implying a reciprocal presence of God] if it takes place before the lifting of the veil; they call it disclosure [*mukāshafa*] if it takes place after the lifting of the veil. . . . Once the veil is lifted, those who progress along the way know with certainty in their hearts that God is present with them. . . . This degree of attachment they also call inferior. And if, after the lifting of the veil and after disclosure, there is something like the radiance of Essence, those who are on the way reach the mystical station of highest contemplation [*mushāhada*], the highest of which they call superior attachment. For people such as these, the first station is to be present to God; then comes disclosure, then contemplation. . . . Being present to God is for those who have knowledge of certitude; disclosure, for those who have the eye of certitude; contemplation, for those who possess the reality of certitude."

The Moroccan Sufi Ibn ᶜAjība, in his *Miᶜrāj*, adds a few details to this picture and reworks it. J.-L. Michon has given us a profound study of the *Miᶜrāj*. Ibn ᶜAjība says that presence before God takes place through "the power of *dhikr* when it rules the heart." *Dhikr* is the act through which one thinks of God by constantly keeping Him in one's memory. It introduces, after the station of disclosure, that "intimate encounter [*musāmara*]" in which the secrets of the divine essence appear: "The servant is then removed from his own existence and plunged into the ocean of Unity [*bahr al-aḥadiyya*] for an hour or two. Whenever he returns to self-consciousness and to his senses, he is like a swimmer who returns to the surface yet for the most part remains under water. It is then that the ecstatic encounter [*wijdān*] begins, and the light of contemplation begins to shine."[47] As for contemplation, "it is the uninterrupted succession of epiphanic lights [*anwār al-tajallī*] in the heart, which are never obscured by a veil." And Ibn ᶜAjība adds: "Let us imagine a dark night in where lightning brightens the sky again and again—a kind of night that is made into day. Such is the heart that perpetually receives theophanic illumination."[48]

Qushayrī, for his part, distinguishes three degrees that coincide with the three levels of human life of which we have spoken: the level of the soul (self-consciousness), that of the heart, and that of the intimate secret. He examines three terms that share a common root: *tawājud*, *wajd* and *wujūd*. The first, by virtue of its "form," implies an effort: "The *tawājud* consists of wanting ecstasy (*wajd*) to come, through a kind of free choice." It characterizes the state of beginners. But in fact, ecstasy is a gift of God. It consists in the soul's being removed from the whole set of qualities that characterize a human being, when the mark (*sima*) of divine essence is impressed upon it. Certain mystics, such as Junayd, claim that it is accompanied by joy (*surūr*). Others, such as Ibn ᶜAṭāᵓ, say sadness (*ḥazn*). Tahānawī explains this difference by saying that joy can be related entirely to God, as to its source, while sadness is a quality that relates to the heart that feels it; consequently, joy is more appropriate to ecstasy. Nevertheless, the point of view of Ibn ᶜAṭaᵓ is justified by the fact that joy touches the heart as much as does sadness, and it is normal for the heart, which while it doubtless exists for God, is not yet totally submerged in God, to feel pain at being cut off from its human attributes. So sadness is a living sign of its uprootedness.

Be that as it may, ecstasy is not the end point of the mystical journey. The mystic attains existence (*wujūd*) "after being raised up beyond ecstasy." But contemplation of the existence of God is only possible after "the extinguishing of the humanity" (*khumūd al-bashariyya*) within a person. Junayd said: "What rightfully pertains to contemplation is that the destruction of self [*maᶜa fiqdānika*] accompany the existence of God." Abū ᶜAlī al-Daqqāq said: "The quest for existence makes it necessary for human beings to be wholly taken up [*istīᶜāb*]; ecstasy necessarily requires that they be submerged [*istighrāq*], and [true] existence demands that they be lost in non-being [*istihlāk*]."

If we take these texts literally, it seems that mystics, upon reaching the highest level of their journey, are engulfed in the ocean that they contemplate. Are we then in the presence of a Hindu-type system? We can be sure that the answer is no. In fact, the first thing we can say is that all the quotations we have provided relate to the idea of attachment, and not the idea of union. Islam could no more tolerate the union of human nature with divine nature than could Judaism. We note moreover that even in Christianity, Christ's hypostatic union, while it can ground the mystical experience ontologically, in no way results from a mystical journey or grace: we have seen that it rests on the fact that the Father has created all things through the Son, in the Son and for the Son. We need not return to that.

Absolutely speaking there is, for the three monotheisms, no measure common to creator and creature. In Islam, the word *ittiḥād*, which means "union," is defined in the following way by Tahānawī: "It is the intuitive vision of a single and absolute existence, inasmuch as all existing things exist through the existence of this One, while in themselves, they are non-existent. But it is not as though that which is not God could have a particular existence through which it then becomes united to God." This definition removes from the word *ittiḥād* any sense that would make it a synonym for "fusion." Human beings never become one with God through a kind of fusion by which their nature, their created essence, would be confused with the divine nature and essence. If human beings return to God, as the Qurʾan says in numerous verses (for example 2:28), it is not because there is but a single existence to which everything will be restored, according to the doctrine of existential monism (*waḥdat al-wujūd*); it is because God, who created human beings to worship Him, summons them to eternal worship.

Now, there can be no doubt that the condition of the mystics in their contemplation here-below is a kind of anticipation of what will be in their vision beyond, in paradise. Christians also share this point of view. We can therefore conclude that *ittiḥād* becomes identical to *ittiṣāl*, of which it is nothing more than the highest form, which is realized in contemplation, although we have seen that it exists in inferior forms of attachment—in *tawājud* and *wajd*.

But what does the mystic contemplate who has reached this summit? The divine Essence, no doubt, but not in itself. The mystic contemplates it in its radiance, or as translators sometimes put it, in its epiphanic illuminations (*tajalliyāt*). In order to comprehend what can then happen, we must recall what Plotinus wrote: one must have the form of the sun in order to see the sun. What happens to this idea among our mystics? It is at once preserved and transposed. Preserved—because it remains true that like cannot be known, seen, or grasped except by like. Transposed—because here, all initiative reverts to God. When God lifts the veil that covers over the heart of a person who has set out on the way (*al-sālik*), so that God is thereby disclosed, divine light bursts upon this person and this heart becomes radiant; once the eye of the heart becomes pure vision, the highest kind of attachment—in other words, union as we have seen it defined—is realized in contemplation.

What then disappears in human beings? Their soul or self-consciousness, together with their attachments to the world. The heart itself, when it makes its presence felt, clouds a person's vision, just as when our eye calls attention to itself, through tears or a speck of dust or any irritation whatsoever, and we see poorly. At the same time, the intimate sense of our own created existence disappears, for it would place a screen between us and God: contemplatives only apprehend their existence as it bathes in the creative light of divine existence.

To use another image, one could say that contemplatives are like artists, devoted to beauty, who contemplate a beautiful work without reflecting on themselves. Entirely forgetting themselves, they are totally absorbed by what they see and at the same time are filled with what they see—as if they were now only what they saw and existed only through their joy in seeing it. In this sense, an Arab poet has said: My existence is to be without existence, in the vision that shines upon me.

THE MONOTHEISTIC MEANING OF PANENTHEISM

There is no need to make hasty accusations of pantheism against the mystics, and even less need to imagine that they hold to Hindu or Buddhist conceptions that they have camouflaged under the cloak of monotheistic teachings or references to texts said to be revealed. Indian mysticisms and monotheistic mysticisms cannot be reduced to one another. Certain historians, among them Gershom Scholem, have proposed replacing the term "pantheism," with that of "panentheism." Though everything is not God, everything is in God; though God is not everything that exists, God is in everything that exists.

This is certainly an idea that has struck the mystics of the three monotheistic religions. Furthermore, it finds support in their texts, especially the biblical texts. The most famous is that of Isaiah 6:3: "Holy, holy, holy is the LORD Sabaoth. His glory fills the whole earth." This verse sums up and resolves the whole mystical problematic. God is holy (*qādôš*), and sanctity (*qôdeš*) is what separates from the profane; it is the mark of divine transcendence. But then, immediately after this first affirmation, a second, apparently contradictory affirmation is added: that of divine immanence. All that is not God is filled with the glory of God—that is to say, of God's radiance and God's living presence. The sanctity of God does belong to a created being, taken by itself; it includes all the overflowing richness that the goodness of God wishes to give.

Thus God is simultaneously transcendent and immanent to the world; what logical reason cannot reconcile the living experience of the contemplative unifies in an ineffable vision. That is why philosophers and speculative theologians, when they seek to comprehend what the mystics are saying, either interpret them to mean that absolute transcendence absorbs the world in a God where all else is dissolved, or to mean that immanence bathes everything in the divine. We end up, in either case, with similar formulations that can pass as pantheistic, with all the vagueness that the notion involves.

But verses justifying some kind of panentheism are not rare. Thus one reads in Jeremiah 23:24: "Do I not fill heaven and earth?" Obviously we must rule out any thought of localization, though such language can scarcely express these things without employing prepositions and terms implying place. Yet one will have the option of saying that God could not be a stranger to what exists and what He has created. This idea is expressed, in the holy books, with the image of royalty and possession.

"God is a great king" (*melek gādôl*) affirms Psalm 95:3. "In his power are the depths of the earth, the peaks of the mountains are his," the next verse continues. Present to the whole universe, God is particularly present to His people: "And you will know that I am among you in Israel" (Joel 2:27). God dwells on the holy mountain, in His abode. Nevertheless, the Bible says very specifically that the temple does not contain God, in the sense of localization. Solomon asks in 1 Kings 8:27: "Yet will God really live [*yēšēb*] with human beings on earth? Why, the heavens, the highest of the heavens, cannot contain you. How much less this temple built by me!" But God does dwell there through His glory, which fills it, and through His name. In fact, God Himself commands "to have a temple built where my name should be" (*lihyôt šĕmî šām*; 1 Kings 8:16). It is in these dwellings (*miškĕnôt*, cf. *šekînâ*), in these "courts of the Lord" that the soul encounters God. Writing from a messianic perspective, Ezekiel transmits the following words from the angel of the LORD: (43:7): "Son of man, this is the dais of my throne, the step on which I rest my feet. I shall live here among the Israelites for ever" (*ʾăšer ʾeškān šām*, cf. *šekînâ*). One should note that Solomon, when wondering if God dwells on earth, employs the verb *yāšob* which means: to rest, to stop on a journey, and not the verb *sâkân* from which *šekînâ* is derived. Finally, Ezekiel again announces (48:35): "The name of the city in future must be: The-LORD-is-there [*YHWH šāmmâ*]."

Correspondingly, one finds numerous verses saying that all existing beings are in God, for if they did not have this divine "bulwark," they would sink into nothingness. "You fence me in, behind and in front" (Psalm 139:5). God is called a tower, a fortress, a refuge. Certainly one could object that these are no more than images. No doubt. But even if they signify only the protection that human beings find in God, they still imply that this protection cannot be reduced to aid that comes from on high, but that it embraces those who are protected, to the very depth of their being.

There is also the matter of God's "shadow": it is a reality that promises to preserve the creatures whom it envelops. In Psalm 91:1, we read of those "who live [*yōšēb*] in the shelter [*bĕsēter*] of the Most High, who abide in the shadow of the Almighty [*beṣēl šadday yitlônān*]."[49] Isaiah speaks of the hand of God that covers Israel (49:2; 51:16). Another image is that of the shadow of God's wings. We find this image particularly in two Psalms, with interesting contexts. "So the children of Adam take refuge in the shadow of your wings. . . . [I]n you [*ʿimmĕkā*] is the source of life, by your light we see the light" (Psalm 36:7–9). This last expression brings to mind the al-Nūr sūrah: "Light upon light" (Qurʾan 24:35). It may seem strange that the shadow of a wing should be associated with the light of God. But if this shadow is the veil that protects us from the false glitter of the world, it is entirely normal that the true light should shine in and through it. We may recall the dark night (*al-laylat al-ẓulmā*) in which the lightning flashes on and on, as the Muslim Sufi says, and indeed the *noche oscura* of Saint John of the Cross—the night of senses, and above all the night of the soul, wherein "even though this happy night darkens the spirit, it does so only to impart light concerning all things."[50] A second important text is that of Psalm 63:7–8: "in the shadow of your wings I rejoice; my heart clings to you" (literally: behind you) *dābqâ ʾahăre(y)kā*, which carries the idea of attachment or holding fast, *dĕbeqût*).

In Islam, the Qurʾan frequently expresses both the idea of divine royalty and God's possession of all things. "Then exalted by God, the True King! [*al-Ḥaqq*]" (20:114). In other verses (59:23; 62:1), God is called "the Sovereign Lord, the Holy One [*al-quddūs*]." Certainly the Qurʾan says nothing about God dwelling in the heavens or on the earth. In the Qurʾan, the verb *ḥalla* is never taken to mean coming down upon a place to dwell there, and Islamic theologians have generally condemned theories of *ḥulūl* (inhabitation) according to which God comes to inhabit an *imām* descending from ʿAlī in order to guide and illuminate the community. (This is the thesis of Shiite extremists [*Ghulāt*], as with a "Knower" [*ʿArif*] who has reached the summit of gnosis [*maʿrifa*], according to the thinking of certain esoteric mystics.) Muslims have often more or less confused this conception of *ḥulūl* with the Christian doctrine of Incarnation. Nevertheless, it must be pointed out that God calls the temple of *Kaʿba*, in Mecca, "My House" (*Baytī*, 2:125; 22:26). It is also said concerning the human being (50:16): "We are nearer to him than his jugular vein."

Be that as it may, the idea of divine immensity is qurʾanic and is expressed with the adjective *wāsiʿ* (vast, large, ample, spacious), which appears in seven verses accompanied by the adjective *ʿalīm*, which is translated, since it concerns God, as "omniscient." Neither person nor thing can be hidden from the eyes of God. *Wāsiʿ* is also associated with *ḥakīm* (sage). The commentators have concluded from this that God is omnipresent through His knowledge and His action. Fakhr al-Dīn al-Rāzī distinguishes three meanings. According to the first, God is immense through His power and through the administration of His Sovereignty. According to the second, God is immense through the abundance of His benefits, "which clearly reveal what is good for men, in order that through it they come to give their consent (*riḍwān*) to God." According to the third, God is immense through mercy (*Raḥma*).

This last exegesis, which concerns profoundly spiritual values, is that of Ibn al-ᶜArabī. We have seen how he conceives of the nature and active power of the divine names. *Wāsiᶜ* is a name that is linked with Mercy. Ibn al-ᶜArabī also cites verse 7:156: "and My mercy embraces [*wasiᶜat*] all things." Thus the reason for *Raḥma* is to cause being to persevere, in consequence of the name *al-Wāsiᶜ* through which God envelops all things in mercy and knowledge. The presence of God is that of His name, which molds beings into the image of its function. Now, the function of a divine name is to manifest the Essence. Divine immensity is therefore linked to the mercy that comes "from next to God" (*min ᶜindiʾllâh*). "He is the One who gives [*al-Wahhāb*] always [*ᶜalāʾl-dawām*], the one who overflows [*al-Fayyāḍ*] for ever [*ᶜalāʾl-istimrār*]," writes Ibn al-ᶜArabī in the *Futūḥāt*.[51]

Now we should note here a curious, but extraordinary commentary on the introductory sūrah of the Qurʾan, the *Fātiḥah*. It is written there (1:1–2): "Praise be to God, Lord of the Worlds, the Beneficent [*Raḥmān*], the Merciful [*Raḥīm*]." A bit later, God speaks of a way that is straight and narrow: "The path of those whom You have favored, not (the path) of those who earn Your anger" (1:6–7). Here is the interpretation of Ibn al-ᶜArabī: "From the beginning, God brings mercy [*Raḥma*] to pass. . . . Then, in the second place, he brings anger to pass, in such a way that mercy precedes anger at the very first beginning of existence." Thus Adam was from the beginning heaped with this mercy, before having to take on the punishment of his disobedience." After that, he again received mercy. There are therefore two mercies, with anger placed between them. "Now, the two mercies ask to be united because they are entirely similar, in such a way that they inter-penetrate and the anger that stands between them is annulled."[52] Ibn al-ᶜArabī concludes: "Consequently the word *Raḥma* is an expression of the primary existent,"[53] in that it (mercy) orders all the gifts bestowed from the beginning of creation. But if the first mercy is at the origin of all that exists, from the primal foundation through the beings of the sub-lunar world engaged in the vicissitudes of becoming and haunted with non-being, the second mercy restores all things in the heart of that divine immensity which preserves all being. God is therefore present in the worlds through His first mercy, and the beings of the world which are in His image—human beings—are present in God through the second mercy.

If we now turn to Christianity, we must state once more that its doctrine of Incarnation places it in a more favorable position in this respect. Along with the fullness that Christ has from the Father, he has received in himself all creatures, even though he was "emptied" of his divine majesty in order to humble himself to the point of living in them. But the problematic is always the same. And this is what matters to us. We note, moreover, that the entire teaching of the Bible—on the presence of God in the world, and on the human being as microcosm in God—is at the heart of the meditation of Christian mystics. To be sure, the magisterium of the Church has fought off every formulation that could pass for pantheism, and has often exercised an excessive vigilance. For this reason ecclesial authority has often been unable to acknowledge the panentheistic formulas supported by scriptural texts of the kind we have quoted. Unfortunately, that same authority has not always distinguished between a panentheism that is acceptable and conforms to scripture, and what would actually amount to an existential monism. One of the most famous cases of this confusion is that of Meister Eckhart.

THE CASE OF MEISTER ECKHART

At the level of philosophy Meister Eckhart followed the Aristotelian tradition through Arab commentaries, and his thought was very close to that of Saint Thomas. But at another level, he had come under the influence of Saint Augustine, Pseudo-Dionysius, and, through them, Plato and Plotinus. God does not have being: God is being or, rather, the principle of being as its creator. It is in this sense, as we have seen, that Meister Eckhart speaks of God as no-thing, since God is beyond all that our rational understanding can grasp as being. It is not through reason, therefore, nor indeed through anything which is human, that human beings can find God.

But the mystic does not stop with this negative theology. "God has such a close union [*Einung*] with the soul that it is past belief: and God is so lofty [*erhaben*] in Himself that neither understanding [*Verstand*] nor desire can attain to Him. But desire reaches further than anything that can be grasped by the understanding. . . . All that understanding can grasp, all that desire can desire, that is not God. Where understanding and desire end, there is darkness, and there God shines."[54] In another sermon, Meister Eckhart cites Saint Paul (1 Timothy 6:15–16), who speaks of the manifestation of Jesus Christ "who at the due time will be revealed by God, the blessed and only Ruler of all, the King of kings and the Lord of lords, who alone is immortal, whose home is in inaccessible light, whom no human being has seen or is able to see. . . ." Nevertheless, God, as the superabundant (*überschwenglich*; cf. Plotinus's *huperplēres*) Being, grants superabundant knowledge, for being and knowledge (*Sein und Erkenntnis*) are something that is absolutely one. But then we are dealing with mystical knowledge, the true knowledge that rests upon the perfect likeness (*Gleichheit*) between the known and the knowing. It is realized where "the soul is in-formed in the highest purity, in the impress of pure essence, where she tastes God before He assumes truth or cognisability, where all naming has been dropped: *there* she knows Him most purely—there she receives being on an equal footing."[55]

On many points, we can compare this text to a passage in the Fifth Ennead in which Plotinus asks how plurality emerges from the One: "It is precisely because there is nothing within the One that all things are from it. . . . Seeking nothing, possessing nothing, lacking nothing, the One is perfect and, in our metaphor, has overflowed, and its exuberance has produced the new: this product has turned again to its begetter and been filled and has become its contemplator and so an Intellectual-Principle."[56] One can also relate the idea of nothingness, in Meister Eckhart, to that of the *ʾên Sôp* in the kabbalists. The problem for all of them—Eckhart, Plotinus, and the kabbalists—is to account for the union of the soul in contemplation with this absolutely transcendent One-who-is-nothing.

But if God is no-thing, this is relative to what *we* think of as being. But in reality it is this being in relation to us which is no-thing (*Nichts*). Creatures, taken in themselves and apart from God who created them, are nothing. But, just as for Plotinus, this is because God, the source of all being, is nothing that can be determined or defined that creatures to the degree they are determined, defined, and hence finite, are, from this angle, strangers to all true being. We could say that for human beings who consider themselves to be beings, God is no-thing, while human beings who consider themselves non-beings, God is Being. Just as Plato had seen in *The Sophist*, defined being is being that has a limit, and the limit is non-being—or as Meister Eckhart says, a "not" (*nicht*). To be this is *not* to be that. This is why he says that one must be stripped of the "not" (*entblöszt stehen vom "Nicht"*).

In this regard, Meister Eckhart uses the example of hellfire. What exactly burns the damned? The "not," he replies. What makes a glowing coal burn the hand? The fact that the hand is not glowing coal, is not fire: "But if my hand contained all that the coal has or can effect, it would be all of the nature of fire. Then, if anyone were to take all the fire that ever burnt, and poured it out on to my hand, that could not hurt me."[57] The punishment of the damned comes because they are separated from God and deprived of all the richness of being that is in Him, from the fact that they are nothing but themselves. If the soul, instead of clinging to external, created things and to its own being as a creature, turned to its foundation (*Grund*), which is the "foundation without foundation," God himself, where God brings union with Himself—if it returned to the "nakedness" (*Bloszheit*) of true human nature, if the heart purified itself by annihilating all that bears the mark of the created (*alle Geschöpflichkeit*)—then the whole world would be present (*gegenwärtig*) to the soul. "There is one power in the soul that is not only power but being [*Wesen*], and it is not only being but it frees from being: it is so pure, so high and so noble in itself that no creature can enter it—only God dwells there."[58]

An extraordinary conclusion: insofar as I cling to myself as a creature, I cannot find myself, I cannot dwell in myself. "God is closer to me than I am to myself."[59] This closeness of God is not just what Saint Paul says, but it also evokes, *mutatis mutandis*, the words of the Qurʾan, telling us that God is closer to us than is our jugular vein.

But God is also present to things: "God is equally near in all creatures."[60] "I have sometimes said before that God's life and God's being are in stone or in a bit of wood, or in other creatures that are not blessed."[61] At the same time, all things, in what they share of reality, are plunged into the Fatherhood of God. Eckhart writes: "Here all blades of grass, wood, stones, and all things are one. . . . Therefore, all that nature can produce concentrates on this, plunging into the Father-nature [*das musz in die Vaterschaft stürzen*] so as to be one and one Son."[62] An expression of extraordinary force that was bound to scandalize! But it says nothing more than what Saint Paul teaches in his letter to the Ephesians, that it is in Christ, in the Son, that all things have been created. All things can therefore be thought of as linked to him in his sonship, participating in his being as Son, in perfect unity and equality: "In God, no creature is nobler than another."[63]

We see, then, to what an extent these thoughts of Eckhart present analogies with others we have examined here, apart from the constant and indeed essential reference to Christian doctrine. We may also note their close relationship to scriptural texts. But the censors confused panentheism with pantheism and, without looking closely, condemned the formula, "all that is, is in God." Meister Eckhart protested that he had never held to anything like pantheism, and had simply written: "All that is in God is God." Some may object that his response is nothing but subterfuge and that it even hurts his case. In fact, if, as he wrote, all things are plunged into the Fatherhood of God, they enter into God's very intimacy, into His mystery, and then they are God, that would be pure pantheism. But the truth of the matter is that he never claimed that created things, insofar as they are spread throughout space and time, are God. They are only in God through their unity, which is not at all the unity of their multiplicity in the world, but an essential unity within divine thought, prior to their dispersal within the becoming of their generations here below.

Eckhart gives us the foundation of his teaching in this revealing text: "And since the soul has the potentiality of knowing all things, therefore she never rests till she gains the primal image where all things are one; and there she rests, there she is in God."[64] What is this image? It must be perfectly one, beyond all the partial forms from which we must in fact separate ourselves entirely. This image is the Word (*das Wort*) of God, as Saint Paul explains to the Colossians. It is the Son in his perfect unity with the Father, though not in his relation to the Father the way speculative theology might grasp it, using concepts of fatherhood and sonship. That is why Eckhart speaks of the primordial image, without calling it the image of God, which would introduce a duality from the start. It is a unifying image in which all creation discovers or rediscovers its unity. It is the Word, and as Saint John taught: "In the beginning was the Word: and the Word was with God and the Word was God" (John 1:1).

There seems to be no doubt about the orthodoxy of Meister Eckhart, therefore, and J. Ancelet-Hustache had reason to affirm in his book on the *Treatises* that in the very places where the great mystic uses his most audacious expressions, he remains in complete agreement with the teaching of Saint Paul—in particular with the verse in his letter to the Galatians (3:26–27): "every one of you . . . has been clothed in Christ."

We can also discern the clear influence of Pseudo-Dionysius. We read in *The Celestial Hierarchy* a kind of commentary on James 1:17, "all that is good, all that is perfect, is given us from above; it comes down from the Father of all light." Pseudo-Dionysius makes the following reflection on the procession of light revealed to us: "[I]n its power to unify, it stirs us by lifting us up. It returns us back to the oneness and deifying simplicity of the Father who gathers us in [*pros tēn tou synagōgou patros henotēta kai theopoion haplotēta*]."[65] And the author returns to the Epistle to the Romans (11:36): "Everything there is comes from him and is caused by him and exists for him."

We could find traces of panentheism, thus conceived, in all the Christian mystics, as well as among Jews and Muslims. We can note it in Saint John of the Cross, but in a different atmosphere, in the pervasiveness of love.

It seems obvious, therefore, at the end of this long investigation (too short for all that could be said, but adequate to sustain the conviction) that by means of the language of neoplatonism, mystics of the three monotheisms have expressed, in analogous ways—often quite similar and always very akin to each other, despite dogmatic differences—the same spiritual problematic, the same type of solution. Although we can say nothing about the experience as such, it does not appear to be entirely foreign to any of them, whatever their dogmatic differences. But, as Muslims often conclude difficult discussions, God alone knows what is the case: *Allāhu aʿlam.*

5

EXPRESSIONS OF MYSTICAL EXPERIENCE: THE LANGUAGE OF LOVE

Neoplatonism furnished both a framework of thought and a language. A framework of thought—because it presented a metaphysical vision of the world, concerned with the problems of the One and the many, of Being and non-being, of transcendence and immanence, of the Absolute and the relative. Its language, however picturesque, was at root philosophical. In particular it was the language of a theory of knowing, of supra-rational, intuitive knowing. That is why the monotheistic mystics, to the extent that this thought touched them, have tended to insist on the cognitive aspect of mystical experience.

The contemplation they evoke is presented, above all, as a knowing of God, in a way that is certainly sublime—a gift of God, bathed in divine light—but still a knowing, or better, a "vision." Love is not absent, since all Jewish, Christian, and Muslim spiritual writers admit of God's love for human beings, and human beings' love for God. But this love is, in the neoplatonic climate, a certain glow of knowledge in the heart. In contrast, disciples of pure Love believe that knowledge depends on love, or more precisely, that love is knowledge—indeed the only means of knowing this God who is entirely beyond the reach of the created mind.

THE SONG OF SONGS AND THE BOOK OF SONGS [*ISFAHANI*]

The Bible, which is a fundamental source of inspiration for both Jews and Christians, stresses the commandment to love. God loves His people, and Israel must love its God: the Torah, the books of the prophets, and the Psalms are filled with this notion. But we must make a unique place for the Song of Songs, which read literally is truly a love song, and its images are those of human love:

As an apple tree among the trees of the wood,
so is my love among young men.
In his delightful shade I sit,
and his fruit is sweet to my taste.
He has taken me to his cellar,
and his banner over me is love.
Feed me with raisin cakes,
restore me with apples,
for I am sick with love [*kî ḥôlat ʾahăbâ ʾāni*].

(2:3–5)

We note, moreover, that similarities exist with pre-Islamic Arabic poetry. For example, the Bridegroom compares the one he loves to his mare (1:9), as does the Bedouin poet when he compares a young beauty to an antelope or gazelle:

Her neck is like that of a white gazelle, slender
when she extends it in her swift race . . .

(*Muʿallaqa* of Imruʾ al-Qays, v. 34)

The style here and there reflects the same sensibility and the same source of inspiration:

. . . your hair is like a flock of [black] goats
surging down Mount Gilead.

(Song of Songs 4:1)

Her hair is bejeweled upon her shoulders, dark and black like coal,
Thick like the cluster on a palm tree, laden with dates.

(Imruʾ al-Qays, v. 35)

We may mention yet another example:

Your teeth, a flock of sheep to be shorn
when they come up from the washing.

(Song of Songs 4:2)

She smiles with her red lips: like chamomile in bloom
Piercing through the sand on a knoll moist with dew.

(*Muʿallaqa* of Tarafa, v. 8).

The difference is that the poetry of the *Jāhiliyya*, from before the arrival of Islam, is foreign to the Qurʾan, while the Song of Songs forms part of the Bible. Jewish and Christian religious people felt constrained to give the Song of Songs a symbolic meaning. Yet once they had done so, they had at their disposal a whole vocabulary which could be transposed for expressing mystical love.

In Judaism, as Georges Vajda writes,[1] the phraseology of the Song of Songs expresses the love of God for Israel. This is especially the case in the poetic work of Ibn Gabirol, who, according to Hayyim Schirmann, seems to have been the first to make use, in Jewish literature, of the popular love song style to describe relations between God, Israel, and the Messiah.[2] The bride of the Song is then the community of Israel, and the union of love tends to be conceived in the eschatological perspective of the restoration (*tiqqûm*) of the people chosen in divine friendship after the time of Exile (*gālût*). But the question is disputed as to whether the redemption of Israel will liberate individual souls or, on the other hand, whether one must present "the ethical-religious act of the individual as converging with the coming of redemption," as Martin Buber said.[3]

A movement in favor of this latter conception began around the middle of the sixteenth century. From this perspective, the final salvation of Israel, and through Israel, of all humanity, would be at least partly the fruit of the work of the mystics. Whatever the role of these messianic visions, Jacob Anatoli, in the thirteenth century, certainly was thinking of the individual soul when he referred to the Song of Songs, explaining that the beloved "desires to make an effort to apprehend and to discover [the object of his love] in the way of all passionate love, wherein all thoughts and aspirations incline toward his beloved." And he cites verse 3:1: " . . . I sought the one whom my soul loves; I sought but could not find him!" That, he said, is because she did not search the way the precept prescribes: "You shall seek him with all your heart and all your soul." Baᶜal Shem Tov, at least if one follows Buber's interpretation, provides a mediating solution: ecstasy is solitary, but worship (*ᶜăbōdâ*) is communal: worship that expresses itself in prayer is to the final ecstasy what the search for relationship is to its consummation. In summary, it is because Israel is beloved by the Bridegroom that the souls who serve and pray in Israel can become his brides.

We recall, moreover, that the communal interpretation is based on texts of the Bible. The infidelities of the people of God are called prostitution: " . . . for the country itself has become nothing but a whore by abandoning the LORD" (Hosea 1:2). Hosea's spiritual heir, Jeremiah, takes up the same theme: "Yet on every high hill and under every green tree you have sprawled and played the whore" (2:20). But nuptial symbolism still remains the most pronounced: "The LORD says this: 'I remember your faithful love [*ḥesed*], the affection of your bridal days, when you followed me through the desert" (Jeremiah 2:6). Ezekiel (16:1–43; 59–63) draws on the same language. But the most beautiful text is no doubt that of Isaiah (54:4–8), in which God consoles Jerusalem: "Do not fear, you will not be put to shame again, do not worry, you will not be disgraced again. . . . For your Creator is your husband. . . . Yes, the LORD has called you back like a forsaken, grief-stricken wife, like the repudiated wife of his youth, says your God. . . . I did forsake you for a brief moment. . . . But in everlasting love [*ûbĕḥesed ʿôlām*] I have taken pity on you."

So it is utterly consonant with the biblical revelation of the love of God to consider the bride in the Song of Songs as representing the community of Israel. Nevertheless, it is important to note that after the exile, as historians explain, Israel, purified by trials, understands the importance of each human heart. Israel thus discovers that God does not merely love His people as a whole, but each of its members in their faithfulness to the Law: "The LORD loves the upright" (*ʾōheb ṣaddîqîm*, Psalm 146:8; a verse that, to the letter, carries over into the Qurʾan, 5:42; 49:9). Another verse is still more valuable from the point of view of the mystic: "But know that the Lord has set apart the faithful [*ḥasîd*] for himself" (Psalm 4:3).[4] In recent translations, the text of this verse has been corrected with reference to Psalm 31:22: "Blessed be the LORD, for he has wondrously shown his steadfast love [*ḥasdô*, from *ḥesed*] to me."[5] In either case, the relationship is interesting. The word *ḥasîd*, which designates the person of deep piety (and from which Hasidism draws its name), comes from the same root as *ḥesed*—grace, love.

The two verses only express the same idea in two different ways. The second is very important, because it speaks of the love of God "for me" (*lî*). It concerns an individual person, the object of predilection; the word "dilection" in fact comes from the Latin *diligere*, which means: to choose, distinguish, and finally, to love with an affection that results from a choice. It corresponds exactly to the Hebrew verb *hiplîʾ* employed in these two verses. So the human being becomes the object of a vocation of love: God loves each one through a choice that sets each person apart. Each person is called to respond through an exclusive love of God, the purest love that one can bring forth—as Ibn Paquda said, "an offering of the soul." This love cannot be bought: human beings have nothing to give in exchange, unless it be themselves. Ibn Paquda returns to the Song of Songs (8:7): "Were a man to offer all his family wealth to buy love, contempt is all that he would gain." But God "calms" the soul that gives itself, and it "is quenched by the cup of love." If God "fills it, it gives thanks; if He overwhelms it, it is patient and only receives with more love and abandon."[6] And here, once again, Ibn Paquda evokes the Song of Songs (1:13): "My love is a sachet of myrrh lying between my breasts."

There is a very important expression in verse 8:6 of the Song, an image that was to play a major role in the lexicon of mystical love: "For love is strong as Death. . . . The flash of it is a flash of fire, a flame of the LORD himself [*lĕhebet-yâh*]." The latter term comes from the root *lāhab* which means "to be consumed." The form *hitlahôb* means "to be set ablaze" and provides the noun *hitlahābût*—that which blazes—which designates the fervor of ecstasy, according to Baᶜal Shem Tov. This fervor is also "the cup of grace." The book of Genesis (3:24) reports that after having expelled Adam and Eve from paradise, God placed cherubim wielding "the fiery flashing sword, to guard the way to the tree of life." To Baᶜal Shem Tov, as soon as the *hitlahābût* touches this sword, it flashes sparks and the way becomes free. This fervor bears joy within it. It restores human beings to the primordial love of their Creator.

Many are the Christian mystics who have meditated on the Song of Songs and who have nurtured their spiritual life from it. Not only does the reading of the Bible as a whole draw their attention to love, but they find in Saint John the revelation that "God is love" (1 John 4:16). The most famous among such Christian mystics is certainly Saint John of the Cross, the author of *The Living Flame of Love* (a title that evokes *hitlahābût*) and *The Spiritual Canticle: Stanzas between the Soul and the Bridegroom.*

"*Where have You hidden, Beloved, and left me moaning?* . . ." In this first stanza the soul, enamored of the Word, her Bridegroom, the Son of God, longs for union with Him through clear and essential vision. She records her longings of love and complains to Him of His absence, especially since His love wounds her. Through this love she departed from all creatures and from herself, and yet she must suffer her Beloved's absence. . . .[7] This first stanza is related to Song of Songs 1:7, as quoted from the Latin translation: "Show me where you pasture [your flock] and where you rest at midday."[8] But one can find here a theme from erotic love poetry: absence and return, separation and reunion. It also appears among Muslim mystics. Saint John of the Cross interprets this verse as a prayer addressed to the Father: "In requesting Him to disclose His place of pasture, she wanted Him to reveal the essence of the divine Word, His Son. For the Father does not pasture in any other than His only Son, since the Son is the glory of the Father. And in begging that He show her His place of rest, she was asking to see that same Son. The Son is the only delight of the Father, Who rests nowhere else, nor is present in any other than in His beloved Son. He rests wholly in His Son, communicating to Him His essence at midday, which is eternity, where He ever begets Him and has begotten Him."[9] We see how the biblical text is stretched along the lines of the Christian belief in the Trinity. Since God is love, God's love for human beings cannot help but relate to that essential love through which God engenders the Word. But, at the same time, the love of human beings for God can only be true if it enters into the hidden mystery of this essential Love.

In order to be able to find this Bridegroom, insofar as that is possible in this life, "It should be known that the Word, the Son of God, together with the Father and the Holy Ghost, is hidden by His essence and His presence in the innermost being of the soul. A person who wants to find Him should leave all things through affection and will, enter within himself in deepest recollection, and regard things as though they were nonexistent."[10] One is reminded of those episodes in romance novels where the lover hides in order to meet his beloved, lest he be seen by anyone and betray his secret.[11] One also thinks of the popular saying: lovers are alone to the world — *la soledad de amor.*

Along with images of fire and flame, we find still others that evoke secular love poetry. Thus, the "touch of a spark" *(el toque de centella)* is "a very subtle touch which the Beloved sometimes produces in the soul . . . , which inflames her in the fire of love. . . ."[12] Saint John of the Cross draws the idea of this touch from a suspect translation of the Song of Songs (5:4: "My love thrust his hand through the hole in the door; I trembled to the core of my being." The text is difficult to interpret; in any case, it does not actually speak of "touching." Dhorme translates: "and my bowels are moved for him" (literally: upon him, *ʿâlâyw*). The motive to supply a biblical reference is obvious. The Latin translation reads: *Dilectus meus misit manum suam per foramen, et venter meus infremuit ad tactum ejus*: my bowels quivered at his touch; "at his touch" is a paraphrase of the Hebrew *ʿālāyw.* After this touch, which ignites a fire flaring up like a blaze that does not continue, then comes the intoxication of love under the influence of a spiced wine (*el abodado vino*). "It should be known that this favor of sweet inebriation, because it has more permanence, does not pass away as quickly as the spark. . . . [A] person feels in his intimate substance that his spirit is being sweetly inebriated and inflamed by this divine wine. As David says: 'My heart grew hot within me, and in my meditation a fire shall be enkindled' [Psalm 39:4]."[13]

Saint John of the Cross returns, moreover, to the Song of Songs 8:2, where the Bride says to her Beloved: "[Y]ou would teach me! I should give you spiced wine to drink [*yayin hā-reqaḥ*]. . . ." This wine signifies "my love spiced with Yours, transformed in Yours. . . . The meaning is that when I was put in His love, He gave me love to drink. . . . He put His charity in order in me, accommodating and appropriating His own charity to me. Hence the soul drinks of the Beloved's very own love, which He infuses in her."[14] Thus the wine that the Bride pours out is actually received from the Bridegroom. In fact, "the drink of highest wisdom makes her forget all worldly things."[15] Thus, she cannot conceive of offering anything other than what she has been given, and what is not of this world.

In the state of inebriation and forgetfulness in which she now is, "it seems that her previous knowledge, and even all the knowledge of the world, in comparison with this knowledge is pure ignorance."[16] That is because "the bride in the Canticle, after having treated of the transformation of her love into the Beloved, refers to this unknowing in which she was left by the word, *nescivi* (I did not know)."[17] We note that Saint John of the Cross here makes use of the biblical text (Song of Songs 6:12) in an entirely arbitrary fashion. The text is in fact very difficult to understand in its current state; but be that as it may, he places in the mouth of the Bride the *lōʾ yādaʿtî* (I did not know) that is actually spoken by the Bridegroom. The liberty taken vis-à-vis the context perhaps allows us to think that, without being indifferent to its overall meaning, Saint John of the Cross is looking most of all in this love song for words and images that he can put to use. Even though he often refers to the Song of Songs, he finds support there without actually writing a commentary.

Because God is love and loves His creatures, it is perfectly normal for Christian mystics to believe that they will be united with God through love. We already sense this clearly in the preceding quotations. But a final one expresses this hope with extraordinary power: "It is noteworthy, then, that love is the soul's inclination, strength, and power in making its way to God, for love unites it with God. The more degrees of love it has, the more deeply it enters into God and centers itself in

Him. . . . A stronger love is a more unitive love. . . . Hence, that the soul be in its center—which is God, as we have said—it is sufficient for it to possess one degree of love, for by one degree alone it is united with Him through grace. Should it have two degrees, it will have become united and concentrated in God in another deeper center. . . . But once it has attained the final degree, God's love will have arrived at wounding the soul in its ultimate and deepest center, which is to transform and clarify it in its whole being, power, and strength, and according to its capacity, until it appears to be God."[18]

Saint John of the Cross is the lyricist of God's love *par excellence*, so in speaking of Christian mystics we have begun with him. His blazing soul leaps like a flame to the dizzying heights. Saint Teresa of Avila, who penetrated the mysteries of union no less than he, remains, so to speak, more human, more accessible to the ordinary religious women, her "daughters" whom she sought to enlighten.

In Saint Teresa's *Meditations on the Song of Songs*, in the first chapter, she evokes the book's opening: "Let him kiss me with the kisses of his mouth, for your love-making is sweeter than wine." She admitted that she did not understand the switch from third to second person, as if the Bride were addressing two different people. But above all, she is sensitive to the effect that such words could have on those who have a base and vulgar conception of love. She recalls a sermon that she had heard from a priest who was a religious, "most of which was an explanation of those loving delights with which the bride communed with God. And there was so much laughter, and what he said was so poorly taken, that I was shocked."[19]

Saint Teresa writes in this regard: "It will seem to you that there are some words in the Song of Songs that could have been said in another style. In light of our dullness such an opinion doesn't surprise me. I have heard some persons say that they avoid listening to them. Oh, God help me, how great is our misery! Just as poisonous creatures turn everything they eat into poison, so do we."[20] But she responds to those who deride this style or who, with more hypocrisy than virtue, take offense: "[W]e, little exercised in love, go where they always go and cease to think of the great mysteries this language, spoken by the Holy Spirit, contains within itself. What more was necessary than this language in order to enkindle us in His love and make us realize that not without good reason did He choose this style."[21] And she concludes that "you should never dwell on what you do not understand in Sacred Scripture or the mysteries of our faith more than I have said, nor should you be startled by the lofty words that take place between God and the soul. Being what we are, the love that He had and has for us surprises and bewilders me more; for knowing that He has such love I already understand that there is no exaggeration in the words by which He reveals it to us, for He has shown this love even more through his deeds."[22]

So then, returning to the text of the verse—"Let him kiss me with the kisses of his mouth"—Saint Teresa writes: "O my Lord and my God, and what words are these that a worm speaks them to its Creator! . . . [W]ho will dare, my king, utter these words without Your permission? . . . But the soul that is enkindled with a love that makes it mad desires nothing else than to say these words. Indeed the Lord does not forbid her to say them."[23] So she does not hesitate to employ the language of love with the same ardor as Saint John of the Cross. But we see that she is deeply conscious of what, in his case, seemed at first glance exorbitant.

Besides providing expression for such ardent flights of soul, the Song of Songs has often offered Christian mystics themes for reflecting about union with God. To be sure, in many cases the Latin translations are inexact; they lent themselves to figurative commentaries that were quite arbitrary. There is no point pausing to examine these. But sometimes the biblical text suggested and supported important reflections. For example, Saint Bonaventure, in his work on *The Mind's Journey to God*, says that the soul which believes, hopes in Christ and loves him, acquires the spiritual senses of interior sight, hearing, smell and taste, which disposes it to attempt three "raptures of mind" (*mentales excessus*): devotion, admiration, and exultation. Devotion makes the soul "like a column of smoke, breathing of myrrh and frankincense" (Song of Songs 3:6). Above the quality of its admiration, the soul becomes like the sunrise, the moon, and the sun, as the Song of Songs (6:10) lyricizes: "Who is this arising like the dawn, fair as the moon, resplendent as the sun . . . ?" Through the overflowing of exultation, "the soul, resting totally on its Beloved, pours out delights for the sweetest enjoyment." This final degree of spiritual rapture is expressed in the Song of Songs in these terms (7:7 and 10): "How beautiful you are, how charming, my love, my delight! . . . [May] your palate [be] like sweet wine, flowing down the throat of my love."

Finally, however, Christian mystics have not needed to refer to the Song of Songs alone to find very strong expressions of love. Yet, perhaps encouraged by the "style" of the biblical song, they have dared to use a language that evokes the language of human love. Thus Tauler, in one sermon (no. 44) on verse 1:7 of John—"He came as a witness, to bear witness to the light"—explains that this witness is received in diverse faculties of the soul until it is returned through its highest faculty, the will, to the power to love. Tauler then speaks of delirious "enraptured love" and the "tempests of love."[24] One could cite many other examples.

EXPRESSIONS OF LOVE IN MUSLIM MYSTICISM

If we now turn to the mystics of Islam, we must immediately note that there is nothing even close to the Song of Songs in the Qurʾan. We must also recall that Muslims, who consider love to be far too human a sentiment, have had an attitude of suspicion toward it and balk at including it among the relations that can exist between God and human beings, or between human beings and God. Only the mystics have retained the proper sense of those verses where the word appears. The word may be *hubb*, or *maḥabba*, from a root that we also find in the Hebrew *ʾahăbâ*. Its presence is enough to legitimate a mysticism of love, despite interpretations that lead away from that meaning. But it is another term that has, without doubt, acted most profoundly upon the meditation of the spiritual writers. It is in fact said (4:125): "God chose Abraham for friend [*khalīlan*]." While this distinction may seem unique to Abraham, we may nonetheless understand that the faithful who love God can desire to attain such high favor.[25]

From the word *khalīl* comes the word *khulla*, which *Tahānawī* in his *Dictionary of Technical Terms* defines in this way: "The word *khulla* is more particular than *maḥabba*: it is the penetration [*takhallul*] of dilection [*mawadda*] in the heart, where it does not allow any space relative to divine secrets, knowledge, and hidden mysteries, which it does not fill when it penetrates there. For God then occupies the heart completely and prevents it from being moved by any sight that would turn it toward something other than him." For the mystic who has set out on the way (*al-sālik*), there is a difference of level between the station (*maqām*) of *khulla* (friendship) and that of *maḥabba* (love). But there is no agreement on their hierarchical order.

Some hold that *maḥabba* is superior and find evidence in a *ḥadīth* transmitted by Bayhaqī: God says to Muhammad, on his night journey:

"Ask, and it will be given to you." The Prophet responds: "Lord! You have taken Abraham for a friend and You addressed yourself to Moses in speaking to him." God says: "Have I not given you something better than that? . . . I have chosen you as a beloved [*ḥabīb*]." Surely the point of view of the *ḥadīth* is driven by the desire to place Muhammad above Abraham and Moses, although the Qurʾan does not say that God chose him as *khalīl*. Yet it is written in fact (6:76): "Thus did We show Abraham the kingdom [*malakūt*] of the heavens and the earth," while it is said of Muhammad, concerning his ascension into heaven (53:9): "Till he was (distant) two bows' length or even nearer." Consequently the beloved reaches God "without an intermediary;" the friend passes through a vision of the divine kingdom. Now, Muhammad is an example for every believer, and in particular for the Sufis who have meditated at length on the two bow lengths and on that even closer proximity which is, for them, the final goal of their mystical quest. Nevertheless, others think that *khulla* (friendship) is a higher station than *maḥabba* (love), because it empties the heart of all love except for the love of the uniquely beloved. It is the perfected form, the most sublime form, of love.

Be that as it may, we must bring together the term *khulla* with the word *uns*, which is not qurʾanic, but which the Sufis often employ. *Uns*, or *muʾānasa* is the act of being familiar with someone. It is often associated with *jalīs*, one who sits in the company of other people in order to take part in a "council" (*julūs*) where one then discusses various things. Through *khulla*, therefore, the human being is admitted into familiarity with God and converses with God by discussing secrets and intimacies. This is *musāmara*, which means precisely to discuss at night. Perhaps the word carries a vestige from nocturnal encounters between lovers, a frequent theme of erotic poetry. Thus ʿUmar b. Abī Rabīʿa recounts in one of his poems that he is party to the search for the one he loves, for she had followed her family when they moved their encampment. He finds her again as evening comes.

> When we again met one another, she bade me welcome and smiled
> The smile of one who is happy: whoever is satisfied is happy!
> O sweetness of the joy that I tasted there,
> Inclining my ear to her words! O beauty of the object that brought joy to my eyes!

In the same way, the mystics define *uns* as a state of great nobility which consists of the joy they experience before "the perfection of

Beauty" (*kamāl al-jamāl*). Yet it also carries, in their lexicon, a note of reverential fear (*hayba*). Nevertheless, this does not exclude joy, for the one who is familiar with God continues to revere God. Junayd said that *uns* suppresses timid reserve (*ḥishma*) while allowing reverential fear to emerge. It has also been said that it is a state in which hope prevails against fear, yet without eliminating it entirely. This describes the mystical condition of Moses when the Lord addressed him in a familiar fashion.

One of the first and most famous lyricists of divine love in Islam is the great mystic Rābiᶜa al-ᶜAdawiyya of Baṣra, who died in 801.[26] She made a crucial place for *khulla*, which she seems moreover to place on the same level as *ḥubb* and *maḥabba*. The following verses are attributed to her:

> My rest, oh my brothers, is in my seclusion,
> And my Beloved [*ḥabībī*] is constantly in my presence.
> I find nothing to replace the passion [*hawā*] that I have for Him
> And to love Him with passion in the midst of creatures is a trial for me.
> Wherever I am, I see His beauty.
> He is my *miḥrāb*, the direction of my prayer . . .
> Oh sweetness of heart! Oh meeting of all desires!
> Exercise Your generosity, that a union coming from You might heal my soul.
> Oh my joy, my life, perpetually,
> My flowering comes from You and my inebriation as well!
> I flee all creatures, and I await
> From you a union, the summit of my desire.

Indeed it is *uns*, and with it *khulla*, that Rābiᶜa describes in two verses that are so technically compact that translation is almost impossible. Here is their sense:

> Yes, yes, I have made You, at the depth of my heart, the confidant who speaks to me [*muḥaddithī*]
> And I let my body appear to those who wish to associate in my company [*julūsi*]
> For the body, to me, is a close friend [*mu'ānis*] for those who converse in my company [*jalīs*]
> While the Friend of my heart [*ḥabīb qalbī*] is a familiar friend [*anīs*] at the depth of my heart [*fu'ād*]

We find important terms brought together here that we have pointed out before: *julūs* and *jalīs*, *ḥabīb* (cf. *ḥubb* and *maḥabba*), *anīs* and *muʾānis* (cf. *uns* and *muʾānasa*).

But the most famous of Rābiʿa's poems is the one about two loves:

I love You with two loves: the love of passion [*hawā*]
And a love that comes because You are worthy to be loved.
As to the love which is that of passion,
May I set out to think only of you, of nothing except for You.
As to the love for which You, You alone are worthy,
May You disclose Yourself from behind Your veils that I might see You.
To praise which clings to this and to that I do not dedicate myself,
But to You, the Praise that dwells in this and that.

The first love corresponds to the concept that Saint Augustine had when he wrote, at one point in his *Confessions*: "I loved to love, and I loved to be loved" (3.1). Evoking the thought (*dhikr*) of the one loved so fills with joy the heart of one who loves that it is this evocation that one loves. Rābiʿa does not repudiate this form of love; but she discovers within it another, purer love in which no passion invades the loving subject, and that instead involves total forgetfulness of self in single-minded consideration of the object of one's love. This second love seems superior therefore to the *khulla* in which human beings remain aware of divine favor; it is perfectly disinterested love—indifferent to favors themselves—which all mystics consider to be authentic love. Christian and Muslim spiritualities agree completely in this assessment.

We can easily allow that the language of God's love can hardly keep from being inspired by the language of human love. The rich poetry of Arabic not only provides a vocabulary, it also provides dramatic situations that can easily be transposed. For example, Umar b. Abī Rabīʿa, though renowned for his debaucheries, experienced true and exclusive love, like the *khulla* of the mystics, when he met Zaynab:

She does not leave any room for other women in my heart,
In spite of what my lips say to them in jest.
She is worthy of my vow of sincerest love, a love able to cherish her.
My passion moves toward her; friends, do not speak ill! . . .
Yes, after what I have received from her, my heart is like one blind to other women.

And here is another verse that can easily be transposed to express mystical values:

The glance that I cast toward her when she appeared, was dazzling and so
remains,
To the point where I see, in that very look, how much it lacks.

The body has its appetites to satisfy and it can submit to an exclusive love. But:

My hearing, my sight, are allies of what I love, in league against my body.
How could I live without what makes me understand and hear?

Love alone counts; the sufferings that the Beloved can provoke matter little, for she becomes the center of all things. A poet from the Abbasid epoch, Abūʾl-Shīṣ, clearly expresses this sentiment:

Passion contains itself within me, there where you remain. For me,
nothing follows it, nothing precedes.
Blame for my passion feels pleasant to me.
For I love everything that recalls you. Let them blame me then.
"You are like my enemies"—do they say that of you?
Then I love my enemies, if I receive from them what I receive from you!

The look of love is often compared to an arrow. But its sharp point, which wounds the heart, merges so intimately with what the victim holds most deeply in his being that it is no longer possible to separate the two. The poet Ibn Muṭayr al-Asadī has written these verses:

Oh Asmaʾ! God has decreed that I never cease to love you
Until they close my eyes.
Love is a trial; but even though that is so,
I could never take joy in hating you.

But it is a trial that purifies, that raises those who suffer it beyond themselves, giving their life its true value, its authentic reality.

On the other hand, the love of God presents itself through seasons of favor and abandonment, of union and separation, of drawing close and becoming distant. All mystics, though especially Christians and Muslims, have described these interior experiences. Yet human loves are subject to the same oscillating rhythm. The loves of ancient Bedouins were linked to the vicissitudes of nomadic life. The essential theme of ancient pre-Islamic tales (*qasīda*), in the part dedicated to love (*nasīb*), is that of the poet who stands before the remains of an abandoned camp—the *aṭlāl*—and evokes the memory of the one he loved in this now deserted site. Very sensual passions were involved here of course; but through transfiguration of memory, the *dhikr*, they took on spiritual tones, wrapped in a sadness that always bears within itself a moving nobility of feeling. The poems describe the preparations for departure, the scene of separation, the distancing of the caravan, as they move through the lover's thoughts. Alternating between hope and despair, he dreams of the moment when they can meet again. In the interim, absence strengthens feeling and purifies it, so long as absence does not involve forgetting. Absence idealizes the image of the beloved; it excites a desire to be worthy of her. The lover seeks to prove his valor through martial exploits.

We are far from mysticism here, of course. Nevertheless, we should not forget that Islam enjoins the great *jihād*, that great struggle against passions that degrade the soul. There is no doubt that *mufākhara*, which consists of gaining respect by boasting of one's own merits and that is characteristic of the Bedouin mentality, is entirely opposed to the humility of the Sufis. But the love-struck poet elevates himself only in order to be noticed; he then humbles himself before the woman he loves by acknowledging that he has become a slave of love (*mutayyamim*). We may quote a few verses drawn from the *Muʿallaqa* of ʿAntara, verses that are particularly remarkable from this point of view.

> Greetings, vestiges of an era ancient and done!
> A place deserted and desolate now that ʿAbla has departed!
> She has departed for a land ferocious and hostile,
> It is so hard for me to reach you, Daughter of Mukhram!
> You abide in my heart, think of no other.
> Within me, you are the object of love and respect.
> How shall I visit you? Only in springtime.
> You camp with your people at ʿUnayza, and I at Ghaylam.
> Is there a camel of Shadan that will take me on the journey to ʿAbla?
> If you lower your veil to hide from me,
> Then I, I know the art of seizing the horseman armed with steel.

Though Islam, in principle, is hardly enthused about this sort of poetry, Muslims have adopted it and taken it up. Initially it represented to them a model of pure Arabic, so that studies of the Qurʾan often referred to it, which becomes important to us because it helps us see how the mystics were able to draw an entire vocabulary from it. But then, very quickly, Muslims considered the fact that God was the Creator of love in the human heart and that He was the guarantor of its value: thus, while remaining ordinary, love ceased to be thought of as a suspect feeling, foreign to the life of a believer. Even though the Qurʾan does not discredit sexual relations in any way, the kind of love that is at issue here could not have anything to do with carnal love.

According to one *ḥadīth*—transmitted under the authority of the very serious Ibn ʿAbbās, a very serious authority, though perhaps composed to make a particular point—the Prophet supposedly said: "Whoever loves [*ʿashiqa*], is chaste and dies, enters into paradise." This tradition has several variants; among others: "Whoever loves, is chaste, hides their secret, controls their love, and dies, dies as a martyr." The important word, in this revealing text, is the verb *ʿashiqa*: to be in love, from which comes *ʿishq*, another word for love, *ʿāshiq*, the lover. The idea expressed through this root word is that of violent passion. None of these terms is found in the Qurʾan, and understandably, they unleashed a lively protest when certain mystics introduced them into their vocabulary.

CHASTE LOVE IN THE ARAB TRADITION

But the words *ʿāshiq* and *ʿishq* received a quite unique meaning in the *ʿudhrī* poetry of love. This poetry represents a very curious phenomenon of civilization, whose origin remains obscure, and which may have influenced Western conceptions of courtly love. Stendhal, in his book *De l'amour*,[27] quotes passages on "amorous tenderness" from the *Diwān al-Ṣabāba*, by Ibn Abī Ḥajala (whom Stendhal calls Ebn-Abi-Ḥadglat). Here is one passage, which we present in the author's system of transcription:

> Sahid, son of Agba, asks an Arab one day:—What people are you from?—I am from the people among whom one dies when one loves, responds the Arab.—So you are from the tribe of Aszra? adds Sahid.—Yes, through the master of the Caaba! replies the Arab.—So why do your people love in such a way? Sahid then asks.—Our women are beautiful and our young men are chaste, responds the Arab.

Henrich Heine has also evoked this love linked to death. This conception gave rise, in Arabic writing, to an abundant literature, to numerous treatises on love, filled with poems. The attributions to such-and-such a legendary "hero" that accompany these works are often suspect, but even if they are false, the treatises exist nevertheless and are no less well-known and appreciated. There were great treatises, other than the *Diwān*, mentioned above, extending over a long period.[28] The *Kitāb al-Aghānī* (The Book of Songs) by Abū'l-Faraj al-Iṣfahāni (875–967) collects, among its numerous stories about poets and abundant quotations from poems, a large quantity of love poems. As long as we neither overstate the case nor forget other related "literary" influences which inspired Muslim mystics, we may compare the importance of this collection to the role that the Song of Songs has played in the meditation of Jewish and Christian mystics.

ᶜ*Udhrī* love involves heroic couples who incarnate and illustrate it. The most famous are Majnūn-Laylā, Lamīl-Buthayna, Qays-Lubnā, Kuthayyir-ᶜAzza. Some of them actually existed, others are largely fictional characters. Especially in Persian mysticisms, these figures became pure symbols of religious love. D'Herbelot, in the *Bibliothèque orientale*,[29] spoke of it several times. We cannot improve upon his observation:

> All Muslims regard these two lovers [Majnūn and Laylā] in much the same way that Jews have regarded the Bride and Bridegroom of the Song of Songs, allegorizing their history and using it to elevate the most spiritual Muslims into contemplation of divine mysteries.

Indeed, we see another couple celebrated, Joseph and Zulaykha, the daughter of Pharaoh and the wife of Potiphar. One group of Muslims from the sect of the Kharijites, moved by a rigid pietism, felt that because of the unseemly story recounted in the sūrah of Joseph, this sūrah should be excluded from the Qur'an as unworthy to be the Word of God. In fact, it is Zulaykha (whose name is not given in the text) who tries to seduce the young man (*rāwadathu* ᶜ*an nafsihi*, 12:23) once he reaches puberty (*lammā balagha ashaddahu*), because she was "smitten to the heart with love" (*shaghafahā ḥubbaan*, 12:30). But Joseph remained faithful to the ideal of chastity, and she herself recognized that he was able to preserve himself from evil (*ista*ᶜ*ṣama*). Withal, she did not repent.

Is it the continence of Joseph that allows the account to be transfigured and that gives it a religious value? That is possible. But there is an instructive commentary by Ismāᶜīl Ḥaqqī on verse 12:30: *shaghafahā ḥubban*: "Her love for Joseph split the membrane of her heart [*shaghāf al-qalb*] and penetrated to its depth. . . . Know that love [*maḥabba*] is an inclination toward what is beautiful. When it becomes excessive, it is called ᶜ*ishq*, and when ᶜ*ishq* breaks all bounds, it is called inebriation [*sukr*] and wild love [*hayamān*]. Whoever experiences an excessive love [ᶜ*ishq*] is excusable and cannot be blamed, for it is at the heavenly horizon, just as are madness and disease, for example. Love [*maḥabba*] is the principle and cause of the existence that God gives to creatures, so that God says of it (in the *ḥadīth qudsī*): I was a hidden treasure and I loved [*aḥbabtu*] to be known."

Here Ismāᶜīl Ḥaqqi recalls that ᶜAbd al-Razzāq al-Qāshānī, a famous Sufi of the school of Ibn al-ᶜArabī (died in 1327), said that ᶜ*ishq* is a unique form of love, because it is excessive *maḥabba*; that is why one cannot apply this word to God, because excess has no place among the divine attributes. We note that, if it is applied to human beings, that is because for them God is the object of an infinite love. Haqqī further reports that Junayd, in one pericope, recounted the story that one day Fire said: "Oh my Lord! if I do not obey you, will You punish me through something that is more powerful than I? Yes, said God, I will master you through My most intense Fire, which is the most intense. — Is there a Fire greater than I? — Yes, said God, it is the Fire of My Love [*nār maḥabbatī*], which I cause to dwell in the heart of My friends, the believers." The term that we have translated as "friends" is *al-awliyā*ᵓ, which is sometimes rendered as "saints." The fire of divine love cleanses every stain from imperfect human loves; these undergo the trial of suffering, which causes whatever in them that is authentic to emerge. Ḥaqqi writes: "The love [ᶜ*ishq*] of Zulaykhā [for Joseph], even though it was not love in the proper sense of the word, drew her toward the goal, when she had really and sincerely experienced its true reality." He quotes a verse from ᶜAttar:

> Whoever has reached love pure and true
> The Beloved whom they love reaches the secret of their heart.

This same ᶜAttar, in the *Divine Book* (*Elahi-Nameh*), tells a story about Joseph and Zulaykhā that explains how the seduction episode was spiritualized. One day Joseph encountered Zulaykhā: "Disease and poverty were overwhelming her with a hundred sufferings. . . . She was undergoing, because of Joseph, a suffering without measure." But he, for his part, wished she would disappear. Then God sent the angel Gabriel, who declared on behalf of the Lord:

> We will not take away her life.
> For she retains within her an abundance of love for the one who loves Us.
> Since she has not stopped loving you, for your sake I count her among the company of my friends, . . .

I have made her bear a life of pain, but I will rejuvenate her for your sake.
She has given the treasure of her life for you; therefore I will bless her so that she might be yours.
For our Joseph she is full of tenderness; none will meditate on her death out of hatred.

There is only one authentic love, then, and God loves those who love Him and whom He loves. D'Herbelot is justified, therefore, to write concerning Joseph and Zulaykhā: "Muslims . . . often use their names and their example to lift the hearts of men to a love more exalted than vulgar love, claiming that the two lovers are only the figure of the faithful soul who rises, through love, to God." That is what made Hafez say in his *Divan*: "I understand quite well how the excellent beauty of Joseph can and should transport the heart of Zulaykhā beyond the bounds of ordinary love." After all, according to commentators on this poet, Joseph is a figure of the Creator, and Zulaykhā, of the creature. Thus we return to the context of the Song of Songs.

Perhaps ʿAttār, more than Saint John of the Cross, accents the notion that authentic and pure love of creatures is part of the soul's love for God and corresponds to God's love for the soul. Nevertheless, such an idea is not absent from the thought of Christian mystics, because their faith implies the value of love for neighbor in Christ. Nevertheless, such love does not express itself through the image of worshipping the Beauty of a beloved; instead it concerns love for every neighbor, not a particular being of the heart's choice.

Saint Teresa of Avila, like the Muslims we have been discussing, denounces whatever is called improperly by the name of love. In the *Way of Perfection* she writes: "Now it seems to me that those whom God brings to a certain clear knowledge, love very differently than those who have not reached it. . . . [T]hey care little about being loved. . . . It will seem to you that such persons do not love or know anyone but God. I say, yes they do love, with a much greater and more genuine love, and with passion, and with a more beneficial love; in short, it is love. . . . I say that this attitude is what merits the name 'love,' for these other base attachments have usurped the name 'love.' . . . It is true that what they see they love and what they hear they become attached to; but the things that they see are stable. As soon as these persons love, they go beyond the bodies and turn their eyes to the soul. . . . [E]ven if [such a soul] dies with love for them and does all the good works it can for them and possesses all natural graces combined, their wills will not have the strength to love it or make this love last. . . . For it is a love that must end when they die if the other is not keeping the law of God. . . . O precious love that imitates the Commander-in-chief of love, Jesus, our Good!"[30]

One grasps the differences; but how can one help from noting profound resemblances? In the essential reality of love, one loves God and neighbor out of the same love, for both grow from the love with which God loves His human creatures. Saint John, inspired by Christian faith, expressed these thoughts so well: "My dear friends, let us love each other, since love is from God and everyone who lives is a child of God and knows God . . . because God is love" (1 John 4:7–8). "God is love, and whoever remains in love remains in God and God in him" (1 John 4:16).

Muslim mystics have also been able to take up themes of separation (*farq*) and union (*jamᶜ*), absence (*ghayba*) and presence (*ḥuḍūr*), sobriety (*ṣaḥw*) and inebriation (*sukr*). But these notions receive a much more interior meaning. *Farq*, for example, is no longer separation within space. That would not make any sense when it concerns relations with God. According to Abū ᶜAlī al-Daqqāq, *farq* is "that which is torn away from you" and *jamᶜ* is "that which is brought near to you." The human being is a creature in the midst of creatures. Persons can be as attached to them as to themselves and are thus in a state of ignorance (*jahl*), which is evil. *Farq* is not an evil, for it is of utmost importance that human beings recognize themselves as creatures at the heart of creation (*khalq*), projected into the immanence of this world through the creative act of the transcendent God who gives being superabundantly without being impoverished and while remaining within His own Self. We see therefore that *jamᶜ* stands out within *farq*. There is no separation, for human beings, without union. For, says Qushayrī "those for whom there is no separation [*tafriqa*] do not have any *ᶜubūdiyya* [i.e., adhesion to the state of servitude in adoration of the *Rubūbiyya*, divine Lordship]. But those for whom there is no union, do not have knowledge [*maᶜrifa*]." It is therefore the same with the pairing of *farq* and *jamᶜ*, as with other pairs that we have already encountered: fear and hope, reverential fear and familiarity, to which one can add the constriction (*qabḍ*) and dilation (*basṭ*) of the heart.

Qushayrī finds support in the *al-Fātiha* sūrah, to show how the two states are linked. When the Qurᵓan says: "You (alone) we worship" (1:4), God indicates separation; when the Qurᵓan says "You (alone) we ask for help," God indicates union. "When human beings address a word to God in the language of trust and confidence (*najwā*), whether asking of God, invoking God, praising God, thanking God, in making honorable amends, in humbly and fervently beseeching God, they remain at the level of separation; when they strain their ear to listen in the very depth of their heart to what their Master speaks to them in confidence (*mā yunājihi bihi*), when they understand in the secret of their being the word that God addresses to them . . . , then this is evidence of union." We again find the very terms that define *khulla.*

As for the term *ghayba*, it does not designate, as it does in erotic poetry, the absence of the loved one, for God could not be absent from His creation. It relates to the heart that absents itself from the world of creatures, refusing to acquaint itself with the conditions of their being, even renouncing every personal feeling. In this state, human beings experience a feeling of emptiness, of bewilderment, of uprootedness. It is like being exiled from themselves while not yet existing in God. But for them this is a stage through which they come into the presence of their Lord, the Creator. The bewilderment of absence leads to an inebriation that is sometimes compared to folly (*junūn*); like drunkenness caused by wine, it leads to total forgetfulness both of all surrounding reality and of oneself. The state of sobriety is a return to lucidity that brings with it true knowledge of God.

THE CASE OF ḤALLĀJ

Among Muslim mystics, the one who has given love (*ʿishq*) the place of fundamental value is Hallāj. Perhaps he was not the first to introduce this term into mystical vocabulary. Louis Massignon has pointed out a *ḥadīth qudsī* of al-Ḥasan al-Baṣrī where a verb from the same root appears and applies to both God and human beings: "When what rules in my servant is the concern of attending to me, I lead him to find his well-being and joy in remembering Me. And when I have led him to find his well-being and his joy in remembering Me, I love him and he loves Me [*ʿashiqanī wa ʿashiqtuhu*]." One can also see a precursor in Nūrī. Massignon writes on this subject: "Nūrī is the first to have preached the notion of pure love . . . ; like Sarī, he even stresses the idea of that desire (*ʿishq*) that God inspires in the fervent soul; this was moving toward the Hallājian thesis of union with God through love."[31] Massignon translates *ʿishq* as essential desire and stresses the fact that Ḥallāj defined divine essence as essential desire. In doing so, he went farther than most or all of his predecessors.

We must limit ourselves to a few quotations, which the preceding remarks clarify perfectly. It is reported that Ḥallāj said: "Oh You, who have made me drunk on Your love, and made me wander, perplexed, through the spaces of Your presence; You are Isolated in Eternity, and it is for You alone to occupy the throne of Truth."[32] In the same sense, we highlight this invocation: "I beseech You, through the light of Your Face . . . , that you not allow me to wander through empty spaces of perplexity, but deliver me from the abysses of reflection, detach me from the world, and make me Your confidant by secret conversations."[33] We again find in this text all the terms we have already encountered, along with the ideas that they connote: bewilderment [or perplexity], familiarity, confidential discussions in the secret of the heart.

Ḥallāj too speaks of alternating seasons for coming near and distancing, which mark relationships between the soul and God: "Oh people! God converses with His creatures in all kindness: He reveals Himself to them, then He steals away, always with a view to their instruction. In fact, if He did not manifest Himself, all people would fall into impiety, just as, if He did not conceal Himself, they would all be dazzled [*futinū*]."[34] One must understand that they would be dazzled in the sense that they would forget their creaturely condition by which they must serve God in the obedience that is *ʿubūdiyya*. In fact the passive verb *futina* means "to be tested through trials." Human beings would therefore be dazzled by divine favor, as would happen here-below by glory or fortune. That is why, adds Ḥallāj, "God does not allow either of these two states to remain permanently for them."[35]

Nevertheless, when the faithful have been purified in their heart by undergoing these coupled states (which in their alternations exclude yet attract one another), and when the faithful reach pure love, then they transcend these alternations in an abiding—at least, more or less abiding—mystical state, which is the final goal of the spiritual quest. That is what Ḥallāj explains in a few verses on the subject of *fatā*. This term, which means "young man," has taken on a particular meaning among the mystics: one who is adept at *futuwwa* or spiritual knighthood. We could therefore translate the term, as Henri Corbin did, as "spiritual knight" and recall the *fityān* (plural of *fatā*) of the "Faithful in Love."

When a man in love reaches perfection within *fatā*
And inebriation makes him forget his union with the Beloved,
He witnesses in truth to the point that passion makes him attest,
That the prayer of those who love [*al-ʿāshiqīn*] releases from impiety.

In fact, prayer, even of praise, supposes a distance between the one praying and God, a distance that pure love has overcome. But in this world, this ideal state cannot be perfectly attained, and when the soul has a taste of it, it longs for death to deliver it.

> My death, this is survival; my life, this is death.

After the experience of what is called the union of union, in which the soul is united in God to the totality of being, the only prayer that can be addressed to God is to be withdrawn from this exile in the midst of beings who are only partially real.

> I have caught fire, all of me, in the All of Your All, Oh my Sanctity!
> You have unveiled Yourself to me as though You were in myself.
> I have turned my heart once more to what is not You, and there I have not seen
> Anything but my exile, while You, in my exile—You are my closest intimate [*unsī*]
> Alas! I myself am in the prison of life, kept away,
> Far from intimate fellowship. Seize me, then, to draw me from prison and to Yourself.

The verb *qabaḍa* means "to seize by the hand, to arrest." From it comes the word *qabḍ* which is the opposite of *basṭ*, as we have seen. The roots of these terms are qurʾanic. It is written (2:245): "God closes His hand [*yaqbiḍu*] and opens it [*yabsuṭu*]."[36] God tightens His hand upon the heart in order to compress it and take out what is attached to creatures, only to open it again in order to fill it with all His favors. Without *qabḍ*, there would be no *basṭ*, just as without death there would be no Life.

Interestingly enough, Ḥallāj describes the development of such a sublime love in terms quite near to those frequently employed in ordinary poetry. Anṭakī conveys the following verses:

> The beginning of love [*ḥubb*] is an inclination that maddens
> The heart of the lover so completely that he meets death as a game.
> Its origin is a haphazard glance
> Or a flirtation that ignites the heart like a flame,
> Like a spark thrown from a flint
> That kindles then burns the largest bonfire.

Ḥallāj in turn writes:

At first, ecstasy is only a hint, then a look
That makes a flame surge up in the intimacy of hearts.

This flame (*lahab, lahīb*) recalls the flame of love in Saint John of the Cross and the *hitlahabût* of Hassidism.

We end by pointing out a very curious teaching on the relation between divine nature (*al-Lāhūt; al-Lāhūtiyya*) and human nature (*al-nāsūt; al-nāsūtiyya*). The thought of Ḥallāj is particularly difficult to grasp here, but there is an initial text that is rather clear: "Just as my humanity loses itself in Your Divinity without being dissolved, Your Divinity takes hold of my humanity without entering into contact with it." The context is so obscure that Massignon translated it two different ways, which only serve to reveal his hesitations.[37] Be that as it may, it is clear that union with God does not cause human nature to disappear.

A second text defies all translation and what Massignon proposes[38] leaves one perplexed. We shall risk a translation whose only advantage is that it follows the text as closely as possible: "You manifest Yourself as You wish, just as you manifest yourself according to Your will, beneath the most beautiful of forms, the form in which dwells the Spirit that speaks by offering Knowledge, Witness, Power, and Proof. Then, You have given orders to Your witness who says *I* in Your Essence, which is a *He*. Whatever may be said of You, when You present Yourself in the form of myself in the wake of my repeated returns, You cast an appeal to myself through myself, while I am lifted up in my ascensions to the very throne of my pre-eternities before the words of my creatures."

What meaning are we to give this passage? First of all there is the idea that God manifests Himself in a human form, which is the most beautiful of forms, as it says in the Qurʾan (95:4): "Surely We created man of the best stature." Therefore the *nāsūt*, before being the humanity of a particular person, is the pre-eternal Human Form of the manifestation of God. Now, in the Qurʾan, which is the eternal and uncreated Word of God, it is prophets and, in general human beings, to whom God addresses himself and who respond to Him. Consequently, Divinity converses eternally with Humanity. When the humanity of Ḥallāj is lifted up into this pre-eternal Humanity, he reaches "the throne of his pre-eternities," where creatures, enveloped in *nāsūt*, speak with their Creator—particularly where the whole race of Adam, in the "pre-eternal covenant" (according to the translation that Massignon gives to the word *mīthāq*), before being born into time, recognized that God was its Lord.

At this level, Ḥallāj can speak for God, because God calls to him through himself. He becomes, so to speak, the mouth-piece of God and expresses himself in His name. That is why he can say: "*Anāʾl-Ḥaqq*," I am the creating truth, I am God. And so too, in our text, he says: "my creatures." In the transcendence of His Essence, God says "I" for *nāsūt* and through *nāsūt*. This is what God loves as the object of His intimate and eternal discussions; in this, human beings can love God and become God's friends and confidants.

Certainly, in order to become acquainted with Ḥallāj, one must read the work of Louis Massignon, just as, to become acquainted with Ibn al-ʿArabī and the Iranian mystics, one must read the works of Henri Corbin.[39] In the same way we refer back, for Jewish mysticism, to all that Scholem, Buber, and André Neher have written. As for Christian mysticism, it requires study of a great many works. As we have said, if one goes into detail, resemblances besides those we have highlighted will emerge, but at the same time, so will differences. Our intention was not to make them seem unanimous, which is impossible, even within one and the same monotheistic religion.

Moreover, if there were unanimity, monotheism would take on an impoverished monotony. We can be content to have reached the point where, without hiding the differences—indeed the oppositions—we can delineate fundamental, analogous tendencies, similar problematics and converging expressions which allow us to affirm that the three messages are akin on the spiritual plane and that the three messengers are creatures and masters in a single spiritual family.

CONCLUSION

At the end of this investigation, it seems clear to us that the three monotheistic messages have concurred in creating a religious humanism that promises spiritual values to humanity regarding its situation in the world and its relation to God. Throughout multiple variations, this humanism continues to present a very original character.

What is characteristic about these values, once discovered, is that they always remain current. That is why we have limited our study to the interior aspect of the monotheistic cultures, focusing our attention on the heart. The heart is the home where the messages of the three messengers centered and encountered each other. Certainly there are other interesting aspects of the messages which are more likely to pique historical curiosity. Speculations about legal, ethical, and social questions that derive from these lend themselves to numerous comparisons, above all between the Talmud and the Muslim treatises of *Fiqh* but perhaps also with ecclesiastical canon law.

Such comparisons are particularly rich in the field of philosophy, where collaboration between Jews, Muslims, and Christians was active in the Middle Ages. Averroës, Maimonides, St. Thomas Aquinas stand as symbols of this happy meeting of minds. Their philosophical theology found common ground naturally, to the extent that it reflected upon the One God, on His attributes, His creative act, and His governance of the world. The works on this point are numerous and well known. Still, on the one hand, the agreement of all these thinkers was based upon a notion of God conceived as First Cause—in other words on a single God closer to the God of the philosophers than the God of revelation. As soon as one turns to the truths of faith, which a theologian or even a philosopher can hardly avoid doing, divergences begin to appear. Moreover, a fundamental concern was to know whether philosophy is the servant of theology (*philosophia ancilla theologiae*), as is clearly the case for St. Thomas and Maimonides (who sees in philosophy, as A. Chouraqui has said, "a necessary element in mystical knowledge"), or whether it is an independent discipline that restricts revelation and faith to those domains where questions are posed that cannot be resolved through demonstrative proof, as Averroës thought might be the case. On the other hand, this medieval philosophy, brilliant as it was, remains marked by its epoch and ought to be renewed.

It would certainly be desirable if Jews, Christians, and Muslims, following the example of their illustrious ancestors, were to collaborate today in examining the philosophical problems of our time. Through such mutual assistance they might propose solutions that would certainly not be foreign to one another, solutions that our world sorely needs. Unfortunately, there is reason to fear that this is only a devout hope, at least for the immediate future. On the other hand, it would be important to initiate a Judeo-Islamic-Christian dialogue concerning the values of spirituality. This would be very useful and, it seems to me, more immediately feasible.

Henri Corbin believed, in this regard, that such a dialogue should begin at the level of the *gnoses* that have developed within the three religions. But besides the irreducible specificity of the different communal *gnoses*, it is certain that they retain only the messages they can integrate, through their hermeneutic, with *a priori* systems that are quite foreign to the messages and revelations that constitute the living faith of the faithful in the three religions. Besides, this would mean asking the Muslim gnostic not to believe any more in the Imāms (seven or twelve), or the Jewish gnostic to forget the historic conditions in which the kabbalah was born and which have marked it over centuries, and the "Christian" gnostic, Basilidian or Valentinian, to renounce the doctrine of the demiurge, chief of the evil angels and god of the Jews. Indeed this could be done, provided that the gnostic systems are reduced to a simple schema of an "imaginal" world of angelic intermediaries between the First Principle which is One in its transcendence and the world here-below of humanity. In other words by emptying the gnostic systems of all that is properly theirs, one could reach agreement among all those who hold to what is generally termed gnosis. But then it would no longer remain the authentic faith of monotheistic believers. The messages would no longer impose themselves except as something disfigured by what claims to be the authentic interpretation, either figurative or symbolic. Consequently, those who have received the message of the three messengers cannot, without denying their proper faith, hope to find some kind of unity among themselves if they follow the proposal of Henri Corbin. On the contrary, they will certainly meet as brothers and sisters if they meditate on their own spirituality and that of other monotheistic mysticisms, even if on other points they are fraternal enemies. This is what we have attempted to show, as it represents our personal conviction.

We have been discussing a Judeo-Islamic-Christian humanism. We investigated some of its elements by examining, through their own testimony, the most representative spiritual adepts of the three monotheisms, because we wanted to define this humanism in itself and not in relation to other visions of the human person, the world, and God (or some other Absolute) foreign to the messages of the three messengers. In fact, the danger lies in defining them by what they are not—in function of the Other. This is not the right way to discover their authentic identity. But all the same we can note that with respect to other products of the human spirit, revealed monotheism has produced and ripened original fruit on its branches. Above all, we think of the Brahmanic religion and of Buddhism.

The East has often been distinguished from the West. It is evident that geographically these two notions are quite relative—anything East being West of its East and anything West being East of its West. In what sense, therefore, should we employ these terms? Must we arbitrarily decree that certain things belong to the East and others to the West? Certainly not. Two peoples who lived on the eastern shores of the Mediterranean, the Hebrews and the Greeks, have each played a unique role in the history of humanity. The encounter of the Greek miracle and monotheistic revelation launched a movement of civilization that first developed in that eastern region but was then transported westward, to the Roman Empire of the West, to Italy, Gaul, Spain, England, and Germany, until it constituted what we now call, for this simple reason, Western civilization. In effect, this movement hardly spread eastward from the Mediterranean East: Persia was touched but India resisted, thanks to its mass as a subcontinent. The invasion of Alexander, like the later invasion of the Islamic generals, did not manage to penetrate it deeply. So one can call the civilization of this immense country situated to the east of the Mediterranean East, Eastern. This having been made clear, one must conclude that Judeo-Islamic-Christian religious humanism is a Western humanism, that it was at the origin and remains an essential element of Western civilization. The three messengers created a world; they engendered a type of humanity. (We will not speak of China, which has been still more impenetrable to the spirituality of the West.) Nevertheless, wherever Jews, Christians or Muslims settle, they always bring their values, which are those of the West, although they sometimes take on some indigenous contours.

It is true that exchanges took place between India and the West, either on the scientific or the philosophical level (for example, during the epoch of the Vedanta), or even on the level of mystical ideas. But here the contrasts have always remained strong. Certain historians have wanted to see Indian influence in the origin of *taṣawwuf*, the doctrine of the Sufis. This is more than exaggerated. The resemblances one may detect are altogether superficial: they touch on the practice of asceticism, charity, and alms, as well as the search for wisdom. Louis Massignon and Louis Gardet have tried to find more precise rapports, but these remain at the level of concepts apparently interchangeable, in that one need not transpose them to understand them in their inextricable systemic complexity and to comprehend their exact meaning (to the degree that they have one, for Indian thought seems quite allergic to univocal definitions). Indian thought slips away and eludes every attempt of a Western mind to capture it, and specialists themselves confess their difficulty in finding a foothold.

Oliver Lacombe's work, *L'Absolu selon le Védānta* concerns the pure and simple non-dualism of Shankara and the non-dualism of various others such as Rāmānuja. He cautions that "before comparing, it is necessary to know adequately the two terms of comparison. But one must certainly render immediately intelligible to philosophers each of these parallel sketches of the twin Indian teachings. To this end, a basis of comparison was necessary, which we wanted as simple as possible so that the reader might at once be provided with a system of fixed and familiar references and cautioned, by the very diversity of proposed landmarks, against any oversophisticated or jejune assimilation."[1] The warning is clear. In fact it is often possible to find analogies with the types of thought with which we are familiar. This is the case when one reads in the RgVeda: "At first was neither Being nor Nonbeing. . . . There was no death then, nor yet deathlessness. . . . The One breathed without breath, by its own impulse. Other than that was nothing else at all" (RgVeda X, 129).[2] This text, taken in itself and outside of any vedic context, makes one think of Plotinus. But one loses one's footing upon reading in the *Brhadāranyaka Upanishad* (III.9,1–9): "Then Vidagdha Sākalya asked him: 'How many Gods are there, Yājñavalkya?' He replied according to the Nivid [a ritual formula], quoting the number mentioned in the Nivid of the All-Gods: 'Three hundred and three and three thousand and three.' 'Yes,' he said, 'but how many Gods are there really, Yājñavalkya?' 'Thirty-three.' To succeeding questions the responses give a decreasing number of Gods: six, three, two, one and a half, finally One. And when Vidagdha Sākalya asked: 'Which is the only God?,' Yājñavalkya replied: 'Life Breath; he is Brahman, which they call "that" [*tyad*].'[3] It is not even conceivable that such conceptions could enter into any of the mental categories of a Western person.

Strictly speaking the thought of Rāmānuja could be more easily linked to Western religious conceptions than that of Shankara, which is very distant from them. In a work written in collaboration with Louis Gardet on the experience of the self, Lacombe concluded his study in these terms: "So far as India is concerned, our attention has been directed, as it should be, to those schools of spirituality guided by the search for the experience of the Self and through the practice of Yoga organized into a complete system of thought. We should not forget, however, that at the very heart of this religious culture, where the quest for a transpersonal mysticism of immanence predominates, the ample development of *bhakti* attests to the presence of a fundamental and fully self-conscious aspiration for a spiritual life in which a personal God is the center and which exalts the loving response of the created person to the gracious initiatives of Divinity."[4] He speaks in *L'Absolu selon le Védānta* of the teaching of Pāñtcharātra, resolutely opposed to that of Shankara, which was the point of departure for a new vedantic school, that of Rāmānuja: "Pāñtcharātra is the expression of a powerful religious movement centered on worship and love—*bhakti*—of a single personal God."[5] One could think therefore of a monotheistic religion (*ekantika dharma*). The name of Vāsudēva, patronym of its central figure, Krishna, attests to the existence of this religion in the three or four centuries that proceeded the Christian era. These faithful are called Bhāgavatas, worshipers of the Blessed One. The Bhagavad Gītā, "vigorously recapturing the teaching of the Upanishads . . . , organizes it around ten major themes of the *ekantika dharma*, religion of the single divine personality, and its corollary, the *bhakti*, which was certainly not absent from the vedic or vedantic religion, but was not prevalent there." According to Lacombe, "the Bhagavad Gītā appears simultaneously as the literary expression of the more ancient of the *ekantika dharma* and as least particular, least sectarian. It did not want to be the book of a particular school, but the book of all the orthodox schools." Lacombe continues: "Vishnuism will include other elements which the Pāñtcharātra has ignored: the cult—and not simply the theory—of the *avatāra*, that of Rāma primarily."[6] In fact these schools have not succeeded in liberating themselves from a complex mythology where one becomes lost among the names of Vishnu (or Nārāyana) and of Krishna; the *vyūha*, which are forms or hypostases of the Bhagavat and cosmic manifestations; the divine, individuated (avatars) "descents;" and finally the apparition of Rāma.

As a result, so far as one can judge, the loving devotion that is *bhakti* certainly moves intentionally toward a unique and personal being. But this determination and this conception remain very distant from that of the one God revealed through the Bible. Doubtless specialists in Indian thought, in command of a thousand and one subtle nuances, would reject this point of view as inspired by a caricature. Only after long and patient studies can the nuances of such a text be grasped and its complexity dominated, a complexity which at first glance seems made of contradictions. But that is the point: if they are so difficult for a Westerner to comprehend, they throw into relief a totally different mentality—and that is all we wanted to show.

The communication of cultures has limits. If "to comprehend" is, as Saint Thomas Aquinas thought, to become the other *as* the other, it is clear that one cannot become just anyone or anything. Only raw material is capable of receiving any form whatsoever—even truly contrary forms—precisely because it is without form. But the human mind is not a *tabula rasa* on which the Veda could be written as easily as the Bible, with perfect and equal indifference. One cannot learn to understand in total indifference: a certain natural sympathy is necessary, one not at our command. It is true that the most characteristic ideal of Indian thought involves a certain "vacuity" that is not solely absence of all self-consciousness, of all attachment to self. We have spoken of this void with reference to the monotheistic mysticisms of the West. This ideal involves emptying the very reality of the self which is conceived of as a "subject" in constant relation with the objects of this world, in function of the postulate that a subject is inevitably related to objects. But if the being of the self is not only denied but disappears, what would fill the void which remains is of no interest at all. If this ideal of Indian thought becomes something other than words—if it takes on reality—it cannot interest anyone, because no one any longer exists, since no self is left. As a result, if in order to comprehend Indian thought I must not so much open myself to another and find a way of sympathetic understanding, but rather cease to be myself, according to the ideal in question, there is no longer any reason any use for my self to understand that ideal.

Wanting to "enter into the thought of others" doubtless is a worthy project. But it must be me, myself, who enters, and enters from the outset. For, I can deprive myself of many things, but not of my own self in my personal being. I can overturn the "idols of the tribe" and the "idols of the forum," as Francis Bacon said. I can make an effort to bracket my habits of thought, my tastes, my desires, my prejudices and those of my times. But something irreducible will always remain: my self. And if I then claim to comprehend Indian thought, chances are that it will be because I have manipulated it in order to make it enter into my own, instead of making mine enter into it. India is another world.

Nevertheless, certain Indian systems speak to us more propitiously and offer themselves better than others to our comprehension. But one must be very prudent and not claim victory too quickly. In her remarkable work on the two branches of the school of Rāmānuja, Suzanne Siauve studied *prapatti* in particular, that surrender to God by which the faithful rely totally on God's grace, from which comes all initiative and all protection.[7] One normally thinks of quite similar Western values such as the *tawakkul*, the *taslīm* and the *tafwīd* of the Muslim mystics. "The state of *prapanna*, of someone who makes the act of *prapatti*, the *prapadana*, is a determined and definite norm, a state of consecration that introduces one into a new relation with God, a surer relation than that of *bhakti* itself. For *bhakti*, or devotion, is cultivated with effort. It is a *yoga*, *bhaktiyoga*, depending on study and mental concentration; it uses the terms of the Upanishads in order to penetrate the grandeur of the divine attributes; it is *upāsana*, devout meditation, *dhyāna*, contemplation, *jñāna*, knowledge, *vidyā*, knowing, according to the equivalent expressions that Rāmānuja and his followers provide. This *bhakti*, permeated knowledge, culminates in direct vision, which is known as a perfect concentration on the 'recollection on God.' But the *prapanna* is one who discourages such efforts and feels unworthy of them. . . ."[8] Most of the ideas expressed in this text surface in the accounts we have given of Western monotheistic mysticism. Note especially the question of the relationship between knowledge and love, or later, the importance of the study of the Bible in the spiritual progress of Jewish mystics, or the value of recollecting God, *dhikr*, among the Muslim mystics.

Siauve recalls that the Lord Himself discloses the "secret" of His love in the Bhagavad Gītā (XVIII, 66): "When you have abandoned all the *dharmas*, taking recourse in Me alone, I will deliver you of all your sins, fear not."[9] This means that "God alone is the means of His own attainment," as the *Katha Upanishad* (II, 23) already taught: "By him whom he chooses is the *ātman* attained. To him the *ātman* reveals his own being."[10] This teaching obviously makes one think of quietism. But Siauve senses the differences deeply: "This however involves surrendering not only the fruits or the desire for fruits, but also oneself and one's own destiny, to the good pleasure of God. The difficulty proper to Hinduism is that of reconciling such an attitude with the personalist character of the teachings of the *bhakti*: the personal subject must subsist in order to be in relationship with a personal God, and as long as the feeling of self subsists, how can we truly be delivered from egotism? The idea that the entire being of the subject can be taken up into a relationship to the divine Person, that the finite subject would be nothing more than a relation to the Other, is not a perspective that spontaneously emerges within the Hindu world, for which renunciation of self is manifest above all in the state of *yogin*, of having become "pure subject," totally indifferent and at the same time empty of its own substance and its relations."[11]

These teachings show, nevertheless, that it is possible to extract from the vedic and upanishadic texts, or from the later Bhagavad Gītā, ideas that relate very much to our own, and indeed to a problematic that is familiar to us. However, as Siauve underscores, Hindu thought accommodates itself to the tendencies of this genre only with difficulty.

What are we to say about Buddhism? We could simply pass over it in silence, since it has nothing to do with the idea of God revealed in the three monotheisms. We should point out, however, what could be quite incomprehensible for a Western mind. For example, in his work on the idea of *prajnā*, Guy Bugault, who has thoroughly studied the problem of knowing and unknowing in Buddhist anagogy, writes: "To what extent does the notion of a return to one's self, even if uncontaminated by notions of introspection and reflection, still in fact make sense within a perspective that generally refuses the notion of a 'self'? What does the practice of *dhyāna* [recollection] as *pratyātmavedya* [inner-directed regard, introversion] mean, if at the same time one professes the negation of all substance and, conspicuously, of all personal substance, if one professes *nairātmya* [absence of 'self,' insubstantiality]?"[12] In turn, how is one to speak of a transmigrant individuality (*pudgala*) if one affirms its insubstantiality (*pudgala-nairātmya*)? The destiny of my self, reduced to a series of (*samtāna*) events, or in other words, to a connection of atoms, should be as indifferent for me as that of my body, which will dissolve and be eaten by worms. Why fear transmigration? Why speak of awakening (*bodhi*)? Awakening of whom? Awakening to what? There is an intimate link between *bodhi* and *nirvana*: "To take up again the metaphor of wind and fire, . . . what is to be extinguished is not the flame, but rather the wind: the absence of breath (nir-VA) is closely related to awakening by the light."[13] Final recollection happens at the point where all intentional thought is rejected. "Concerning *nirvana*, properly speaking it is beyond this perspective, as negative as this may be. It presumes the rejection of this rejection. Rather than being the rejection of all intentional thought, it is the absence of it, and it is the absence of intentional thought (*acitta*), rather than the absence of all thought."[14] For such intentional thought always envisages an "earthly region," even if it is a thought of self within a reflection on one's self. "To return to the Sanscrit term '*acitta*,' it is necessary to see in non-thought a thought so punctiliar, so cut off from itself, so ab-solute, that it no longer comprises even the margin of intentionality characteristic of *citta*. *Acitta* is a thought that is not vectorial, does not signify, and a thought from which signs and marks . . . are effaced. According to our familiar points of reference, it therefore seems insignificant to us. It is simply the brilliance of the absolute. To our eyes, therefore, it is a thought that has been smashed to pieces, annihilated, broken, yet when lived from within, it is precisely uninterrupted thought."[15] The absence of thought, therefore, is not the privation of thought. It is thought that is "like that." The fact of being "like that" is called *tathatā*, a term which takes on an absolute meaning. Thought which is "like that" is neither thought of some thing, nor thought about itself, nor any thought, nor in any general way "thought about. . . ." It is simply thought.

These few remarks — and one could multiply them — show to what extent the idea of absolute vacuity which characterizes Buddhism is distant from the preoccupations of the monotheistic mystics of the West, even when they speak about nothingness, *nada*, *Nichts* or *fanāʿ*. For them, it is certainly necessary to employ one's self; but the void, when realized, is made in order to be filled by God. So we may note in a certain sense that Buddhism only carries to their extreme limits tendencies that seem connatural to all Indian thought.

So one can affirm *a priori* that if monotheistic mystics had been able to become familiar with the works of one or another school of India, they would have been incapable of entering into it, and would have extracted at best only very approximate and altered ideas. On this point we have an important witness, the great scholar Bīrūnī, who lived in India, read Sanscrit and was probably able to carry out his inquiries in the vernacular. He wrote the *Livre de l'Inde*, in which he demonstrated a keen intelligence, which did not prevent him, however, when speaking of Indian philosophy and beliefs, from seeing them under a single aspect or from interpreting them in the light of his formation as a Muslim thinker.

A fundamental question to clarify on this subject is that of the reality and the nature of the I. We have tried to show that, for any of the monotheistic mystics, the human I does not disappear in God at the moment of ecstasy and union, even where God is considered as the absolute One. What then happens to this I within Indian thought? There are several teachings. It would be hard to do better than to cite a passage from the conclusion of Michel Hulin in his important work on the principle of the ego in classical Indian thought:

> On one hand, an inert absolute. . . . encompassing all finite manifestations, all modes, but neither aware of itself nor conscious of its own character as the Encompassing One. On the other hand an absolute capable of denying itself, rending itself apart, but of reconstituting itself beyond this rending. On one hand the *sānti*, the peace of the depths, immutable, indifferent to agitation on the surface. On the other hand, a veritable uneasiness on the part of the absolute, a "bacchic delirium where there is no member that is not drunk, but that is at the same time translucid and in calm repose." On one hand, a cosmic manifestation based only on illusion and on the other hand, a free engagement of Shiva (Absolute Spirit) within the cosmic unfolding. . . . We would in this way possess in the Advaita Indian version the most restrictive conception of individuality: *omnis determinatio est negatio*. The only possible meaning of individual existence would be to work for one's own destruction, to end the kind of metaphysical scandal that it constitutes. In the tantric perspective, however, the sense of individual existence would be one's own enlargement: to loosen the hinges, the anchors of bodily and mental *habitus*, to reinject the feeling of I into all the zones of being that have become deathlike under the effect of inertia.[16]

Monotheistic mysticism has nothing to do with such alternatives.

One remembers the famous formula that inspired Schopenhauer: *Tat tvam asi*: Thou art That. It has been the object of numerous interpretations, which Hulin studied in his book.[17] It is quite possible for a Westerner to be misled regarding its meaning. But what strikes him is the kind of identity that is stipulated between a Thou, which can only think in a personal way, and a That, which is neuter. Now Ernst Müller, in his book on the *Zohar*, pointed out that the name of Elohim designates "a being who, in becoming object, is still entirely subject." It is to this idea that the *Zohar* relates the phrase: *mî bārâ ʾeleh*: Who has believed this? With the letters *mî* and *ʾeleh*, one forms the name of Elohim, "signifying thereby an act of creation in which the objective world of *This* releases the eternal principle of *Who*." Is it the *this* that poses the question of *Who*? In the same way Philo of Alexandria, instead of employing *to on* (to be, being, in the neuter), spoke of *ho ōn* (He who is, Being, in the masculine). By meditating on these nuances one may come to grasp—we believe—the specificity of Western conceptions concerning the human person, the world, and God.

In his magnificent work *I and Thou*, Martin Buber writes: "Spirit is not in the *I*, but between *I* and *Thou*."[18] Later he says that "the *I* is as indispensable to this, the supreme, as to every relation, since relation is only possible between *I* and *Thou*. It is not the *I*, then, that is given up, but that false self-asserting instinct. . . ."[19] Although one really ought to read the whole book, we may give one final citation: "[T]o step into pure relation is not to disregard everything but to see everything in the *Thou*; not to renounce the world but to establish it on its true basis. To look away from the world, or to stare at it, does not help a man reach God; but he who sees the world in Him stands in His presence. 'Here world, there God' is the language of *It*; 'God in the world' is another language of *It*. But to eliminate or leave behind nothing at all, to include the whole world in the *Thou*, to give the world its due and its truth, to include nothing beside God but everything in Him—this is full and complete relation."[20] One could not mark the contrast with *Tat tvam asi* better than this.

In a period when each group claims its identity even while wanting to open itself to others—something which at first looks like two contradictory desires, but which life itself will conciliate—it is good to avoid every kind of syncretism, to know what one is in oneself, and then to know how one differs from others, in order to know exactly what one can offer to others helpfully as well as helpfully receive from others.

But there remains something still more important. In the West itself, several philosophies persist in our day, under the pretext of scientific relativism, in denying to human beings anything of value or of irreducible originality. They see only an anonymous objective structure in the human being, or—to speak a language that has become fashionable—the result of some kind of electronic programing in which the programer is unknown (but one dare not pose this metaphysical question, now devoid of interest). It suffices to know the code in order to know all that can be known about the programer.

We can also note that a movement has been launched that is resolutely hostile to Judeo-Christian thought and culture. Nietzsche is praised to the skies, and one interprets him in any way that suits one's thesis. But one overlooks the treasures that the three monotheisms carry within themselves and one exploits their dogmatic divergences, in order to dismiss them back to back. (We are not speaking of those who go about seeking, in the practices of certain sects which have more or less assimilated or supposedly assimilated Indian doctrines, a justification for a life they no longer know how to direct.)

That is sad. It is high time to study Judeo-Islamic-Christian humanism, to know it, to spread it, and to defend it.

NOTES

1. THREE MESSENGERS AND THREE MESSAGES

1. [For a more extensive study, see Joel L. Kraemer, *Philosophy in the Renaissance of Islam: Abū Sulaymān al-Sijistānī and His Circle* (Leiden: E. J. Brill, 1986).]

2. [Translated from French text.]

3. [Translated from French text.]

4. [French: "Et Nous fimes alliance" or covenant. . . .]

5. [Translated from French text.]

6. [Translated from French text.]

2. MESSENGERS, MESSAGES, AND ADDRESSES

1. [French: "God can do without the world."]

2. [English translation is from the New Revised Standard Version.]

3. [Translated from French text.]

4. [Translated from the French.]

3. UNDERSTANDING FAITH, THE LIFE OF FAITH

1. Saint Teresa of Avila, *The Book of Her Life* 10.7, in *The Collected Works of St. Teresa of Avila*, vol. 1, trans. Kieran Kavanaugh and Otilio Rodriguez (Washington, D.C.: Institute of Carmelite Studies, 1976–1985): 77.

2. Saint Teresa of Avila, *The Book of Her Life* 10.8: 77–78. On the role of theologians in the expression of Saint Teresa, see the work of Jeannine Poitrey, *Introduction à la lecture de Thérèse d'Avila* (Paris: Beauchesne, 1979), 44–47.

3. Gershom Scholem, *Origins of the Kabbalah*, ed. R. J. Zwi Werblowsky, trans. Allan Arkush (Princeton: The Jewish Publication Society, Princeton University Press, 1987), 246.

4. Scholem, *Origins of the Kabbalah*, 276.

5. Meister Eckhart, *Meister Eckhart: German Sermons & Treatises*, vol. 2, trans. with an introduction by Maurice O'C. Walshe (London: Watkins, 1979–): 332.

6. Meister Eckhart, *Meister Eckhart: The Essential Sermons, Commentaries, Treatises, and Defense,* trans. with introduction by Edmund Colledge and Bernard McGinn, preface by Huston Smith, The Classics of Western Spirituality (New York: Paulist Press, 1981), 85.

7. [Arnaldez is here citing a work which was included in the 1937 French translation of John of the Cross but which is now recognized to have been a spurious addition to the Spanish *Obras Completas* at that time. That it was mistaken as genuine, however, attests to the general fidelity of the sentiments expressed to those of John of the Cross.]

8. Scholem, *Origins of the Kabbahah,* 20.

9. Scholem, *Origins of the Kabbahah,* 475.

10. Philo [of Alexandria], *De specialibus legibus* [On the special laws] 1, 8–10, trans F. H. Colson, in *Philo,* vol. 7, Loeb Classical Library (Cambridge, Mass.: Harvard University Press; London: William Heinemann Ltd., 1938): 105.

11. [42:19b translated from the French.]

12. [New Jerusalem Bible: "Who so blind as the friend I have taken to myself . . . ?"]

13. Martin Buber, *Hasidism and Modern Man,* ed. and trans. Maurice Friedman (New York: Horizon Press, 1958), 99.

14. Vajda, *L'Amour de Dieu dans la théologie juive du Moyen Age,* Etudes de philosophie medievale, no. 46 (Paris: J. Vrin, 1957), 103.

15. Gershom Scholem, *The Messianic Idea in Judaism, and Other Essays on Jewish Spirituality* (New York: Schocken Books, 1971), 48. Cf. French edition, *Le Messianisme juif: essais sur la spiritualité du judaïsme,* trans. Bernard Dupuy (Calmann-Lévy, 1974), 101.

16. Scholem, *The Messianic Idea,* 46.

17. Saint Augustine, *The Lord's Sermon on the Mount* 1.2.8, trans. John J. Jepson, Ancient Christian Writers: The Works of the Fathers in Translation no. 5 (Westminster, Md.: Newman Press, 1948), 15.

18. Augustine 2.1.1, pp. 92–93.

19. Saint Teresa of Avila, *The Book of Her Foundations* 6.18–21, in *The Collected Works of St. Teresa of Avila,* vol. 3: 131–33.

20. See note 7 above.

21. The citation is inexact. The idea of prayer is drawn from the end of verse 7, and Tauler gives to the *omophrones* of verse 8 the sense of "having one soul," instead of "being of one mind" [agreeing among yourselves—NJB; or being unanimous—literal translation of the French text].

22. Johannes Tauler, *Sermons,* trans. Maria Shrady, introduction by Josef Schmidt, preface by Alois Haas, The Classics of Western Spirituality (New York: Paulist Press, 1985), 137, 140.

23. Martin Buber, *The Legend of Baal-Shem,* trans. Maurice Friedman (New York: Harper & Brothers, 1955), 25–26.

24. Scholem, *Origins of the Kabbalah*, 415.

25. Scholem, *Origins of the Kabbalah*, 416.

26. Saint Teresa of Avila, *Meditations on the Song of Songs* 2.28, in *The Collected Works of St. Teresa of Avila*, vol. 2: 235.

27. Saint Teresa of Avila, *Meditations on the Song of Songs* 3.1, in *Collected Works* 2: 236.

28. Saint Teresa of Avila, *The Interior Castle* 5.3, in *Collected Works* 2: 349.

4. EXPRESSIONS OF MYSTICAL EXPERIENCE: THE LANGUAGE OF NEOPLATONISM

1. Saint Teresa of Avila, *The Book of Her Life* 8.5, in *The Collected Works of St. Teresa of Avila*, 1:67

2. Saint Teresa of Avila, "A Satirical Critique" 5, in *Collected Works* 3:360.

3. Gershom G. Scholem, *Major Trends in Jewish Mysticism*, 3rd ed. (New York: Schocken Books, 1954 [1941]), 44.

4. Plotinus, *The Enneads* II 9.2, trans. Stephen MacKenna; 3rd ed. revised by B. S. Page, with an introduction by Paul Henry (London: Faber and Faber Limited, 1962), 134.

5. Plotinus, *The Enneads* II 9.6: 137.

6. Plotin, *Ennéades*, trans. and ed. Emile Bréhier, Collection des Universités de France (Paris: Societe d'Edition "Les Belles lettres," 1924–1938), 2:108–110, notice.

7. Gershom Scholem, *Origins of the Kabbalah*, 83.

8. Louis Massignon, *Essai sur les origines du lexique technique de la mystique musulmane*, 2nd ed. (Paris: Librairie Philosophique J. Vrin, 1954), 145–53. This work has been translated as: *Essay of the Origins of the Technical Language of Islamic Mysticism*, trans. Benjamin Clark (Notre Dame, Ind.: University of Notre Dame Press, 1995).

9. [See note 7 in chapter 3.]

10. Saint Teresa of Avila, Toledo, to P. Jerónimo Gracián, Seville, 23 October 1576, letter 122 in *The Letters of Saint Teresa of Jesus*, trans. and ed. E. Allison Peers, from the critical edition of P. Silverio de Santa Teresa (Westminster, Md.: Newman Press, [1950]), 1:318.

11. Saint Teresa of Avila, Toledo, to Don Lorenzo de Cepeda, 10 February 1577, letter 168 in *The Letters of Saint Teresa*, 1:426–27.

12. Saint Teresa of Avila, "A Satirical Critique" 6, in *The Collected Works of St. Teresa of Avila*, 3:360–61.

13. Plato, *Gorgias* 505b, trans. Terence Irwin (Oxford: Clarendon Press, 1979), 82.

14. Plotinus, *The Enneads* V 7.1: 419.

15. Plotinus, *The Enneads* V 7.1: 419–20.

16. Plotin, *Ennéades*, trans. and ed. Emile Bréhier, 5:121, notice.

17. Avicenna, *Ishārāt* II (Cairo: ed. S. Dunya, 1957–58), 213.

18. Avicenna, *Kitāb al-Najāt* III, p. 247.

19. [Translated from French. NJB reads: "disordered bodily desires, disordered desires of the eyes, pride in possession."]

20. Scholem, *Major Trends in Jewish Mysticism*, 140.

21. Scholem, *Major Trends in Jewish Mysticism*, 208.

22. Scholem, *Major Trends in Jewish Mysticism*, 209.

23. Scholem, *Major Trends in Jewish Mysticism*, 215.

24. Scholem, *Major Trends in Jewish Mysticism*, 224.

25. Scholem, *Major Trends in Jewish Mysticism*, 224–25.

26. Scholem, *Major Trends in Jewish Mysticism*, 216–17.

27. Scholem, *Major Trends in Jewish Mysticism*, 216.

28. Ibn ᶜArabī, *Futūḥāt*, book III, part 16, chapter 23, p. 152, §124.

29. [Translated from the French.]

30. [English translation taken from *The Confessions of St. Augustine*, trans. John K. Ryan (New York: Doubleday Image Book, 1960).]

31. Martin Buber, *Hasidism and Modern Man*, ed. and trans. Maurice Friedman (New York: Horizon Press, 1958), 115.

32. Plotinus, *The Enneads* I, 3.1: 37.

33. Plotinus, *The Enneads* I, 6.7: 61.

34. Plotinus, *The Enneads* I, 6.9: 63–64.

35. Plotinus, *The Enneads* I, 6.9: 64.

36. Plotinus, *The Enneads* I, 6.7: 62.

37. Plotinus, *The Enneads* V 5.13: 414 and 413.

38. Plotinus, *The Enneads* V 5.6: 408.

39. Emile Bréhier, *The Hellenistic and Roman Age*, trans. Wade Baskin, vol. 2: *The History of Philosophy* (Chicago: University of Chicago Press, 1965), 196.

40. Gershom Scholem, *The Messianic Idea in Judaism*, 205–6.

41. Scholem, *The Messianic Idea*, 214.

42. Scholem, *The Messianic Idea*, 214.

43. Scholem, *The Messianic Idea*, 214.

44. Scholem, *The Messianic Idea*, 218.

45. Scholem, *Major Trends in Jewish Mysticism*, 262.

46. Scholem, *Major Trends in Jewish Mysticism*, 261.

47. Jean-Louis Michon, *Le soufi marocain Aḥmad Ibn Ajība (1746-1809) et son Miᶜrāj: glossaire de la mystique musulmane*, Etudes musulmanes 14 (Paris: J. Vrin, 1973), 246.

48. Michon, 247.

49. [English translation from New Revised Standard Version.]

50. Saint John of the Cross, *The Dark Night* II 9.1, in *The Collected Works*

of St. John of the Cross, trans. Kieran Kavanaugh and Otilio Rodriguez (Garden City, N.Y.: Doubleday, 1964), 346.

51. Ibn ʿArabī, *Futūḥāt* I, p. 256, §434.

52. Ibn ʿArabī, *Futūḥāt* I, pp. 190–91, §270.

53. Ibn ʿArabī, *Futūḥāt* I, p. 191, §271.

54. Eckhart, serm. 80: *Adolescens, tibi dico: surge* on Luke 7:12, in *Meister Eckhart: German Sermons & Treatises*, vol. 2, trans. and ed. Maurice O'C. Walshe (London: Watkins, 1979): 235–36.

55. Eckhart, serm. 25: *Nunc scio vere quia misit Dominus angelum suum* on Acts 12:11, in *Meister Eckhart: German Sermons & Treatises*, vol. 1, trans. and ed. Maurice O'C. Walshe (London: Watkins, 1979): 199.

56. Plotinus, *The Enneads* V 1.1: 380.

57. Eckhart, serm. 13b: *In hoc apparuit caritas Dei in nobis* on 1 John 4:9, in *Meister Eckhart: German Sermons & Treatises*, 1: 116–17.

58. Eckhart, serm. 80: *Adolescens, tibi dico: surge*, 2:238.

59. Eckhart, serm. 69: *Scitote, quia prope est regnum Dei*, 2:165.

60. Eckhart, serm. 69: *Scitote, quia prope est regnum Dei*, 2:166.

61. Eckhart, serm. 58: *Euge serve bone et fidelis etc.* (on Matthew 25:23) 2:90.

62. Eckhart, serm. 83: *Haec dicit Dominus: Honora patrem tuum, etc.*, 2:251.

63. Eckhart, serm. 25: *Nunc scio vere quia misit Dominus angelum suum*, 1:199.

64. Eckhart, serm. 25: *Nunc scio vere quia misit Dominus angelum suum*, 1:199.

65. Pseudo-Dionysius, *The Celestial Hierarchy* 1.1, in *Pseudo-Dionysius: The Complete Works*, trans. Colm Luibheid, foreword, notes, and translation collaboration by Paul Rorem, preface by René Roques, introductions by Jaroslav Pelikan, Jean Leclercq, Karlfried Froehlich, The Classics of Western Spirituality (New York: Paulist Press, 1987), 145.

5. EXPRESSIONS OF MYSTICAL EXPERIENCE: THE LANGUAGE OF LOVE

1. Georges Vajda, *L'amour de Dieu dans la théologie juive du Moyen Age*, Etudes de philosophie medievale 46 (Paris: J. Vrin, 1957), 91.

2. Hayyim Yefim Schirmann, *Ha-shīrāh ha-ʿibrīt bi-Sefarad ube-Provāns* [Hebrew poetry in Spain and Provence] (Jerusalem-Tel Aviv, 1955), 182; cited in Vajda, *L'amour de Dieu*, 88, note 3.

3. Martin Buber, *Die chassidischen Bücher* (Hellerau: Verlag von Jakob Hegner, 1928), 119.

4. [New Revised Standard Version.]

5. [New Revised Standard Version.]

6. Bahya Ibn Paquda, *Introduction aux Devoirs des Coeurs*, trans. and ed. André Chouraqui, with an introduction by J. Maritain (Paris, 1950), 183.

7. Saint John of the Cross, *The Spiritual Canticle* 1.2, in *The Collected Works of St. John of the Cross*, trans. Kieran Kavanaugh and Otilio Rodriguez (Garden City, N.Y.: Doubleday & Co., 1964), 416.

8. *Indica mihi . . . ubi pascas, ubi cubas in meridie.*

9. Saint John of the Cross, *The Spiritual Canticle* 1.5, pp. 417–18.

10. Saint John of the Cross, *The Spiritual Canticle* 1.6, p. 418.

11. To keep his secret [*Kitmān al-sirr*] is the foundational rule of the law of love, in Arabic poets.

12. Saint John of the Cross, *The Spiritual Canticle* 25.5, p. 507.

13. Saint John of the Cross, *The Spiritual Canticle* 25.8, p. 508.

14. Saint John of the Cross, *The Spiritual Canticle* 26.7, p. 512.

15. Saint John of the Cross, *The Spiritual Canticle* 26.13, p. 513.

16. Saint John of the Cross, *The Spiritual Canticle* 26.13, p. 513.

17. Saint John of the Cross, *The Spiritual Canticle* 26.14, p. 514.

18. Saint John of the Cross, *The Living Flame of Love* 1.13, in *Collected Works*, 583–84.

19. Saint Teresa of Avila, *Meditations on the Song of Songs* 1.5, in *The Collected Works of St. Teresa of Avila*, trans. Kieran Kavanaugh and Otilio Rodriguez (Washington, D.C.: Institute of Carmelite Studies, 1976–1985), 2:217–18.

20. Saint Teresa of Avila, *Meditations on the Song of Songs* 1.5, vol. 2:217.

21. Saint Teresa of Avila, *Meditations on the Song of Songs* 1.5, vol. 2:217.

22. Saint Teresa of Avila, *Meditations on the Song of Songs* 1.7, vol. 2:218–19.

23. Saint Teresa of Avila, *Meditations on the Song of Songs* 1.10, vol. 2:220–21.

24. Johannes Tauler, *Sermons*, trans. Maria Shrady, introduction by Josef Schmidt, preface by Alois Haas, The Classics of Western Spirituality (New York: Paulist Press, 1985): 150–51.

25. [In fact, the entire verse from the Qurʾan suggests this: "Who is better in religion than he who surrenders his purpose to Allah while doing good (to men) and follows the tradition of Abraham, the upright? Allah (Himself) chose Abraham for friend."]

26. Margaret Smith, *Rābiʿa the mystic & her fellow-saints in Islam; being the life and teachings of Rābiʿa al-ʿAdawiyya al-Qaysiyya of Baṣra together with some account of the place of the women saints in Islam* (Cambridge, England: The University Press, 1928 [1984]).

27. Chapter 53.

28. The *Diwān al-ʿāshiqīn* by Muhammad b. Ziyād (died around 845); the *Kitāb al-Zahra* (Book of the Flower) by Ibn Dāwūd (died in 907); the *Kitāb al-Ẓarf waʾl-Ẓurafā* (The Book of the Refinement of the Refined, which also bears

the title of *Kitāb al-Muwashshā*, or Book of the Work of Embroidery) by Ibn Isḥāq al-Washshā (died around 936); the *Ṭawq al-Ḥamāna* of Ibn Ḥazm (died in 1064); *Maṣāriᶜ al-ᶜushshāq* (The Arenas of Lovers) by al-Sarraj (died in 1106), and finally though much later *Tazyīn al-aswāq fi tartīb ashwāq al-ᶜushshāq* (On the Hierarchy of Lovers' Burning Desires).

29. Barthelemy d'Herbelot, *Bibliothèque orientale, ou Dictionnaire universel, contenant generalement tout ce qui regarde la connaissance des peuples de l'Orient . . .* (Paris: Compagnie des Libraires, 1697).

30. Saint Teresa of Avila, *The Way of Perfection* 6.3, 5, 8–9, in *The Collected Works of St. Teresa of Avila*, 2:62–65.

31. Louis Massignon, *The Passion of al-Hallāj: Mystic and Martyr of Islam*, trans. with a biographical forward by Herbert Mason, Bollingen Series no. 98 (Princeton, N.J.: Princeton University Press, 1982), 1:81.

32. *Akhbar al-Hallaj: recueil d'oraisons et d'exhortations du martyr mystique de l'Islam Husayn Ibn Mansur Hallaj. Mis en ordre vers 360/971 chez Nasrabadhi et deux fois remanie publie, annoteet traduit par Louis Massignon et Paul Kraus*, 2nd ed. reconstructed and completed by Louis Massignon (Paris: Libr. Philosophique Vrin, 1975), 108.

33. *Akhbar al-Hallaj*, 111.

34. *Akhbar al-Hallaj*, 112.

35. *Akhbar al-Hallaj*, 112.

36. [Translated from the French.]

37. Cf. Massignon's translation in *Akhbar al-Hallaj*, 103, and in *The Passion of al-Hallāj*, 600.

38. *Akhbar al-Hallaj*, 105.

39. [English readers should consult William C. Chittick, *The Sufi Path of Knowledge: Ibn al-ᶜArabī's Metaphysics of Imagination* (Albany: State University of New York Press, 1989).]

CONCLUSION

1. Olivier Lacombe, *L'Absolu selon le Védānta: les notions de Brahman et d'Atman dans les systèmes de Çankara et Rāmānoudja* (Paris: Librairie Orientaliste Paul Geuthner, 1937), 6–7.

2. [English translation from Raimundo Panikkar, ed. and trans., *The Vedic Experience, Mantramañjarī: An Anthology of the Vedas for Modern Man and Contemporary Celebration* (Berkeley: University of California Press, 1977), 58.]

3. [*Ibid.*, 663–65.]

4. Louis Gardet and Olivier Lacombe, *L'Expérience du Soi* (Paris: 1981), 171.

5. Lacombe, *L'Absolu selon le Védānta*, 25.

6. Lacombe, *L'Absolu selon le Védānta*, 26.

7. Cf. Suzanne Siauve, introduction to *Aṣṭādaśabhedanirṇaya*, critical edition, ed. and trans. Suzanne Siauve (Pondichéry: Institut français d'indologie, 1978): 1.

8. Siauve, 6–7.

9. [Translated from the French. An alternate reading follows, from David White, trans., *The Bhagavad Gītā: A New Translation with Commentary*, American University Studies, Series VII, vol. 39 (New York: Peter Lang, 1988), 236: "Giving up all other duties (*dharmān*), come to Me as your one refuge: do not grieve—I will save you from all evils."]

10. [Translation is from Pannikar, *The Vedic Experience*, 710.]

11. Siauve, 10.

12. Guy Bugault, *La notion de "prajñā" ou de sapience selon les perspectives du "Mahāyāna"* (Paris: De Boccard, 1968), 32.

13. Bugault, 62.

14. Bugault, 151. [Cf. Paul J. Griffiths, *On Being Mindless: Buddhist Meditation and the Mind-Body Problem* (La Salle, Ill.: Open Court, 1986).]

15. Bugault, 179.

16. Michel Hulin, *Le Principe de l'Ego dans la pensée indienne classique: la notion d'Ahamkāra* (Paris: 1978), 357.

17. Hulin, 208ff.

18. Martin Buber, *I and Thou*, trans. Ronald Gregor Smith (Edinburgh: T. & T. Clark, 1937), 39.

19. Buber, 78.

20. Buber, 79.

SELECTED BIBLIOGRAPHY

al-Hallaj, al Husayn ibn Mansur. *Akhbar al-Hallaj: recueil d'oraisons et d'exhortations du martyr mystique de l'Islam Husayn Ibn Mansur Hallaj. Mis en ordre vers 360/971 chez Nasrabadhi et deux fois remanie publie, annote et traduit par Louis Massignon et Paul Kraus.* Reconstructed and completed by Louis Massignon. 2d ed. Paris: Libr. Philosophique Vrin, 1975.

Augustine, Saint. *The Confessions of St. Augustine.* Translated by John K. Ryan. New York: Doubleday, An Image Book, 1960.

———. *The Lord's Sermon on the Mount.* Translated by John J. Jepson. Ancient Christian Writers: The Works of the Fathers in Translation, no. 5. Westminster, Md.: The Newman Press, 1948.

Bréhier, Emile. *The History of Philosophy.* Vol. 2. *The Hellenistic and Roman Age.* Translated by Wade Baskin. Chicago: University of Chicago Press, 1965.

Buber, Martin. *Die chassidischen Bücher.* Hellerau: Verlag von Jakob Hegner, 1928.

———. *Hasidism and Modern Man.* Edited and translated by Maurice Friedman. New York: Horizon Press, 1958.

———. *I and Thou.* Translated by Ronald Gregor Smith. Edinburgh: T. & T. Clark, 1937.

———. *The Legend of Baal-Shem.* Translated by Maurice Friedman. New York: Harper & Brothers, 1955.

Bugault, Guy. *La Notion de "prajñā" ou de sapience selon les perspectives du "Mahāyāna".* Paris: De Boccard, 1968.

Chittick, William C. *The Sufi Path of Knowledge: Ibn Al-ʿArabī's Metaphysics of Imagination.* Albany, N.Y.: State University of New York Press, 1989.

Eckhart, Meister. *Meister Eckhart: German Sermons & Treatises.* Translated and edited by Maurice O'C. Walshe. 3 vols. London: Watkins, 1979.

———. *Meister Eckhart: The Essential Sermons, Commentaries, Treatises, and Defense.* Translated with an introduction by Edmund Colledge and Bernard McGinn. With a preface by Huston Smith. The Classics of Western Spirituality. New York: Paulist Press, 1981.

Gardet, Louis, and Olivier Lacombe. *L'Expérience du Soi.* Paris: Desclée, 1981.

Griffiths, Paul J. *On Being Mindless: Buddhist Meditation and the Mind-Body Problem.* La Salle, Ill.: Open Court, 1986.

Herbelot, Barthelemy d'. *Bibliothèque orientale, ou dictionnaire universel, contenant generalement tout ce qui regarde la connaissance des peuples de l'Orient. . . .* Paris: Compagnie des Libraires, 1697.

Hulin, Michel. *Le Principe de l'Ego dans la pensée indienne classique: la notion d'Ahaṃkāra.* Paris, 1978.

John of the Cross, Saint. *The Living Flame of Love.* In *The Collected Works of St. John of the Cross,* translated by Kieran Kavanaugh and Otilio Rodriguez, 567–649. Garden City, N.Y.: Doubleday & Co., 1964.

———. *The Dark Night.* In *The Collected Works of St. John of the Cross,* translated by Kieran Kavanaugh and Otilio Rodriguez, 293–389. Garden City, N.Y.: Doubleday & Co., 1964.

———. *The Spiritual Canticle.* In *The Collected Works of St. John of the Cross,* translated by Kieran Kavanaugh and Otilio Rodriguez, 391–565. Garden City, N.Y.: Doubleday & Co., 1964.

Kraemer, Joel L. *Philosophy in the Renaissance of Islam: Abū Sulaymān Al-Sijistānī and His Circle.* Studies in Islamic Culture and History series, vol. 8. Leiden: E. J. Brill, 1986.

Lacombe, Olivier. *L'Absolu selon le Védānta: les notions de Brahman et d'Atman dans les systèmes de Çankara et Rāmānoudja.* Paris: Librairie Orientaliste Paul Geuthner, 1937.

Leon-Dufour, Xavier. *Dictionary of Biblical Theology.* Translation of *Vocabulaire de Théologie Biblique.* Translated under the direction of Joseph Cahill. New York: Desclee Co., 1967.

Massignon, Louis. *Essay on the Origins of the Technical Language of Islamic Mysticism,* Translated by Benjamin Clark. Notre Dame, Ind.: University of Notre Dame Press, 1995.

———. *The Passion of Al-Hallāj: Mystic and Martyr of Islam.* Translated with a biographical foreword by Herbert Mason. Bollingen series, no. 98. Princeton, N.J.: Princeton University Press, 1982.

Michon, Jean-Louis. *Le soufi marocain Aḥmad Ibn Ajība (1746–1809) et son Miʿrāj: glossaire de la mystique musulmane.* Etudes musulmanes, no. 14. Paris: J. Vrin, 1973.

Panikkar, Raimundo, ed. and trans. *The Vedic Experience, Mantramañjarī: An Anthology of the Vedas for Modern Man and Contemporary Celebration.* Berkeley: University of California Press, 1977.

Paquda, Bahya Ibn. *Introduction aux devoirs des coeurs.* Translated and edited by André Chouraqui. With an introduction by J. Maritain. Paris, 1950.

Philo [of Alexandria]. *Philo.* Vol. 7–8. *De Specialibus Legibus* [On the Special Laws]. Translated by F. H. Colson. The Loeb Classical Library. Cambridge, Mass., and London: Harvard University Press; William Heinemann Ltd., 1938.

Plato. *Gorgias.* Translated by Terence Irwin. Clarendon Plato Series. Oxford: Oxford University Press, Clarendon, 1979.

Plotinus. *Ennéades.* Translated and edited by Emile Bréhier. 6 vols. Collection des universités de France. Paris: Societe D'Edition "Les Belles Lettres," 1924–38.

———. *The Enneads.* Translated by Stephen MacKenna. Edition no. 3 revised by B. S. Page. With an introduction by Paul Henry. London: Faber and Faber Limited, 1962.

Pseudo-Dionysius, *The Celestial Hierarchy.* In *Pseudo-Dionysius: The Complete Works.* Translated by Colm Luibheid. Foreword, notes, and translation collaboration by Paul Rorem. With a preface by René Roques. Introductions by Jaroslav Pelikan, Jean Leclercq, and Karlfried Froehlich, 143–91. The Classics of Western Spirituality. New York: Paulist Press, 1987.

Scholem, Gershom. *The Messianic Idea in Judaism, and Other Essays on Jewish Spirituality.* New York: Schocken Books, 1971.

———. *Origins of the Kabbalah.* Edited by R. J. Zwi Werblowsky. Translated by Allan Arkush. Princeton: The Jewish Publication Society, Princeton University Press, 1987 [1962].

Scholem, Gershom G. *Major Trends in Jewish Mysticism.* 3d ed. New York: Schocken Books, 1954 [1941].

Siauve, Suzanne, ed. and trans. *Aṣṭādaśabhedanirṇaya.* Critical Edition, Translation and Notes. Pondichéry: Institut Français D'indologie, 1978.

Smith, Margaret. *Rābiʿa the Mystic & Her Fellow-Saints in Islam; Being the Life and Teachings of Rābiʿa Al-ʿAdawiyya Al-Qaysiyya of Baṣra together with Some Account of the Place of the Women Saints in Islam.* Cambridge, England: The University Press, 1928 [1984].

Tauler, Johannes. *Sermons.* Translated by Maria Shrady. With an introduction by Josef Schmidt. With a preface by Alois Haas. The Classics of Western Spirituality. New York: Paulist Press, 1985.

Teresa of Avila, Saint. *The Collected Works of St. Teresa of Avila.* Translated by Kieran Kavanaugh and Otilio Rodriguez. Washington, D.C.: Institute of Carmelite Studies, 1976– .

———. *The Letters of Saint Teresa of Jesus.* Translated and edited by E. Allison Peers. From the critical edition of P. Silverio de Santa Teresa. 2 vols. Westminster, Md.: The Newman Press [1950].

Vajda, Georges. *L'Amour de Dieu dans la théologie juive du Moyen Age.* Etudes de philosophie medievale, no. 46. Paris: J. Vrin, 1957.

White, David. *The Bhagavad Gītā: A New Translation with Commentary.* American University Studies. New York: Peter Lang, 1988.

ANNOTATED LIST OF AUTHORS CITED

Abraham b. Ezra. Jewish thinker of the twelfth century (1092–1167), under the double influence of rabbinic teaching and neoplatonism. For him the heart is the primary vehicle of the rational soul. It is the organ of rational knowledge (*daʿat*). The "great mystery" is the return of the sensible heart-soul to its source, which is to say, adhering to God. He also emphasized communion with God (*dĕbequt*).

Abūʾl-Barakāt al Baghdādī. Philosopher and scientist of Jewish origin who converted to Islam. He translated his name Nathanael as Hibat Allah (Gift of God). Born in the region of Mossul around 470/1077, moved to Baghdad after 560/1165. To Avicenna's system he offered numerous modifications in his *Kitāb al-Muʿtabar* [Book of what can be established through personal reflection], much of which is copied from the *Kitāb al-Shifaʾ*. In particular he thought that each human soul is a single species, in other words, that it differs specifically from all others. He also wrote a commentary on Ecclesiastes. His work exerted a great influence on Fakhr al-Dīn al-Rāzī.

Abūl-Faraj al Iṣfahānī (or Iṣbahānī). Historian, poet and Arab literary figure, born in Isfahan in 284/897, died in Baghdad in 356/967. He was Shiʾite and was favored by the Būyides. He was equally well-received by Aleppo, at the court of Sayf al-Dawla. He is famous for an extensive work, which comes to twenty volumes in the Būlāq edition (1868), the *Book of Songs* (*Kitāb al-Aghānī*). He collected the songs which, upon the order of the caliph Hārūn al-Rashid, had been chosen by the most famous musicians of the era, such as Ibrahīm al-Mawṣilī. He added notations on the Arab poets, cited numerous verses, and gave important information on tribes, customs, and ways of life. Finally he related a great number of anecdotes on the poets and their company: caliphs, vizirs, governors. *ʿUdhrī* love poetry held an important place in this work.

Abūʾl-Shīs. Arab poet, died around 200/915. He lived in the court of Hārūn al-Rashid. He wrote panegryrices and funeral prayers, poems, and bachic songs. Although he was not very original, his elegies on the afflictions of old age, composed toward the end of his life, express personal sentiments that are quite profound.

al-Anṭakī (Dāwūd b. ᶜUmar al-Ḍarīr). Arab physician born in Antioch. Having learned Greek, he studied the original texts o medical science. He died in Mecca in 1008/1599. As questions concerning love had always been considered dependent on medicine, he summarized the work of Muhammad al-Sarrāj (who died in 500/1106), to which he gave the title *Tazyīn al-aswāq fi tartīb ashwāq al-ᶜushshāq*. The work brings together numerous anecdotes, often legendary, on the history of famous lovers.

ᶜAṭṭar (Farīd al-Din Muhammad b. Ibrāhīm). Persian mystical poet. His date of birth is not known exactly. He died in 586/1190. His most famous poem is *The Colloquy of the Birds* (*Manṭiq al-Ṭayr*). The birds, led by the hoopoe (cf. the role of the hoopoe in the qurʾanic story of Solomon and the queen of Sheba in sūrah 27, "The Ant," verse 20 and following), leave in search of Sīmurgh, whom they have chosen as king. All perish en route, except for thirty who in the end recognize divinity in themselves. In Persian, *sī* means thirty, and *murgh*, bird. Thus the *sī murgh*, thirty birds, are identified as Sīmurgh. They are submerged in divine reality by *fanāʾ*. *ᶜAṭṭar* is also the author of a poem in twelve songs, *The Divine Book* (*Ilāhī-nāmā*): a king asks six of his sons what they wish for most in the world. They experience every worldly desire. Their father seeks to inspire in them a sense for the very highest of spiritual values.

Augustine (Saint). Latin Church Father, born in Numibia in 354, famous for his conversion to Christian orthodoxy and known above all through his *Confessions* and his book on *The City of God*. He struggled against the Donatists, the Pelagians, and above all the Manichaeans whose opinions he had shared. In 391 he was consecrated bishop of Hippo. Against Pelagius he emphasized divine grace, for which he is surnamed "doctor of Grace." (See *On Grace and Free Will*.) He made numerous commentaries on the scriptures, wrote the *Soliloquies*, where he discusses relations of love for God, and the *Retractations*, where he judges his works and the errors of his youth. In philosophy he follows Plato. He is at the root of a theology called Augustinian, which had an enormous influence on the thought of Christian mystics of the West and in which the doctrine of the love of God and of knowledge through intellectual intuition plays a preponderant role.

Baᶜal Shem Tov or **Baᶜal Shem:** Master of the Divine Name—a title given, especially in the works of kabbalah and Hassidism, to those who possess secret knowledge of the Name of God expressed by the tetragrammaton YHWH. The founder of modern Hassidism whose true name was Israel b. Eliezer is the best known of all who have borne this title. He lived from 1700 to 1760. He was born in Podolia, a region in western Ukraine, of poor parents, in an era troubled by wars. At twenty he withdrew to the Carpathians, where he prepared for his future task. There he engaged in various crafts in order to live and sustain his family. His renown as a healer and spiritual guide spread. Prayer was his principle means of ecstatic approach to God. He taught that every Jew is a member of the *Shekhinah*. As long as a member remains attached to the body, it can be saved. If it is separated from it, it is impossible to reintegrate. He emphasized the importance of charity. For him spiritual joy in devotion is the proper sentiment for a Jew in every moment of life, but especially in prayer. Against asceticism and the multiplication of fasts that engender melancholy and sadness, he believed that communion with God (*dĕbequt*) does not require retreat from the world. Every action done in the service of God is accomplished in a state of communion. According to him, the salvation of the individual soul precedes the redemption of the world, and his insistence on personal destiny replaces the messianic perspectives that made the final restoration of humanity depend on the coming of the Messiah. On the contrary, the Messiah will come when all human beings become capable of experiencing spiritual ascension.

Bahya b. Paquda. Jewish mystic of Spain who lived in the eleventh century. André Chouraqui describes his subject as a "conversion to the mystery of the hidden life." He lived out his work on *Duties of the Heart* before writing it. He was a "master who initiates his disciples in the depths of the interior life which is entirely love." He presupposed that "exterior knowledge" is spread among the doctors. "The interior way is for Bahya, as for the ascetics and mystics of Islam and Christianity, the theory of relations between the human being and God" (Chouraqui). Pure morality is, in his work, secondary. Long before Ghazālī, with whom he is compared, his thought had been influenced, to a certain degree, by the Muslim Sufis.

Bīrūnī (Abū'l-Rayḥān Muhammad b. Aḥmad al-). One of the greatest scientists of medieval Islam, especially well-known as a mathematician, astronomer, and mineralogist. He was born in 362/973 in a suburb of Kāth in the Khwārizm (delta of the Amū-Daryā), from a poor family of artisans. His life of adventure brought him to India; his knowledge of Sanscrit allowed him to acquire an extensive acquaintance with Indian thought which, nevertheless, he did not grasp in all its complexity. In his work on India (*Kitāb al-Hind*), he set out, among other subjects, the religious and philosophical beliefs of that country, which he understood from a Muslim point of view. He tended to render notions which were quite distant from his own in terms of Islamic theology. In this sense he is a witness of the first order to the reaction of a "Western" mind to Indian thought. On the other hand, his fundamentally scientific mind, for which mathematical language is the only language of science, leads him to criticize the Sanscrit language severely, for its profuse vocabulary more readily conveys myths than it describes from reality. He is opposed to all mysticism, especially when the values and mystical conceptions which for him are "mythical" invade domains of objective knowledge, as is the case in India. He died around 442/1050, probably in Ghazna.

Bisṭāmī (Abū Yazīd al-). One of the most curious mystics of Islam. He spent his life in Bisṭām in the Khurāsān, and died there in 234/857 or 261/874. He wrote nothing, but his maxims were collected and transmitted by those surrounding him. His spiritual master in Sufism was a mystic who did not know the Arabic language, Abū ᶜAlī al-Sindi, but H. Ritter can only say, "it is not impossible that Indian influences may have affected Abû Yazîd through him" (*Encyclopedia of Islam*, 2nd edition, I:162, col. 2). Bisṭāmī had a very advanced sense of divine majesty, and he never ceased in his "travail" to let loose the veils (*ḥujūb*) that separated him from God. "I was my own blacksmith" (*ḥaddād nafsī*). Not only the world, but renunciation of the world, the recollection of God (*dhikr*), and mystic states generally were to his eyes obstacles inasmuch as they are things human which separate one from God. When he thought he had annihilated his Self through *fanāʾ*, "as serpents strip off their own skin," he expressed his transmutation in formulas (*shaṭaḥāt*, "theopathic locutions") such as: "Glory to Me! How great is My situation!" or "I am the Throne [*ᶜarsh*] and the stool (*kursī*); I am the well-kept Table [*al-Lawḥ al-Maḥfūz*]; I have seen the Kaᶜba turn around Me" (whereas it is the pilgrim who makes the trip [*ṭawāf*] around the Kaᶜba). He considered paradise to be a ruse by which God kept the faithful far away from his mystery, filled with delights that are something other than God's own self. All that is not God is illusion. (Cf. L. Gardet, *Expériences mystiques en terres non chrétiennes*, Paris, ch. II, part 3, "Bisṭamī et l'ascèse du vide," pp. 115–30).

Bonaventure (Saint). John Fidanza of Tuscany, "the seraphic doctor" (1221–1274), was the thirteenth century's most eminent representative of the Franciscan school. One of his later works, *The Mind's Journey to God* (*Itinerarium mentis in Deum*), expresses the basics of his doctrine. Concerning the seraphim of Isaiah's vision (6:2), he writes: "Through these six wings, one can adequately understand the six illuminations that sustain the vision and thanks to which the soul is disposed, through stages and journeys, to negotiate its passage to the peace of Christian wisdom through ecstatic transports." Thus, the image of the six seraphic wings suggests the six steps of illumination which begin by way of creatures and lead to God, into whose presence no one is allowed, except through the Crucified One." No one can become one of the blessed, unless one is lifted outside of oneself, "not through bodily elevation, but through an elevation of heart" (*non ascensu corporali, sed cordiali*). Thus, persons need a higher power to elevate them, and that power is the grace of God. Six faculties, corresponding to the six wings placed two-by-two, define three stages in the knowledge of God: the sense and the imagination which allow one to grasp the traces (*vestigia*) of God in creatures external to oneself; reason and intellect which allow one to grasp within oneself and in itself (*intra se et in se*) the image (*imago*) of God; intelligence and the very tip of the soul (*apex mentis*) which is compared to a spark, through which one is elevated beyond oneself (*supra se*) in order to enjoy the sovereign God which is God. The three levels of the human being are therefore the sensible soul (*anima*), the spirit (*spiritus*) and the mind (*mens*). One cannot reach the final level of oneself without prayer (*oratio*) carried out with humility and devotion (*humiliter et devote*) and proceeding from the heart (*ex corde*). Furthermore, creatures cannot be reduced to mere "things": they are "signs" through which one can arrive at contemplation of God and at love of the Creator.

Daqqāq (Abū ᶜAlī al-). Muslim mystic, spiritual master and father-in-law of Qushayrī.

Dārānī (Abū Sulaymān). Muslim mystic who died in 214/830. He was influential in Syria. For him, the mystic journey was a gradation of divine favors adorning the soul. His point of view is the source of the later doctrine of "stages" (*maqāmāt*) which mark the mystic ascension.

Dionysius the Areopagite (Pseudo-Dionysius). Dionysius the Areopagite, converted by Saint Paul, was later held to be the first bishop of Athens. In the fifth or sixth century various writings from the pen of neoplatonic Christians were published under his name. They are *The Celestial Hierarchy, The Ecclesiastical Hierarchy, The Divine Names,* and *Mystical Theology.* These works, in a very obscure symbolic language, were the subject of frequent commentaries by Latin thinkers of the Middle Ages, and exerted a profound influence on the expression of mystical ideas. The *Commentary on the Divine Names* by Saint Thomas Aquinas is one of the most famous. The principle theme of this line of thinking is that of the ascension of the soul according to the negative path (*via negativa*) through the stripping off of sensible impressions, intimate thoughts, and reasonings, until one arrives at "the cloud of unknowing" or is illuminated by "a ray of the divine shadow," beyond all light and beyond being.

Ezra b. Salomon of Gerona. Disciple of Isaac the Blind with whom he was trained in kabbalah at Porquières, near Lunel. Ezra was one of the spiritual masters of the circle of Gerona in the 13th century. He wrote a *Commentary on the Song of Songs.* Among his other works are *The Mystery of the Tree of Knowledge* (*sôd ᶜēṣ daᶜat*) and the *Commentary on Stories of the Talmud* (*pêrûš hā-ʾaggādôt*). The notion of "nothingness" is important in his thought. Job 28:12, "But where does Wisdom come from?" is interpreted to mean it comes from nothingness, the nothingness of thought, "the place where all thought ceases, or rather, where it becomes the divine thought itself" (G. Scholem, *Origins of the Kabbalah* p. 259). In this sense, *dĕbeqût* is presented as a communion with nothingness, for God is beyond all human thought: there is there an "ungraspable" which is identified with the first *sĕpîrâ*.

Ghazālı (Abū Ḥāmid al-). Great theologian and mystic of Islam who lived in the East in the eleventh century (450/1058–505/1111). He is famous for his work *Al-Munqidh min al-Ḍalāl* [The book that guards against error], where he makes a place for doubt (*shakk*) in the quest for God and where he discovers beyond rational intelligence a faculty of intuition that is at work in mystical knowing. He is author of *Iḥyāʾ ʿUlūm al-Din* [Revival of the sciences and of religion] of which the fourth part is designated as *taṣawwuf* (mysticism). He both expounded the philosophy of the Avicenna in *Maqāṣid al-Falāsifa* [The goals of the philosophers] and critiqued it in *Tahāfut al-Falāsifa* [The incoherence of the philosophers]. In theology, he proposed a doctrine of the happy medium, according to the ideas of the Ashʿarite school, between what was considered overly rationalistic in the theses of the Muʿtazilite school, and overly literalistic in the schools that refused to apply any figurative meaning to the anthropomorphic expressions of the Qurʾan. In this spirit he wrote his *Iqtiṣād fiʾl-Iʿtiqād* [The happy medium in belief]. He also attacked the esoteric Gnostics (*al-Bāṭiniyya*).

Ḥallāj (Abū Manṣūr b. Ḥusayn al-). Born in southern Iran around 244/858, he was from a Zoroastrian family. His father converted to Islam. At a young age Ḥallāj felt attracted to the mystical life. He was a "novice" (*murīd*) under a great spiritual master, Sahl al-Tustarī. Later, in Baghdad, he related to various Sufis. He made a pilgrimage in 895. His preaching, through which he sought to touch all people, attracted the hostility of those mystics who did not allow the "secret" to be divulged. His doctrine of spiritual pilgrimage also created conflicts, for although it did not supercede the *ḥajj* to Mecca, it speaks of a mystical Kaʿba. He either introduced or at least generalized the usage of the word *ʿishq* as employed in secular poetry to designate erotic passion. He is the greatest representative of "testimonial monism," as L. Massignon expressed it: God makes the mystic into a free and living organ in order to proclaim His unicity. The Qurʾan, as eternal Word of God, enunciates the formula of *tawḥid*: "There is nothing divine except God," by addressing itself to a humanity (*al-Nāsūt*) which is also the primordial witness to divine unity. But human beings who recite this formula with their lips, or even meditate on it in their heart, are only imperfect witnesses. The ecstatic who is moved by love (*ʿishq*), or as Massignon translates, by essential desire for God, is united to God as part of the primordial *Nāsūt* which recounts the Word of *tawḥīd* through testimony that is authentic because it is identified with that Word. Whence the famous theopathic locution (*shaṭḥ*): "I am God" (*Anāʾl-Ḥaqq*), or "I am the creative Truth." After two arrests and a long legal process, *Ḥallāj* was condemned to death. He was whipped, mutilated, hung from a gallows, and finally beheaded. His body was cremated and his ashes were thrown into the Tigris River in 922 C.E.

Ḥusayn b. ʿAli. Grandson of the prophet Muhammad, son of Fāṭima and of the caliph ʿAlī., he was the third *imān* of the Shiʾites, after his father and his brother Ḥasan. He was killed in the battle of Karbalāʾ in 61/860. His partisans, reproaching themselves for not having defended him adequately during the attempted insurrection against the Umayyad, formed a group of "penitents" (*al-Tawwābūn*). Ḥusayn is considered a martyr by the Shiʾites. His death under atrocious conditions became a theme for meditation and led Shiʾite thinkers to reflect on the value and on the meaning of suffering. Several *ḥadīth* with moral and religious themes are attributed to Ḥusayn.

Ibn ʿAbbās. One of the greatest scientists of the first generation of Muslims, he is the founder of qurʾanic exegesis. Born three years before the *hijra*, he died in 68/687. He is one of the authorities most often cited by commentators on the Qurʾan.

Ibn al-ʿArabī (Muḥyīʾl-Dīn). One of the most important mystics of Islam, called "the greatest Master" (*al-Shaykh al-Akbar*). Born in Murcia in 560/1165, he traveled and lived in the East. He died in Damascus in 638/1240. His doctrine, which owes much to neoplatonism and resembles gnostic systems, rests upon a symbolic interpretation of the Qurʾan. It constitutes a vision of the universe based on the idea that each being is an epiphanic manifestation of God, and is created upon the pattern of divine names. The essence of God remains hidden in its absolute unity. But through God's names and attributes, God is revealed as the Truth (*al-Ḥaqq*) who gives to each created being (*khalq*) the just measure of what it should be. Each creature has a nature composed of matter and form. But God causes a light to shine (*ishrāq*) on it which gives it meaning and value, through which God is manifest. Ibn al-ʿArabī calls that deep meaning of each creature an "angel." To recover one's angel, in union with all other angels who experience God, is the goal of the "journey" toward God and the "journey" in God.

Ibn ʿAṭāʾ. Muslim mystic of the third/ninth century, a faithful disciple of Ḥallāj in whose favor he testified throughout his legal process. Died in 309/922. He said: "Reason is only an instrument for the worship of God [*ʿibāda*]. No one can use it to approach His Lordship." God is knowable through God's creative work. But God makes Himself known to the souls of the elect through God's Word and God's attributes. Finally, to the prophets, God makes Himself known through Himself. Ibn ʿAṭāʾ is a mystic of love, like Ḥallāj. "When the desire of Love is purified and perfect, it lifts one up to that cistern of pure waters where God causes pure water to rain incessantly" (trans. G. Anawati and L. Gardet).

Ibn Bājja (Avempace). Famous philosopher of Spain who lived in the sixth/twelfth century. His *Risālat al-Ittiṣāl* [Epistle of Conjunction] and his *Tadbīr al-Mutawaḥḥīd* [Regimen of the Solitary] are among his most important works. One should isolate oneself from imperfect societies in order to be lifted up to the state of "Blessedness" (*al-suᶜadāʾ*) which is obtained when the human intellect comprehends the intelligibility of its own being. The thought of Ibn Bājja is the least religious of all Islamic philosophy. He himself criticized the mystics. Nevertheless, his views concerning the beatitude of which human beings are capable can take on a high spiritual value in the eyes of a believer.

Ibn Dāwūd. Ẓahirite jurist (one who holds to the apparent meaning of texts), he is especially famous for the work he composed concerning love, the *Kitāb al-Zahra* [Book of the flower, or of Venus]. The first part, edited by Nykl, is a collection of verses that are intended to illustrate a set of themes related to love, leading, in the psychology of lovers, to requisite duties. The work has no religious character whatsoever, but it prompted lively reactions among believers who read it. Besides its documentary value, it is interesting in this sense. L. Massignon, who saw in Ibn Dāwūd one of the initiators of "courtly" ideas, used him to define, by way of contrast, the ḥallajian doctrine of love.

Ibn Abī Ḥajala. Arabic poet and prose writer born in Tilimsān 725/1325. He traveled in the East, made the pilgrimage, returned to Cairo and Damascus and became the superior of a Sufi monastery in the region of Cairo. He was not especially interested in writing mystical works, but he wrote ten poems (*qaṣīda*) in honor of the Prophet. The most important of his edited books is the *Dīwān al-Ṣabāba* (Collection of Amorous tenderness), where he uses materials furnished by previous and contemporary authors, such as Ibn al-Aᶜrabī (*Dīwān al-ᶜAshiqīn*, a collection concerning lovers) and Ibn Dāwūd.

Ibn al-Jawzī. Prolific Arab writer, ḥanafite jurisprudent traditionalist, historian, and preacher, born in Baghdad in 510/1116. He wrote an important study of heresy in his *Talbīs Iblīs*, where in particular he critiqued the mystics and refuted Ḥallaj. He died in 597/1200 in Baghdad.

Ibn Muṭayr al-Asadī. Arab poet of the second/eighth century. His life is not well known. He seems to have traveled throughout Arabia and sojourned in Yemen. Certain passages that are extant treat erotic themes in the style of the pre-Islamic poets.

Ibn Sīna (Avicenna). Disciple of Fārābī and one of the greatest philosophers of Islam. His doctrine is inspired by neoplatonism. God is the Being whose existence is necessary (*wājib al-wujūd*) and who gives all possibilities of existing. Beings emanate from God by means of a procession that, by means of the intellects of the celestial spheres (called angels), reaches the Agent Intellect, from which no other intellect proceeds, but which gives form to material beings in the sublunar world, and then elementary forms, and finally the human form. Human beings are capable of receiving the light of the Agent Intellect and of being elevated by the return to God of which the Qur᾿an speaks. Thus Avicennian thought opens out toward a mysticism. (On this point, cf. Louis Gardet, *La Pensée religieuse d'Avicenne*, Paris, 1951.) Avicenna, born in Afshana, near Bukhārā in 370/980, died in Hamadān in 428/1037.

Ibn ᶜUyayna (Sufyān). One of the great Sunni traditionalists and a jurist of the school of Hejaz. He died in 198/814.

Isaac the Blind. Born around 1165; died in 1232 or 36. One of the oldest representatives of Kabbalistic mysticism. He was surnamed *saggî-nĕhôr*: power in light. From a family of Kabbalists, he lived in Porquières or in Narbonne and was at the center of the Kabbalism in Provence. His influence was considerable; his pupils promulgated and developed his ideas. Certain fragments of this spiritual master cite the *Bahir* book, which has wrongly been attributed to him but which was considered in this milieu as a truly authentic source. There are elements in this book that clearly originate before the twelfth century. The God of Bahir is the God of gnosticism, "the God who wove his powers into the cosmic tree of the worlds, from which all being proceeds and develops" (G. Scholem, *Origins of the Kabbalah*, p. 67). He is a God whose "plentitude" (*mālē᾿*) is benediction (*bĕrākâ*). Inspired by these ideas, the doctrine of Isaac is innovative and frankly symbolic. Elijah is said to have been revealed to him, after having been revealed to his father, Rabed, and to his grandfather Rabbi David. Thus he is called the "Third Elijah." The Kabbalist system of thought would thus be taught by the prophet Elijah. Isaac towers over all his contemporaries though his authority and the enduring influence that he exerts. Nevertheless, his style is obscure. He was a "master of prayer." Scholem wrote: "In his circle, a life of intense prayer is linked to the doctrine of *kawwanah.* Detailed instructions by Isaac concerning the meditations to be performed during the recitation of certain prayers have been preserved" (*ibid.*, p. 257).

Ismāᶜil Ḥaqqi al-Bursawī. Turkish commentator on the Qur᾿an; very influential by way of the mysticism of Ibn al-ᶜArabī, as well as through Persian thought and poetry. He died in 1127/1715.

Jacob Anatoli. Jewish physician, preacher, and philosopher who lived in the thirteenth century in the Jewish community of Narbonne. He traveled to Naples where he enjoyed the friendship of Emperor Frederick II. He translated Arabic works into Hebrew, in particular that of Ibn Rushd (Averroës). His philosophical homilies are collected in his book *malmād ha-talmîdîm* [Instruction for students]. He underscored his doctrine of the Love of God for those who love Him, and of the love of human beings for God. These two loves coexist. One should seek God with all the faculties of the soul subordinated to the rational soul, which is called the heart. But in order to find God, one must observe precepts which delineate this quest for God. That is why the lover of the Song of Songs says, "I have sought the One who loves my soul," then "I have searched and not found." The Torah is called "fire," according to the rabbinic interpretation of Jeremiah 23:29: "Is my word not like fire?" In fact "it incites the natural heat of love for God." Observance upholds faith, and "faith [*ᵓămānâ*] is the truth [*ᵓemûnâ*] solidly established. This intellectualist conception of faith leads therefore to an intellectual love of God.

Jalālayn: the two Jalāl. This is the name for the commentary on the Qurᵓan begun by Jalāl al-Dīn al-Maḥallī and completed by his disciple, the prolific Jalāl al-Din Suyūṭī, who lived from 849/1455 to 911/1505. It is a running commentary that inserts into the qurᵓanic text itself those explanations that are needed to understand it. It is particularly useful for determining the meaning of certain terms.

John of the Cross (Saint). Juan de Yepes y Alvarez, born in Fontiveros in 1542. He entered the Carmelite order in 1563, attended the university of Salamanca and was ordained in 1567. He participated, along with Saint Teresa, in the reform which led to the creation of the monasteries of Discalced Carmelites. John of the Cross, doctor of the Church, was one of the greatest Catholic mystics while also an exquisite poet. His principal works are poems for which he provides a commentary in prose. The most famous are *The Spiritual Canticle*, *The Dark Night of the Soul* and *The Living Flame of Love*. The influence of the Song of Songs on his meditation is considerable. He gives great importance to the purification of the senses and of the spirit (the image of the "dark night") and to the role of "nothing," *nada*, in the ascent toward mystical union. He died in 1591.

Jilānī or Jīlī (ᶜAbd al-Karīm al-). Originally from Baghdad, he traveled in India, which some believe left its mark on his mysticism. Max Horten (*Die Philosophie des Islam*, Munich, 1924) relates the image of the Perfect Man (*al-Insān al-Kāmil*) in the work of Jilānī which bears this title, to the *noētos anthrōpos* of Philo of Alexandria, and the Absolute Man (*al-Insān al-Muṭlaq*) of the Brothers of Purity, but also to the figure of the Buddha according to the philosophy of Mahāyāna (pp. 347–48, note 150). Yet this seems superficial and arbitrary; Jilānī is in the line of thought of Ibn al-ᶜArabī. The Perfect Man is the prototype of humanity, which provides the meaning of all creation. It is the projection of what Ibn ᶜArabī called "Muhammadan light" in which and through which all that comes to be exists as a manifestation of God. (Cf. William Chittick, *The Sufi Path of Knowledge* [Albany: SUNY Press, 1989]: 376–81.) Jilānī died in 832/1428.

Juda b. Samuel Halévi. Jewish philosopher and poet, born in Tudela in 1085. His poetry, marked by the canons of the Spanish school, takes a very personal turn in his *Songs of Zion*, which is inspired by his desire to emigrate to Palestine. Having finally decided to leave Spain and to make a pilgrimage to Jerusalem, he died en route in 1141. He is the author of the famous *sefer ha-kuzari*, written in Arabic around 1130 and translated into Hebrew by Juda b. Tibbon, a work that exerted great influence. He imagines a dialogue between a Jewish doctor and the king of the Khazars, a convert to Judaism. He teaches that no real communion can exist between human beings and God except through the intermediary of Israel's faith, linked to the practices of the revealed Law. "According to Halévi, all nations constitute an organism of which Israel is the heart, and hence must fulfill special duties and functions throughout the course of history" (G. Scholem, *Origins of the Kabbalah*, p. 88). Juda Halévi is famous for his doctrine of the "divine thing," (Arabic: *al-amr al-ilāhī*; Hebrew: *ʿinyān ʾĕlôhî*). The soul of Adam contained this "divine thing" which was at the same time "a supernatural gift and a human disposition" (G. Vajda, *L'Amour de Dieu*, p. 102). The prophetic gift was transmitted from the first man to the Jewish nation; it is a manifestation of the love of God for His elect, but it is only possessed through acts of the elect inspired by their love for God. The Law achieves an equilibrium between three states: fear (*yirʾa*), love (*ʾahăbâ*) and joy (*śimḥâ*). Through each of these, faithful persons can enter into relationship with their Lord. Living prayer is an encounter with God: "When I was going toward You, I found You coming toward me."

Junayd. A mystic of the third century after the *hijra*, born in Nihavand, died in Baghdad in 298/910. He was the *shaykh* of Ḥallāj. His doctrine rests on meditation of the "pre-eternal covenant," the *mīthāq*, in which God is recognized as the Lord of human beings, and which is considered a fundamental expression of God's love for humanity. In return, human beings should, through detachment from all things, accept the will of God and conform to it. This is what Junayd calls *al-fanāʾ biʾl-Madhkūr*, annihilation in the One who is present to memory (through *dhikr*). In this way a return to the origin is accomplished, a return to the condition which was that of the *mīthāq*. According to Junayd, love produces, "by a permutation with the qualities of those who love, a penetration of the qualities of the Beloved" (trans. G. Anawati). In this consists mystical union.

Jurjānī (ʿAlī b. Muhammad al-). Born in Iran in 740/1339, died in Shīrāz in 816/1413. He wrote on logic and grammar, and produced commentaries on theological-philosophical works. He is the author of a *Book of Definitions* (*Kitāb al-taʿrīfaṭ*).

Luria (Isaac b. Solomon Ashkenazi). Jewish mystic, founder of new kabbalah (1534–1572). He was born in Jerusalem of German parents. When still an infant he went to Egypt following the death of his father. At seventeen, already versed in rabbinic literature, he learned of a mystical manuscript and from it read about meditation. He lived in isolation for six years, studying works such as *The Book of the Zohar* while devoting himself entirely to asceticism. Around 1570 he settled down in Safed, in Palestine, which was a center of Kabbalist thought in the East. There he was soon surrounded by disciples, but he was to die of the plague in 1572. Three ideas, formulated like a dialectical movement, govern the cosmological and mystical system of Luria. 1) *Ṣimṣûm* (concentration, contraction, retreat) which is a "retreat by God." "According to Luria, God was compelled to make room for the world by, as it were, abandoning a region within Himself, a kind of mystical primordial space from which He withdrew in order to return to it in the act of creation and revelation." (G. Scholem, *Major Trends in Jewish Mysticism*, p. 261). The Primordial Man (*ʾādām qadmôn*) "is nothing but a first configuration of the divine light which flows from the esense of *En-Sof* into the primeval space of the *Tsimtsum* [*Ṣimṣûm*]. . . . He therefore is the first and highest form in which the divinity begins to manifest itself after the *Tsimtsum*" (*ibid.*, p. 265). 2) The "breaking of vases," which is a difficult idea to interpret. According to Scholem and Tishby, there would be, mixed with the light of the *sĕpîrôt*, before the breaking of vases, forces of evil called "shells" or "husks" (*qĕlîpôt*). The breaking of vases is a process of purification intended to eliminate these shells "in order to give a real existence and separate identity to the power of evil" (*ibid.*, p. 267). Thus evil emerges in a kingdom of its own. 3) *Tîqqûn* is the restoration of the unity of God with the help of human beings and the holiness of their lives.

Meister Eckhart. The foremost master of Rhineland mysticism. He was born near Goth around 1260, entered the Dominican order, and went to Paris to the monastery of Saint Jacques where he finished his theological studies. He obtained the degree of "Master" in 1302, and in 1304 became the provincial of his order in Saxony. From 1314 to 1322 he taught in Strasbourg. Then he became "lector" at Cologne and his fame as a preacher spread throughout Germany. But his mystical ideas drew suspicion as heresy and he was called before the archbishop of Cologne in 1326. He appealed to Pope John XXII. A trial was held in 1327 in Avignon, where he defended himself concerning the errors that were attributed to him yet which did not correspond to his actual thought. He died in 1328, and in 1329 a papal bull condemned twenty-eight of his propositions. Recent research shows that he was unjustly accused of pantheism and has worked to rehabilitate him by testifying to his orthodoxy, founded particularly on the writings of Saint Paul and Saint Augustine. His theology has many affinities to that of Thomas Aquinas, but he is also under the influence of Plato and pseudo-Dionysius.

Nahmanides (Moses b. Nahman). Jewish thinker of Spain born in Gerona in 1194, died in 1270. A disciple of Isaac the Blind, he was one of the medieval masters of talmudic literature and of kabbalah. Until his emigration to Palestine, he was the chief Rabbi of Catalonia. He described, in terms of kabbalah, the ascent of the soul through the worlds toward its homeland in higher spheres. He composed a commentary on the Torah replete with kabbalistic explanations, which itself became the object of commentaries. His uncontested authority did not allow doubt as to the orthodoxy of his ideas, which he presented "as the true mystery of Judaism" (G. Scholem, *Origins of the Kabbalah*, p. 385). He facilitated the admission of traditional kabbalist ideas into official rabbinical circles. His symbolism, which takes up an innovative tradition called "secret" (*sôd*), differs entirely from that of allegory, which presents philosophical ideas under the guise of religious concepts. In this it differs from the thought of Maimonides. Nahmanides does not see any contradiction between the unity of God, according to his incontestably Jewish monotheism, and the manifestions of the *sĕpîrôt* wherein each expresses one of the aspects under which the Glory of God (*kābôd*) is revealed, even to the divine Presence or *šĕkînâ*.

Nūrī. Muslim mystic of the Baghdad school; died in 295/907. Insistence on the relation between love and suffering characterizes his thought, to the point where he tended to love suffering for itself. He depicted ecstasy as a flame that is born, in the intimacy of being, from a passionate desire.

Qāshānī or Qāshī (ᶜAbd al-Razzāq al-). Sufi of the school of Ibn al-ᶜArabī, whose ideas he expounded and defended. His life is not well known. He probably died in 730/1329. He is the author of a large number of works, among which one must highlight his *Dictionary of Technical Terms of the Sufis* (*Iṣṭilāḥāt al-Ṣūfiyya*) and his *Commentary on the Qurʾan* (*Taʾwīlāt al-Qurʾān*), an explanation of the symbols hidden under its literal meaning, in the spirit of Ibn al-ᶜArabī.

Qurṭubī (Abū ᶜAbd Allāh Muḥammad al-). Famous commentator on the Qurʾan, originally from Cordova. He clearly identified the problems of exegesis, made an important place for philosophical explanation, and utilized the *ḥadīth* to determine the weight of judicial sentences. He traveled to the East and died in Minya in upper Egypt in 671/1273.

Qushayrī. Muslim mystic; died in 469/1074. He is the author of an *Epistle* (*Risāla*) which studies the different mystical states and relates them to their qurʾanic source, citing numerous spiritual authors. He sets out to show that Sufism agrees with Muslim doctrine and in particular with Ashᶜarite theology. We have borrowed numerous Sufi citations from the *Risāla*.

Rabbi Gamaliel. Jewish doctor of the first and second centuries C.E. He is the author of a famous prayer that invokes God in His unity within the different *sĕpîrôt*. He distinguishes a world of life above the world of nature, the world of the soul, and the world of intellect.

Rābiᶜa al-ᶜAdawīyya. Famous mystic from the early period of Islam who extolled pure gratuitous love. Once a flute player, she dedicated herself to meditation and lived apart from the world in Basra, where she died in 185/801.

Rāzī (Fakhr al-Dīn al-). Theologian, philosopher, jurist, and qurʾanic commentator, born in Rayy, near Tehran in 543/1149. He was one of the greatest and most accomplished minds in the history of Muslim thought. An Ashᶜarite theologian, he was a disciple of Ghazālī. But as a philosopher he turned toward Avicenna and refused to construct a harmonious synthesis of what he borrowed from these two conflicting masters. In his commentary on the Qurʾan, *Mafātiḥ al-Ghayb* [The keys of the invisible], he examined every aspect of each verse—philosophical, theological, juridical, historical—and laid great stress on mystical perspectives. He died in 606/1209.

Sarrāj (Jaᶜfar b. Aḥmad b. Ḥusayn al-). Born in Baghdad in 417/1026, he is the author of a collection dedicated to love, entitled *Maṣāriᶜ al-ᶜUshshāq* [The arenas of lovers]. He often borrowed from his predecessors and was in turn exploited by his successors. He died in Baghdad in 500/1106.

Suso (Blessed Henry). Born in Constance in 1295 or 1300, he attended the Studium Generale of Cologne together with Johannes Tauler. A Dominican, he does not have the speculative ardor of Master Eckhart, nor the pedagogical clarity of Tauler, but he surpasses them both in precision and profundity of feeling, qualities that permit him to express in a very lively style the doctrine of his masters, Saint Bernard, Saint Thomas Aquinas, and Eckhart. According to him, there is a "first conversion" which is realized through meditation on the mysteries of Christ; the Virgin Mary is also a guide along the path to God; the sufferings of this world bring participation in the suffering of the Son of God. Everything is summarized in three terms: *Entbildet werden von der Creatur, gebildet werden mit Christus, überbildet werden in die Gottheit* (to forsake the form proper to a creature, to be formed with Christ, to be transformed into Divinity). Suso died in 1366.

Tauler (Johannes). Born in Strasbourg around 1300, died in 1361. Tauler was a disciple of Master Eckhart, under whose direction he studied at the Studium Generale of Cologne. A Dominican, he became a preacher in Strasbourg. In Basel (1339–1343) he became the central figure among the "Friends of God." In 1346, he returned to Strasbourg where he directed a group of these "Friends of God." His doctrine synthesizes neoplatonic (pseudo-Dionysian), Augustinian and Thomistic elements in an original and coherent fashion. His doctrine of the purification of the senses and of the mind anticipates the teaching of John of the Cross. This brings renunciation of sensible awareness and of the will according to the practice of mortification. There are three levels to a human being: the sensible, the rational, and the spiritual. The "ground" of the soul is a passivity open to the action of God; the spirit (*Gemüt*) gives to human faculties the possibility of turning toward the infinite. There is only one way of ascent, passing through three stages: the purgative way, the illuminative way, and the unitive way. Tauler recommends sincerity, docility, and moderation. He denounces all forms of pharisaicism. He struggled against the "Brothers of the Free Spirit." This sect, which appeared around the middle of the thirteenth century, especially in the Rhineland, was condemned by the council of Vienna in 1312. Its adherents considered that human beings can attain to such a degree of perfection that they cannot sin. Once reaching this level, there is no longer any need for prayer and mortification; one may permit one's body whatever pleases it; one is no longer held to any human obedience and no longer need observe the precepts of the Church. Human beings can acquire this life of beatitude, because all intellectual nature is blessed in and of itself, and thus has no need for the light of grace. Tauler's struggle against these teachings brought his own position clearly into relief. Finally, we note that he was among those believers who defended Master Eckhart against those who accused him of heresy.

Tawḥīdī. (Abū Ḥayyān al-). One of the masters of Arabic prose in the fourth/tenth century in Baghdad. The place of his birth is not known for certain (Nīshāpūr, Shīrāz, Wāsiṭ, or Baghdad). He was probably born sometime between 310/922 and 320/932, and died at an advanced age around 400/1008. His work is an echo of the Arab culture of his time in Iraq. He engaged in continuous intrigue in order to carve out a place among the powerful, with varying degrees of success. Toward the end of his life, disgusted with men and with society, he burned his books and turned to meditation on religious values. He wrote the *Ishārāt al-Ilāhiyya* [The divine signs], a profoundly spiritual series of invocations. In theology, he always had great affinity for muʿtazilism, and was particularly attracted to the thesis that God only created existences, whereas essences, before existing, are what they are but in the state of nothingness (*fi ḥāl al-ʿadam*), so that once they have received existence they remain a pole of negativity in the creature. Tawhīdī draws from the doctrine the idea that human beings can strive to exist only by clinging entirely to God, the only One who can give them existence (*al-Mūjid*). When they cling instead to themselves — to their own essence — they turn towards nothingness.

Teresa de Cepeda, known by the name of *Teresa of Avila.* One of the greatest mystics of Christianity. She was born in Avila in 1515 and was raised in an Augustinian convent. At eighteen she was admitted into the Carmel of the Incarnation, where the rule was a relaxed one. Disappointed, she finally adjusted to a discipline that did not require a complete break with worldly attachments. In 1554, according to her own account, she experienced a "conversion." Despite the incomprehension of the religious who surrounded her, she abandoned herself to prayer. Her humility led her to submit to the direction of a spiritual director, who was then the provincial superior of the Jesuits. She had several other confessors and gave herself to a rule of perfect obedience. She was favored with numerous visions, yet never thought that they themselves constituted the goal or the summit of contemplative life. Her severity with respect to herself, her lucidity, indeed her sense of humor, make for an authentically human mysticism, without ever undermining the sublimity of her experience. The exceptional favors that she received from God did not distract her from a concern to serve her neighbor. Not only did she direct and sustain the religious who were in her charge, but she intervened in order to rectify religious or even secular situations concerning laity and priests. Despite violent opposition, she reformed the Carmelite order, acting together with John of the Cross. She reestablished the rule of the "Discalced Carmelites" in several convents, and crisscrossed Spain, with adventures of all sorts, in order to found new monasteries. Her account of these activities in her *Book of Foundations* makes for impassioned reading. No mysticism is able to hold action and contemplation together perfectly. Her work is of considerable interest, especially in what she recounts of her personal experience. *The Book of Her Life*, we should highlight *The Way of Perfection* and *The Interior Castle*, with its description of mystical mansions. She died in 1582 in the convent of Alba and was canonized by Gregory XV in 1621. She is a doctor of the Church.

Ṭūsī (Nāṣir al-Dīn al-). Shiʾite philosopher and theologian who died in 672/1273. He wrote a commentary on the *Ishārāt waʾl-Tanbīhāt* by Avicenna. M. A. Goichon, in her French translation of the *Ishārāt*, published under the title of *Directives et Remarques* (Beruit-Paris, 1951), has provided numerous passages from this commentary.

ʿUmar b. Abī Rabīʿa. Famous Arab poet who died around 100/719. He represents the urban poetry of the *ghazal* (erotic poetry). He earned a reputation for debauchery and many of his verses are lighthearted. He even had a sacrilegious side, insofar as he sought to seduce women making the pilgrimage to Mecca. Nevertheless, it seems he also knew true love, of which he sang in a moving fashion.

Washshāʾ (Abūʾl-Ṭayyib Muhammad b. Isḥāq al-). Arab writer and grammarian. Little is known about his life. He taught in an elementary school and also provided lessons in the palace of the caliph al-Muʿtamid. He died in Baghdad in 325/936. He is known for his work entitled *Kitāb al-Muwashshā*, in which he offers several opinions concerning love and sketches a kind of code of love within a society that he carefully describes, that of the "Refined" (*al-Ẓurafāʾ*), who could have been called "precious," had the word been in vogue.

Wāsitī (Abū Bakr Muhammad al-). Disciple of *Ḥallāj* who redirected the doctrine of his master toward an existential monism. He taught the doctrine of the pre-existence of souls, and explained the concurrence of the divine motion of our actions with the absolute transcendence of the divine act, using the notion of an "eternal aspect" to things produced in time (*qidam al-muḥdathāt*). He conceived of union with God as a union in His attributes. He lived in Iraq and in Khurāsān and died in 331/942.

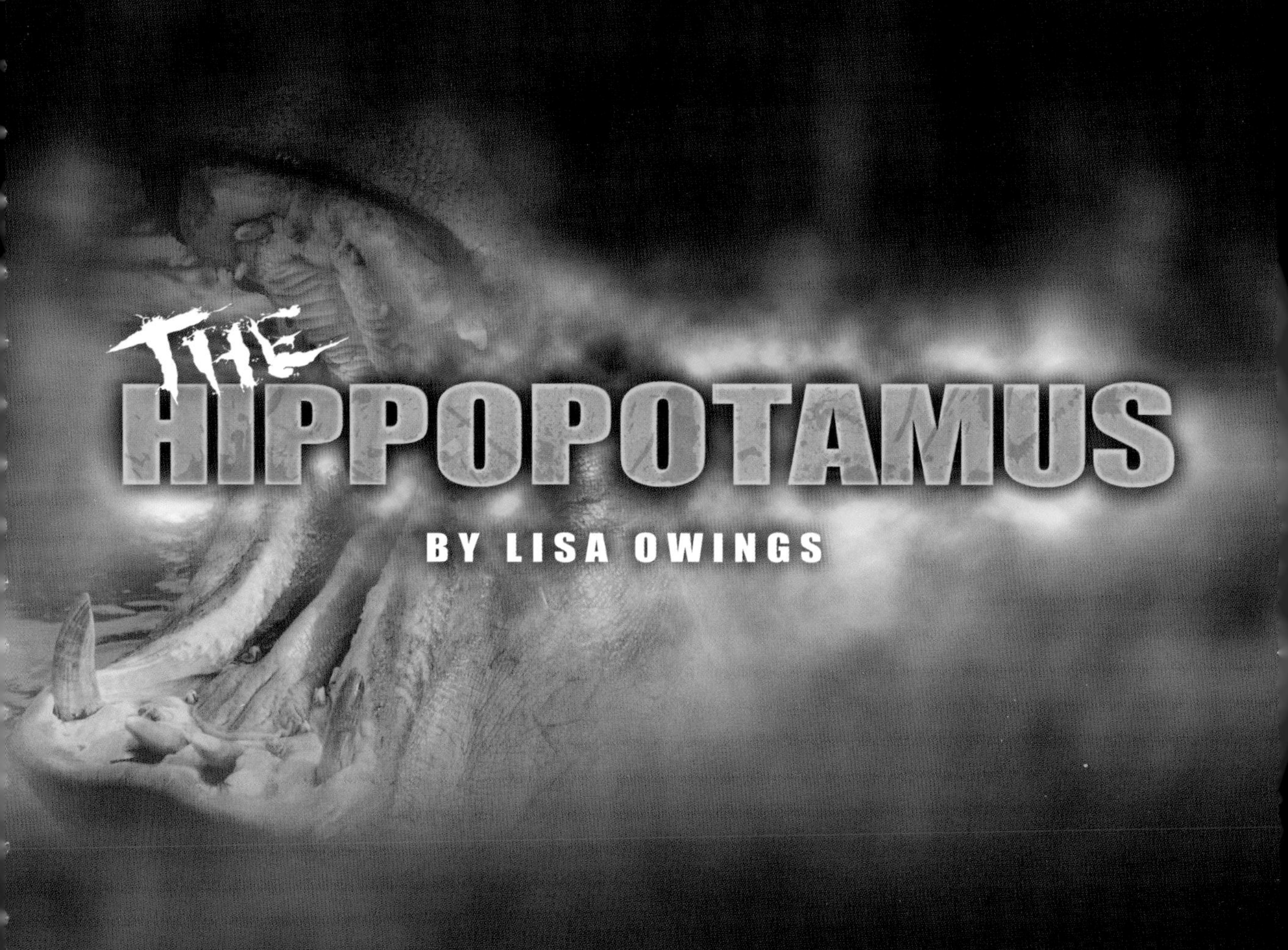

THE HIPPOPOTAMUS

BY LISA OWINGS

BELLWETHER MEDIA • MINNEAPOLIS, MN

Jump into the cockpit and take flight with Pilot Books. Your journey will take you on high-energy adventures as you learn about all that is wild, weird, fascinating, and fun!

This edition first published in 2012 by Bellwether Media, Inc.

No part of this publication may be reproduced in whole or in part without written permission of the publisher. For information regarding permission, write to Bellwether Media, Inc., Attention: Permissions Department, 5357 Penn Avenue South, Minneapolis, MN 55419.

Library of Congress Cataloging-in-Publication Data

Owings, Lisa.
The hippopotamus / by Lisa Owings.
p. cm. – (Pilot books: nature's deadliest)
Includes bibliographical references and index.
Summary: "Fascinating images accompany information about the hippopotamus. The combination of high-interest subject matter and narrative text is intended for students in grades 3 through 7"–Provided by publisher.
ISBN 978-1-60014-666-4 (hardcover : alk. paper)
1. Hippopotamus–Juvenile literature. I. Title.
QL737.U57O95 2012
599.63'5–dc22 2011013159

Printed in the United States of America, North Mankato, MN.

080111 1187

CONTENTS

River of Blood

It was a beautiful afternoon in Zimbabwe. Tour guide Paul Templer was leading a group of canoes down the Zambezi River. Templer saw a female hippopotamus and her calf downriver, so he changed his route to avoid a confrontation. He knew there was a **rogue** hippo on the new route, but he didn't think they would encounter it. Suddenly, he heard a loud thump behind him. He turned to look and saw that one of the canoes had flipped over. His friend, Evans Namasango, was in the water. Templer paddled back to help him. As he reached for Namasango's hand, a hippo lunged out of the water. Everyone watched in horror as Templer's head disappeared into the hippo's powerful jaws. Templer could feel the animal's sharp teeth pierce his back. The hippo dragged him underwater.

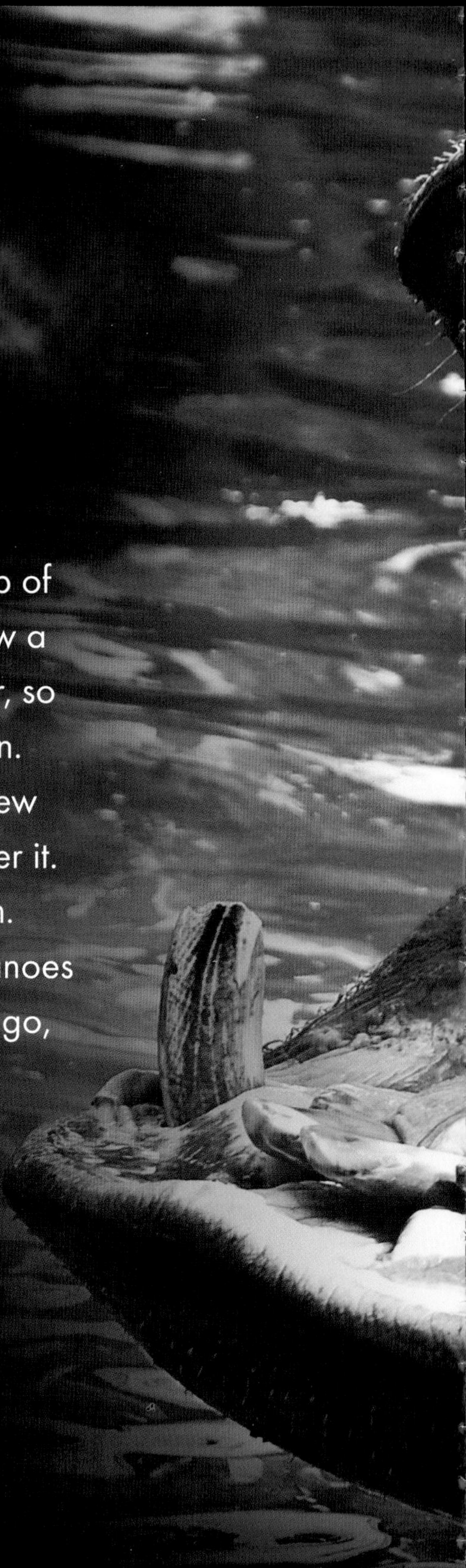

River Horse

Hippopotamus means "river horse" in Greek. However, hippos are more related to pigs than they are to horses.

Templer fought his way out of the hippo's mouth and swam to the surface. He started to pull Namasango toward shore, but the hippo was not through with them. Templer felt the hippo's teeth sink into his foot, crushing his bones. He let go of Namasango and took one last breath before the hippo pulled him back underwater. Templer desperately kicked and scratched at the hippo's nose. The hippo released him, and he swam up for air. He heard someone shout, "Swim to me!" But he was not fast enough. The hippo grabbed Templer around the waist and shook him hard. Templer felt his ribs being crushed. Blood was spraying out of him.

Templer punched the hippo as hard as he could with his free hand. The hippo dropped him into the river. Someone pulled Templer to shore. His left arm was hanging by a thread, and his left foot was crushed. Blood filled his lungs and flowed out of his chest. Templer's friends tried to stop the bleeding. The nearest hospital was hundreds of miles away. He was moments from death when they finally reached it. After seven hours in the operating room, Templer woke up. He had lost his left arm, but he was alive. He later learned that his friend Namasango had not been so lucky.

After the Attack

After two years of recovery, Paul Templer was able to guide tours down the Zambezi River again. Today, he is a famous speaker who inspires people everywhere with his story of survival.

Water Monster

Hippopotamuses have been on the earth for millions of years. Today they live in Africa, in **pods** of 10 to 20 hippos. They spend up to 16 hours a day relaxing in the water. Hippos may seem calm, but they are Africa's deadliest animals.

Hippos are larger than every other land animal except for elephants. They use their size to **intimidate** threats. Male hippos can grow up to 15 feet (4.6 meters) long and weigh more than 7,000 pounds (3,200 kilograms). The largest hippo in a pod is called the **dominant bull**. He controls the pod's territory. Dominant bulls must be aggressive and win fights with other males to keep their position. If a human crosses into the territory of a dominant bull, the result can be death.

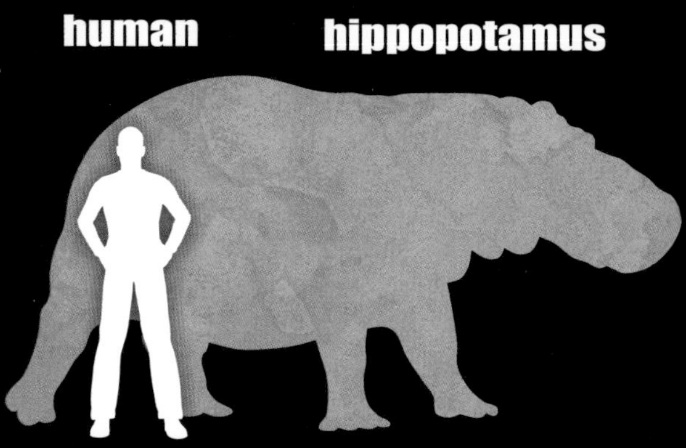

Sinking Hippos

Hippos cannot swim or float. They move through water by walking along the bottoms of rivers or lakes.

Hippos use their enormous teeth when they fight. A hippo can open its mouth up to 4 feet (1.2 meters) wide to threaten an enemy with these deadly weapons. The bottom teeth are the largest. They can grow to be 20 inches (51 centimeters) long. They grind against the top teeth to stay sharp. Hippos can bite with the pressure of almost 2,000 pounds (900 kilograms). That's more than ten times the strength of a human bite! The human body is no match for this bone-crushing force.

When male hippos fight for **dominance**, they lock jaws and shove each other until one backs down. If neither hippo gives up, the battle becomes bloody. The hippos swing their giant heads back and forth and tear at each other's flesh with their bottom teeth. It can turn into a fight to the death.

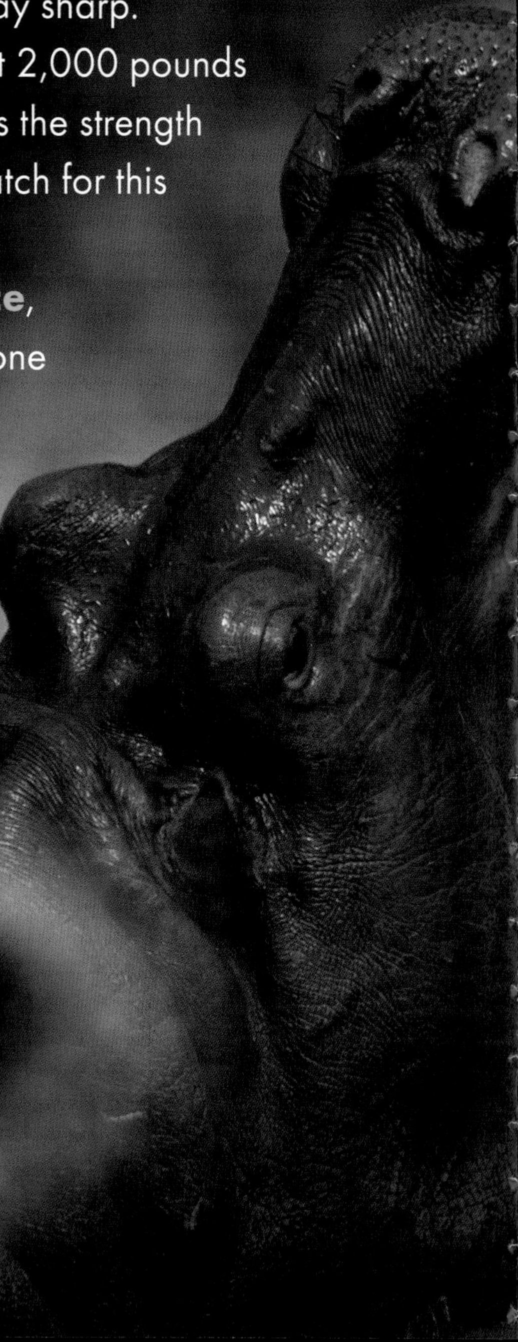

Vegetarians

Hippos eat only plants. They use their strong lower jaws to dig plants out of the ground. A hippo can eat more than 100 pounds (45 kilograms) of plants each day.

Hippos can easily defend their watery homes against humans. Their eyes, ears, and nostrils are all near the top of their heads. This lets them see, hear, and breathe while staying almost completely hidden underwater. By the time a person notices a hippo, it is often too late.

Hippos have webbed feet that help them move underwater. They can also hold their breath for up to half an hour. Their ears and nostrils close as they dip their giant heads beneath the surface of the river. Their eyes even have a clear **membrane** for protection underwater.

Run for Your Life

If you think you can escape hippos on land, think again. Hippos can run more than 20 miles (32 kilometers) per hour!

Hippopotamus Attacks

Hippos attack when they feel scared or threatened. Dominant bulls are the most aggressive. They will do anything to protect their territory. If humans enter a bull's territory, the startled hippo is likely to attack. It can smash intruders under its feet, crush them in its jaws, or hold them underwater until they drown.

Female hippos are just as deadly. They are fiercely protective of their young. Female hippos will charge at anything they think might hurt their calves. Hippo behavior can be **unpredictable** because we don't always know what they see as a threat. A hippo relaxing near shore can turn on you in an instant. People can do little to defend themselves against a hippo's brutal attack.

People can avoid attacks by staying away from hippo territories. Most hippos like shallow, calm waters with gently sloping beaches. People in canoes should paddle slowly to avoid scaring hippos. On land, never get between a hippo and the water. Hippos race for the water when they feel threatened. It is not good to be in their way!

If a hippo charges, try to climb a nearby tree. If there are no trees around, try to find something to hide behind. Running is also an option. Hippos can run as fast as humans, but they can't maintain that pace for long.

Humans kill many hippos each year. Some hippos are illegally hunted for their meat or their **ivory** teeth. Others are killed out of fear or because they damage crops. However, many people are working to protect and better understand hippos.

Observing hippos is a difficult and dangerous job. Hippos are underwater for much of the day. When these huge animals do emerge, people should keep at a safe distance. Scientists are studying how hippos communicate, what they do underwater, and how they affect their environment. The more we know about hippos, the better we can understand why they attack. If we respect these fierce animals, we can avoid future bloody, or even deadly, encounters.

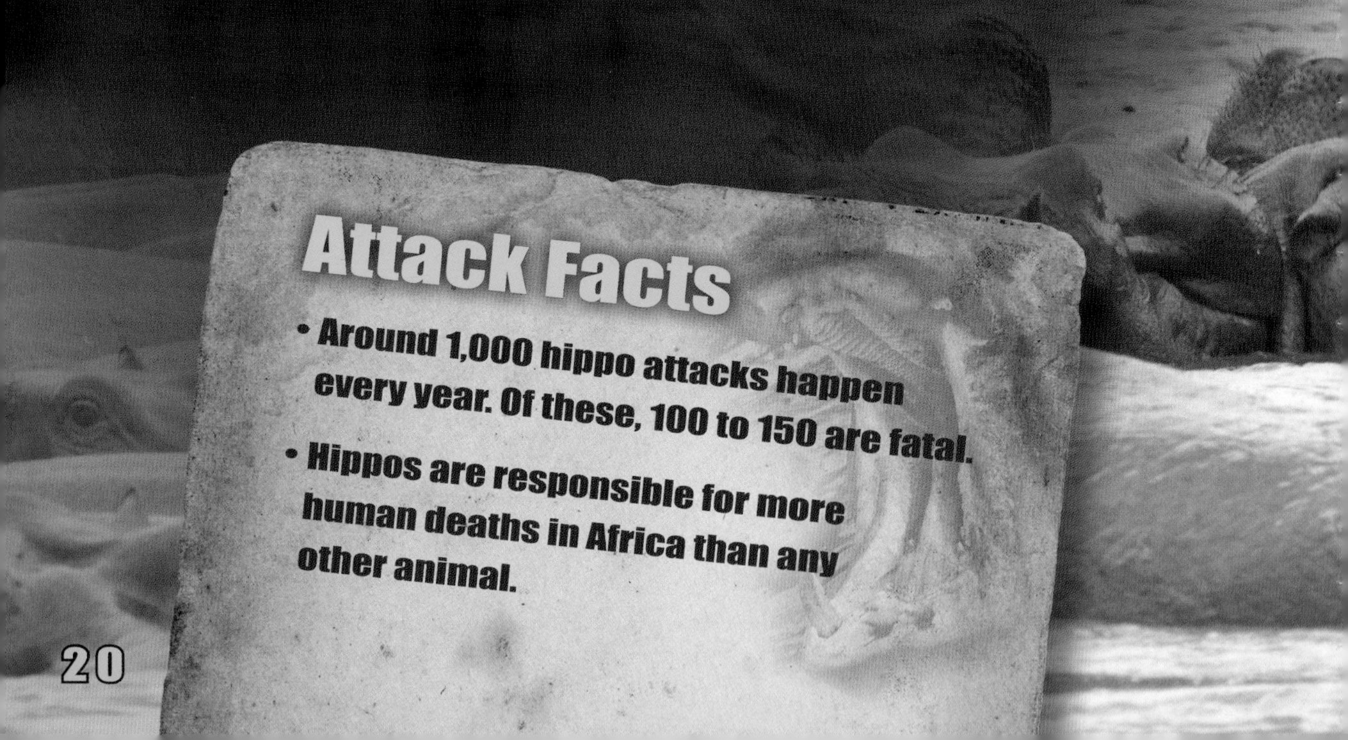

Attack Facts

- Around 1,000 hippo attacks happen every year. Of these, 100 to 150 are fatal.
- Hippos are responsible for more human deaths in Africa than any other animal.

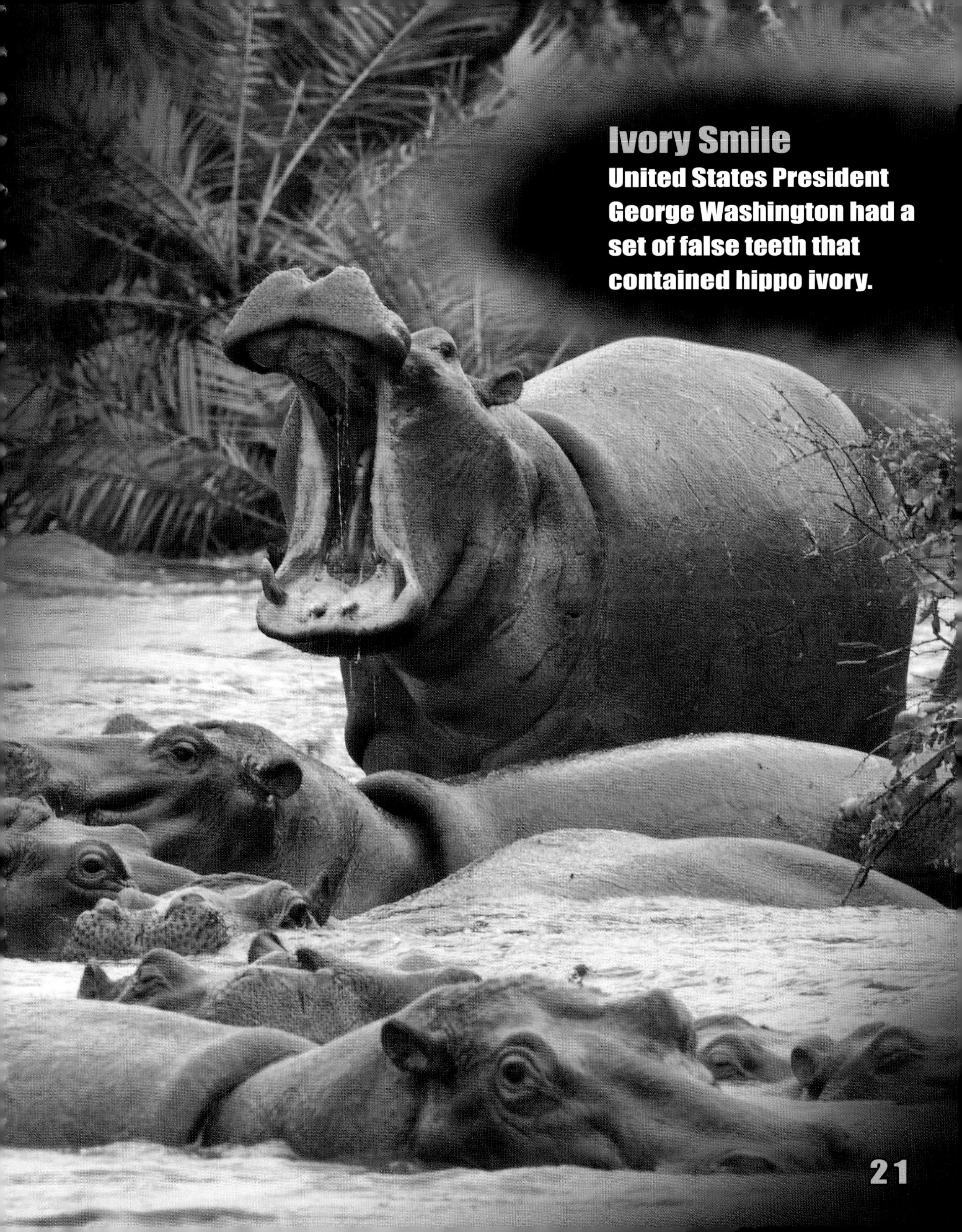

Ivory Smile

United States President George Washington had a set of false teeth that contained hippo ivory.

Glossary

dominance—power or control over someone or something

dominant bull—the large male hippo that is in charge of a pod and its territory

intimidate—to frighten

ivory—hard, white matter that makes up the teeth of hippos and some other animals

membrane—a thin layer of tissue or skin

pods—groups of hippos that live together

rogue—an angry male hippo that has usually been defeated in a battle for dominance; rogue hippos are not part of a pod.

unpredictable—not always behaving in the same way; the behavior of hippos can be very unpredictable.

To Learn More

At the Library

Feldhake, Glenn. *Hippos*. Stillwater, Minn.: Voyageur Press, 2005.

Page, Robin, and Steve Jenkins. *How to Clean a Hippopotamus: A Look at Unusual Animal Partnerships*. Boston, Mass.: Houghton Mifflin Books for Children, 2010.

Zumbusch, Amelie von. *Hippos*. New York, N.Y.: PowerKids Press, 2007.

On the Web

Learning more about hippopotamuses is as easy as 1, 2, 3.

1. Go to www.factsurfer.com.

2. Enter "hippopotamuses" into the search box.

3. Click the "Surf" button and you will see a list of related Web sites.

With factsurfer.com, finding more information is just a click away.

Index

The images in this book are reproduced through the courtesy of: Uryadnikov Sergey, front cover, pp. 16-17; Juan Martinez, pp. 4-5; ZSSD/Minden Pictures, pp. 6-7; Paul Templer, p.8; Roy Toft/Getty Images, pp. 8-9; Warwick Lister, p. 10; Robert Picket/Alamy, p. 11; Shin Yoshino/Minden Pictures, pp. 12-13; Creativ Studio Heinemann/Photolibrary, pp. 14-15; Tony Heald/Minden Pictures, p. 16 (left); Nigel Dennis/Getty Images, pp. 18-19; Carson Ganci/Photolibrary, pp. 20-21.

[illegible]